T0134736

Immersive Education

Paula MacDowell • Jennifer Lock
Editors

Immersive Education

Designing for Learning

 Springer

Editors
Paula MacDowell
College of Education
University of Saskatchewan
Saskatoon, SK, Canada

Jennifer Lock
Werklund School of Education
University of Calgary
Calgary, AB, Canada

ISBN 978-3-031-18140-5   ISBN 978-3-031-18138-2   (eBook)
https://doi.org/10.1007/978-3-031-18138-2

© The Editor(s) (if applicable) and The Author(s), under exclusive license to Springer Nature Switzerland AG 2022
This work is subject to copyright. All rights are solely and exclusively licensed by the Publisher, whether the whole or part of the material is concerned, specifically the rights of translation, reprinting, reuse of illustrations, recitation, broadcasting, reproduction on microfilms or in any other physical way, and transmission or information storage and retrieval, electronic adaptation, computer software, or by similar or dissimilar methodology now known or hereafter developed.
The use of general descriptive names, registered names, trademarks, service marks, etc. in this publication does not imply, even in the absence of a specific statement, that such names are exempt from the relevant protective laws and regulations and therefore free for general use.
The publisher, the authors, and the editors are safe to assume that the advice and information in this book are believed to be true and accurate at the date of publication. Neither the publisher nor the authors or the editors give a warranty, expressed or implied, with respect to the material contained herein or for any errors or omissions that may have been made. The publisher remains neutral with regard to jurisdictional claims in published maps and institutional affiliations.

This Springer imprint is published by the registered company Springer Nature Switzerland AG
The registered company address is: Gewerbestrasse 11, 6330 Cham, Switzerland

Foreword

I have always found learning to be one of the greatest joys of being human—and immersive learning, broadly speaking, to be perhaps the most engaging method for ensuring that the lessons stick. That is, when designed correctly. I have been blessed to collaborate with many researchers, teachers, and designers on *what works* for immersive learning: first through our American Education Research Association (AERA) Special Interest Group from 2007 to 2015, and then to the present day with the broader community we created with the Immersive Learning Research Network (iLRN). It has become apparent to many of us time and again that designing high-quality immersive learning experiences is nontrivial, but achievable. When Paula MacDowell told me about the book that she and Jennifer Lock were putting together, I was intrigued.

The hype and excitement we are hearing about the Metaverse is unprecedented in education. Every day, I hear of the promise and possibilities becoming available for learners with new immersive technologies. Money and marketing in education are transforming the industry. MacDowell and Lock have gathered some of the foremost practitioners and scholars in this emerging multidisciplinary field, who offer design guidelines for both younger and more mature students and strategies to use XR and immersive learning technologies as co-creative tools for teachers and students themselves. Their focus on connecting research to practice is valuable here, and I know you, as a teacher or a designer, will gain from the rich, evidence-based contexts illustrated throughout this book. Within these pages you will find a wealth of situated perspectives on the instructional design process to leverage the capabilities of immersive technologies for achieving enviable levels of learner engagement and connecting students to some of the most meaningful goals educators collectively seek.

Dr. Paula MacDowell has been a key leader for the iLRN network, enabling our growing high-quality research community to be accessible and relevant to teachers, instructional designers, and professionals involved in educational practice. Her knowledge, scope, and enthusiasm have been vital for iLRN to grow conversation and opportunities for instructors and other innovators. Her network of practitioner-researchers has broadened and strengthened iLRN's mission in simply vital ways.

Similarly, Dr. Jennifer Lock brings to this work her experience and expertise in designing learning in technology-enabled learning environments. You will see their vision and drive evident throughout this work from the invited experts that MacDowell and Lock selected for this volume.

I truly believe that sharing *what works* with other teachers is one of the greatest multipliers of good that I know. In this book, you can find inspiring methods to practically engage students of many backgrounds with immersive learning technologies and to use their design capabilities in expert ways. I hope you will try some of these techniques and apply them to your own classroom, museum education program, or group of learners.

In fact, I am personally excited to adventure out into the Metaverse and apply some of this gathered wisdom myself. I hope to find you and your students there!

Sincerely,
Jonathon Richter, EdD
President and CEO
Immersive Learning Research Network

Acknowledgments

We, the editors, respectfully acknowledge the authors for their valuable contributions to the book. Thank you for your professionalism and enthusiasm for designing immersive learning environments and experiences. It has been a positive and rewarding collaboration at all stages of the publication process, including the team Zoom meetings, peer review of colleagues' chapters, three rounds of revisions, and ongoing email communication. We hope readers will find the book as worthwhile and stimulating as its research and development journey has been.

We wish to thank the following colleagues for their valuable time and expertise in reviewing one or more chapters. The peer review process enhanced the quality of the book. We are grateful to the reviewers for their pedagogical insights, technical knowledge, literature recommendations, and constructive critique.

Dr. Lorraine Beaudin, University of Lethbridge, Canada
Dr. Alec Bodzin, Lehigh University, United States
Dr. Kathlyn Bradshaw, Algonquin College, Canada
Ms. Esther Brandon, Brandeis University, United States
Dr. Sunah Cho, University of British Columbia, Canada
Dr. Megan Cotnam-Kappel, University of Ottawa, Canada
Ms. Noeleen De Silva, University of Calgary, Canada
Dr. Irwin DeVries, Royal Roads University, Canada
Dr. Keri Ewart, University of British Columbia, Canada
Dr. Thommy Eriksson, Chalmers University of Technology, Sweden
Dr. Matthew Farber, University of Northern Colorado, United States
Dr. Matt Glowatz, University College Dublin, Ireland
Dr. Cristyne Hébert, University of Regina, Canada
Dr. Yu-Ling Lee, Trinity Western University, Canada
Dr. Yang (Flora) Liu, University of Calgary, Canada
Dr. Daniel Livingstone, Glasgow School of Art, United Kingdom
Ms. Meaghan Moody, University of Rochester, United States
Dr. Yumiko Murai, Simon Fraser University, Canada
Dr. Krystle Phirangee, University of Toronto, Canada

Dr. Luciano Da Rosa Dos Santos, Mount Royal University, Canada
Ms. Roberta Sullivan, University at Buffalo, United States
Dr. Norm Vaughan, Mount Royal University, Canada
Dr. George Veletsianos, Royal Roads University, Canada
Dr. Levina Yuen, Athabasca University, Canada

Contents

Introduction: Meaningful Immersive Learning in Education

Jennifer Lock and Paula MacDowell

Abstract The chapter begins with an introduction to meaningful immersive learning. In the discussion, we examine what it is and how it is taken up pedagogically in K–12 and higher education. We argue there is a spectrum for immersion. Educators and designers may engage in designing across the spectrum to integrate immersive experiences to blend physical and digital realities for meaningful learning. The chapter concludes by introducing the book's four sections: (1) Designing Immersive Learning in K–12 Education, (2) Designing Immersive Learning in Higher Education, (3) Teachers and Students as Designers of Immersive Learning, and (4) The Future of Immersive Learning: Designing for Possibilities.

Keywords Immersive education · Immersive learning · Immersive pedagogy · Learning · Spectrum of immersion · Technology-enabled learning environments

Introduction

Technology-enabled learning environments are ubiquitous in complex contemporary K–12 and higher education classroom contexts. Various digital technologies and applications are being adopted and integrated into teaching and learning. Infrastructures and advances in digital technology create opportunities for more culturally responsive and personalized digital learning experiences. With the recent move to online and hybrid learning because of the COVID-19 pandemic,

J. Lock (✉)
Werklund School of Education, University of Calgary, Calgary, AB, Canada
e-mail: jvlock@ucalgary.ca

P. MacDowell
College of Education, University of Saskatchewan, Saskatoon, SK, Canada
e-mail: paula.macdowell@usask.ca

© The Author(s), under exclusive license to Springer Nature Switzerland AG 2022
P. MacDowell, J. Lock (eds.), *Immersive Education*,
https://doi.org/10.1007/978-3-031-18138-2_1

expectations for learning environments and learning experiences have changed. It is reported that "by 2030, we predict that learners will expect high-quality XR experiences" (Flynn & Frost, 2021). How do we design such learning experiences, and what professional development supports are needed for educators to facilitate augmented, mixed, or virtual reality learnings in these new technology-enhanced learning environments?

Resources have been invested to support educators in learning how to teach using technology-enabled learning environments (e.g., online and blended learning). However, there is a shift away from teaching educators *how* to use the technology (e.g., set up and use a discussion forum in a learning management system) to designing learning experiences. Such exploration opens the question: what do meaningful and engaging learning experiences, look like, sound like, and feel like in technology-enabled learning environments—especially when considering teaching and learning in immersive environments?

Complex concepts can be taught using immersive learning environments where students are able to engage in simulated lived experiences that influence the cognitive, social, and affective dimensions of their learning. As educators, we need to be purposeful in designing, facilitating, and assessing these learning experiences when using immersive technologies to foster deep and meaningful learning. Students may be positively or negatively affected by immersive learning experiences. Teachers need opportunities to engage with immersive technologies to understand the affordances and constraints to help inform how the tools can be used to design meaningful learning.

It cannot be assumed that meaningful learning will occur when using technology. As Dias and Atkinson (2001) argue, "effective integration of technology has everything to do with teaching pedagogy and very little do with technology itself. We should not be impressed with the mere 'use of technology' unless that use is supported by a carefully crafted pedagogy" (p. 10). Rather, we need to understand human experiences within immersive learning environments. Applying immersive technologies requires educators to be intentional in designing learning to support students in meaningfully meeting learning outcomes. As noted by Southgate (2020), it is about how educators "leverage their existing pedagogical knowledge and the signature pedagogies of their specialisations to use the learning affordances of virtual environments in curriculum-aligned ways with diverse groups of students" (p. 25).

The purpose of this chapter is threefold: first, to define the terms immersive technology, immersive learning, immersive pedagogy, and immersive education and examine their similarities and differences; second, to examine what is meaningful immersive learning and discuss how immersive learning is being taking up pedagogically in K–12 and higher education; third, to discuss immersive learning as part of a spectrum. We argue there is a spectrum along which educators and designers may integrate immersive experiences to blend physical and digital realities for meaningful learning.

Vignette

Teri continued to observe students' excitement from another class talking about their augmented and virtual learning experiences as they were learning about marine life. She noticed over the past year that a couple of her colleagues were using various forms of immersive technologies in their classes. Teri often wanted to ask her colleagues where and how to begin but was hesitant to ask, given her lack of technical knowledge and expertise. As students talked more about these various forms of reality and how it is 'just like being there', she became more interested and curious. She could see possibilities for where her students could experience the learning rather than just read and talk about curricular topics. She became more inquisitive about how to make learning come alive in her classroom. This morning, with her cup of coffee in hand, Teri went to talk to her colleague about how she could design immersive learning experiences for her students.

Defining Immersive Education

Learning in Technology-Enabled Environments

For learning to be meaningful, "a learned knowledge (or fact) is fully understood by an individual who can then use it to make connections with other previously known knowledge" (Vergara et al., 2019, p.2). Meaningful learning, according to Mulders et al. (2020), is about the "transfer of knowledge to solve problem-based tasks" (p. 209). Learning occurs best, according to Jacobsen et al. (2013), when learners are "trying to do things that are challenging and of deep interest to them – activities that reflect a close interplay of emotion and cognition in the development of capacity" (p. 14). This interplay is a form of intellectual engagement involves "a serious emotional and cognitive investment in learning, using higher order thinking skills (such as analysis and evaluation) to increase understanding, solve complex problems, or construct new knowledge" (Willms et al., 2009, p. 7). As educators, we need to be intentional about how we design learning that fosters intellectual engagement in support of deep and meaningful learning within technology-enabled learning environments.

As educational technologies continue to evolve and be adopted in K–12 and higher education, we are seeing more opportunities to integrate immersive technologies in teaching and learning. Immersive technology involves the technical capacity to create augmented, virtual, and mixed realities. Augmented reality (AR) allows the exploration "of the real world while adding a digital layer on top that gives the illusion that they have a 3D object" (Donally, 2021, p. 6). AR provides a means "to bring experiential and location-based learning to students by supplementing existing worlds rather than creating new ones. Augmented reality installations can be built to take advantage of existing or low-cost infrastructure" (EDUCAUSE

Learning Initiative, 2005). Virtual reality (VR) involves using a "VR headset or mobile device to create an all-digital view. VR features such as a 360-degree view and surround sound provide a truly immersive experience" (Donally, 2021, p. 6). The computer-generated three-dimensional VR environment "can be a highly imaginative or an accurate simulation of something in the real world (Southgate, 2020, p. 2). In mixed reality (MR), "the AR experience goes beyond an overlay to allow virtual objects to interact with real ones" (Donally, 2021, p. 6). Another term is extended reality (XR) which "encompasses all immersive technologies" (Hinther, 2021). XR technology allows "users to gain concrete experience that might not otherwise be available. By providing *hands-on* experience, XR helps promote student engagement with learning materials and deepens student interaction with complex problems" (Pomerantz & Rode, 2020). XR tools "allow users some type of sensory immersion in their use" (Cheney & Terry, 2018, p. 281). These types of immersive technologies provide new approaches "to present learning beyond our prior limitations" (Donally, 2021, p. 8). Technologies like AR can help "remove barriers to learning and open new opportunities for learning, discovery, and experiences" (Grajek et al., 2021, p. 46). The use of immersive technologies can enhance motivation for learning, allow greater personalization of learning, and provide feedback to inform adjustments or modifications in meeting individual learning outcomes (Dick, 2021).

Immersive Learning and Immersion

Immersive learning involves hands-on educational experience with technology that will "transcend physical space limitations to create educational opportunities that would not otherwise be physically possible" (Dick, 2021). The learner's sense of presence or *being there* in the virtual environment impacts the nature and degree of engagement. The advantages of using immersive technologies are related to engagement, investment, flexibility, creativity, and challenge (Donally, 2021, p.7). For example, immersive virtual reality (iVR) can potentially "enhance immersion, improve spatial capabilities, promote empathy, increase motivation and possibly improve learning outcomes" (Bower et al., 2020, p. 2214). Di Natale et al. (2020) argue that the benefit to learning involves "immersive and interactive properties ... the possibility for users to feel present in the immersive VE [virtual environment] and to use their bodies in a natural way and live sensory experiences similar to those in the real world" (p. 2025). Through engaging in the virtual environment, students learn by practice and first-hand experiences.

Two main views of immersion are distinguished in the literature: psychological immersion (perceived by the user) and technological immersion (capability of the system to immerse the user). Witmer and Singer (1998) view immersion as "a psychological state characterized by perceiving oneself to be enveloped by, included in, and interacting with an environment that provides a continuous stream of stimuli and experiences" (p. 227). In contrast, Slater's (1999) view of immersion focuses on the technology or system, "the extent to which the actual system delivers a surrounding environment, one which shuts out sensations from the 'real world', which accommodates many sensory modalities, has rich representational capability, and so on" (p. 560) In this book, we are interested in how both psychological and technological immersion influence the learning environment to focus attention, minimize distractions, and promote better learning outcomes. Factors that influence how immersion effects learning in virtual environments are articulated by Makransky and Mayer's (2022) immersion principle in multimedia learning: "The immersion principle holds that immersive media per se do not necessarily improve learning; however, implementing effective instructional methods within immersive virtual environments or contextualizing immersive learning experiences within a lesson can improve learning" (p. 5).

Di Natale et al. (2020) propose three levels of immersion with regard to the technology, in particular noting VR. First, the non-immersive involves a "3D world generated on a computer and delivered through a desktop. Interactions provided through a mouse or joysticks" (p. 2008). Second, the semi-immersive can "increase the feeling of immersion by either strengthening sensory inputs (e.g., visual inputs) or enhancing the sense of embodiment by allowing the students to actively interact with the learning environment" (p. 2008). Third, iVR is

> technology that generates environments that perceptually sound the users, increasing their sense of presence and enabling them to experience it as real. This technology represents the highest level of immersion … which allows the users to observe the virtual world from a first-person perspective. (Di Natale et al., 2020, p. 2009)

Knowing these three levels helps us to explore the notion of a spectrum of technology use that supports levels or degrees of immersive learning.

Immersive Pedagogy

Designing, facilitating, and assessing immersive learning requires a change in pedagogical practice, especially given the rapid advances in XR technologies that enable innovative pedagogical approaches based on discovery and inquiry. As such, immersive learning requires a shift away from "designing learning tasks to choreographing learning experiences as a whole, mediated by structured and semi structured social interactions" (de Freitas et al., 2010, p. 82). These learning experiences consist of

> social interactions between members of the learning group, supporting exploratory individual pathways and identification of methods of tutoring that focus more upon mentoring and guiding development. … Also, they may consider the pedagogic approaches needed for the subject area taught, learner group and context of learning. (de Freitas et al., 2010, p. 82)

By designing the learning through a choreographic approach, educators identify what is needed to support the learning. They are responsive in the moment to attend to gaps in knowledge and skills in support of scaffolding the learning. As with any choreography, this process may require practice and modifications to the steps leading to the outcome. Fowler (2014) points out that a "design for learning" (p. 417) approach and "culturally relevant teaching and learning" (p. 420) are defining characteristics of immersive pedagogy. To ensure that immersive technologies are used safely, effectively, and to their full potential, Fowler advocates for developing pedagogical guidelines and best practices "presented in a way that practitioners can understand and apply them in their teaching and learning" (p. 421). Responding to Fowler's call, each book chapter contributes three to five strategies for educators and designers to consider when creating or implementing an immersive learning experience.

Meaningful Immersive Learning in K–12 and Higher Education

Implementing immersive learning in K–12 and high educational contexts begins by checking our assumptions about learning and the use of technology in learning and teaching. First, the focus needs to be on learning and what makes for meaningful and intellectually engaging learning. Considering the learning outcomes creates opportunities to explore pedagogical approaches and the role technology can play in the design of learning. While immersive technologies are rapidly developing, a barrier to widespread adoption is limited high-quality educational content. It is worth noting that immersive experiences do not need to be ultra-realistic to be useful and effective in educational settings.

Second, immersive learning requires more than access to the digital technology. What is the purpose of the immersion? How can the immersive technologies support the identified learning outcomes? What is involved in creating or planning the immersive experience? Creating the immersive experience is a critical component of the learning. "The learning that takes place during the process of building an XR experience—for both the student and the instructor—is arguably more important than the final product" (Pomerantz & Rode, 2020). Professional tools for designing immersive environments need to become simpler to use, affordable, and scalable. Further, both teachers and students need opportunities to experiment and receive ongoing feedback to guide the design process.

As with all planning for learning experiences, purposeful planning is required before, during, and after the immersive experience. Pre-planning the experience requires instructional design work to prepare students for the immersive learning experience, which includes considering the knowledge needed in the subject area and the inquiry questions to guide the immersive experience. When considering the immersive experience (partial or full), we need to ask—what is the nature of the interaction between the students and teacher? What learning outcomes should be achieved through the experience? What topics should the facilitated post-immersive experience learning discussion address? Where and how does assessment play a part in the design of learning?

Third, immersive learning does not equate with full immersion. What does it mean to learn through immersive experiences that may involve various degrees of immersion afforded through the technology? For example, using AR with a tablet may be sufficient to support a particular learning outcome, whereas iVR reality may better align with another learning outcome where students need to engage by embodiment and have a strong sense of presence. The degree of immersion may depend on access, experience, and confidence with a particular technology as well as the learning goals and outcomes. A cost/benefit analysis should also be considered. Immersive experiences should meet several learning outcomes to justify the return on investment and value for learning, compared with using other multimedia or instructional methods.

Through immersive technologies and designing for authentic immersive learning experiences, students are able to engage in learning through experiencing these technological environments. Table 1 provides examples from this book of curricular topics being taken up in rich and robust ways in K–12 classrooms and higher education:

While we observe more educators and students engaging in immersive learning experiences, we also see the need to expand research in this area. More empirical evidence is being reported on the effectiveness of immersive technology for learning. For example, three reports by EDUCAUSE

> demonstrate that XR is an effective technology for active and experiential learning, enabling users to gain concrete experience that might not otherwise be available. ... XR helps promote student engagement with learning materials and deepens student interaction with complex problems. (Pomerantz & Rode, 2020)

However, a gap needs to be addressed regarding the pedagogical practice of immersive learning in classroom contexts for K–12 and higher education. Especially with VR, we need to move the research out of the lab environment and into the classroom. This will enhance the professional development of educators in areas of designing, facilitating, and assessing immersive learning. As we adopt immersive technologies in our classrooms, we need to study their design, implementation, and impact on student learning. Drawing on practitioner inquiry research helps to inform decisions as to why we are integrating immersive learning and how to assess the learning outcomes. An example of research conducted by Cheng and Tsai (2019) focused on immersive virtual field trips in an elementary class. From their study, they found "issues regarding perceptual load when engaging in HMD-based virtual field trips"; that "task-based learning approach can be integrated into the design of immersive virtual field trips in classrooms"; that "pedagogical research to probe how HMD-based VR technology was applied in classroom for teachers to lead their students on virtual field trips"; and the need to "understand how teachers guide their students in the context of educational virtual field trips for attaining perceived involvement in the learning activities rather than in the virtual environments" (p. 13). Another example of necessary research as reported by Southgate (2020) notes that with iVR,

Table 1 Contributions to learning by book chapter authors

Authors	Context	Technology	Contributions to Learning
Quincy Q. Wang	Interactive learning exhibit at science world	AR	Enhancing learning and curiosity about science concepts.
Annie Beaumier and Marguerite Koole	K–12 classrooms	AR/VR	Understanding the impact of natural and human-induced changes on water ecosystems.
Stephanie Wössner	K–12 classrooms	VR; 360 videos	Facilitating intercultural language learning and student agency.
Géraldine Perriguey	K–12 classrooms	VR	Inducing positive emotional states for high-risk situations; preparing students for earthquake risks.
Corinne Brenner, Jessica Ochoa Hendrix, and Mandë Holford	K–12 classrooms	AR/VR	Helping students build STEM skills and develop science identities.
Andreas Dengel, Josef Buchner, Miriam Mulders, and Johanna Pirker	K–12 classrooms; higher education	AR/VR	Integrating immersive educational experiences in the everyday classroom.
Christine Lon-Bailey, Jesse Lubinsky, and Micah Shippee	K–12 classrooms; higher education	AR/VR	Enabling educators to share and collaborate on XR instruction through a common framework.
Sarune Savickaite and David Simmons	Higher education	VR	Improving teaching of complex and abstract psychology topics.
Becky Lane and Christine Havens-Hafer	Higher education	AR/VR	Enhancing lesson planning and offering differentiated instruction.
Paula MacDowell	Higher education; teachers as designers	VR	Empowering teachers as designers of immersive learning experiences for pro-social and environmental change.
Erica Southgate	K–12 classrooms; students as designers	VR	Enhancing student agency to meet learning outcomes through VR content creation.
Camila Lee and Meredith Thompson	K–12 classrooms; students as designers	VR	Managing cognitive load through pretraining and segmenting.
Lorelle VanFossen and Karen Gibson-Hylands	Teachers and students as designers	VR	Integrating immersive storytelling to enhance learning across the lifespan.
David Kaser	K–12 classrooms; students as mentors	VR	Increasing classroom engagement and student empowerment with peer mentoring.

more sustained scholarly attention is required to understand the unique contribution of the technology for learning, how it can be integrated into the curriculum, and the pedagogical underpinnings of effective use in the natural setting of the school classroom. More research is required on how students can use the learning affordances of iVR to master content knowledge, develop higher order thinking, and promote metacognition, problem-solving, and collaboration. (p.15)

Each of these examples emphasizes the need for careful research in terms of designing the learning experience and assessing its impact. To inform best practices, educators engaging in learning design also need to actively study the impact of immersive experiences. Further research and innovation are required to address the various barriers—including cybersickness, access, privacy, and safety issues—that may prevent students from having meaningful immersive learning experiences.

Designing Across the Spectrum of Immersion

There is a spectrum or scope across which educators may begin designing immersive learning experiences. As educators develop their competence and confidence in using immersive technologies for designing learning experiences, they will be able to work toward more advanced levels of immersion (e.g., a fully immersive environment). As educators and designers, we should not be hesitant to begin this work because of lack of expertise or limitation of the technology available in our educational context. As with Teri in the vignette, driving this process is curiosity and interest in designing learning that engages students in a learning experience.

To design the immersive learning experience, students' prior knowledge and experience with technology must be considered. As part of the design for learning, embedded scaffolding supports both the development of content knowledge and the technological skills needed for the immersive learning experience. This work needs to be planned, and the various scaffolding activities may take time to develop student competence and confidence leading to a meaningful immersive learning experience.

A starting point for the design process is Dunleavy's (2014) three design principles for AR learning: 1) "Enable and then challenge (challenge)"; 2) "Drive by gamified story (fantasy)"; and 3) "See the unseen (curiosity)" (p. 29). Educators and designers should be mindful of cognitive overload in immersive learning environments, which can be overwhelming for some students. Connecting to narrative offers personal and cultural relevance while reinforcing learning outcomes. Building on unique affordances of immersive technologies helps to visualize abstract concepts that are challenging to teach. However, Dunleavy (2014) cautions "that designers do not create experiences where the technology becomes a barrier to the environment. Rather the technology needs to drive the students deeper into the authentic observation and interaction with the environment and with each other" (p. 32).

On one end of the spectrum, the immersive experience may involve such technology as a tablet or smartphone. Further along the spectrum, students may be engaged in a deeper level of immersion with iVR. "The key findings are that effective and enjoyable learning does not need high degrees of immersion in most cases, but it profits from guidance and the breakdown of iVR lessons into smaller units" (Mulders et al. 2020, p. 217). Within this immersive spectrum are opportunities to use hybrid platforms; important for inclusion and widespread adoption, these include

2-dimensional screens (e.g., mobile phones, personal computers, and tablets) and VR hardware (e.g., head-mounted displays).

The focus should not be technology-driven; rather, the emphasis should be on the learning outcomes and application of instructional design principles. Mulders et al. (2020) propose an evidenced-based framework that offers guidelines for designing meaningful iVR learning-based (M-iVR-L) key features of VR technology, including immersion, interaction, and imagination. The M-iVR-L framework proposes six recommendations for educators and designers to consider: 1) "Learning first, immersion second," 2) "Provide learning relevant interactions," 3) "Segment complex tasks into smaller units," 4) "Guide immersive learning," 5) "Build on existing knowledge," and 6) "Provide constructive learning activities" (Mulders et al., 2020, pp. 214–216).

As with all meaningful learning across the curriculum, purposeful planning is required before, during, and after the immersive experience. Planning entails applying instructional design principles to prepare and onboard students for the immersive learning experience, as well as considering what knowledge is required in the subject area and the nature of the inquiry questions to guide the learning. When considering the immersive experience (partial or full), we need to ask—what are the interactions between the students and teacher? What learning outcomes should be achieved through the experience? What needs to be taken up in the facilitated post-immersive experience learning discussion? Where and how does assessment play a part in the design of immersive learning? These guiding questions will help educators and designers design and facilitate rich meaningful immersive learning experiences.

Conclusion

The purpose of this chapter was to introduce the concept of meaningful immersive learning, which involves designing across the technological spectrum and across the curriculum. In the following three sections of the book, authors share illustrative examples of immersive learning. In Part 1, **Designing Immersive Learning in K–12 Education**, five chapters feature work and insights on designing immersive learning experiences and environments to meet educational goals and learning outcomes in K–12 educational contexts. Part 2, **Designing Immersive Learning in Higher Education,** comprises five chapters. In the first two, the focus is on frameworks that address the complexity of integrating immersive learning in current educational contexts. The next three chapters showcase examples of immersive learning to enhance the teaching of complex topics and offer differentiated instruction. The first four chapters of Part 3, **Teachers and Students as Designers of Immersive Learning,** share examples of how teachers and students can work as immersive learning designers, storytellers, and world builders. In the concluding chapter, "The Future of Immersive Learning: Designing for Possibilities," we focus on designing for possibilities with immersive pedagogical strategies and immersive learning technologies, grounded by examples and references from chapters in this book. Drawing on this work, we look toward a future of immersive learning in complex contemporary K–12 and higher education classrooms.

References

Bower, M., DeWitt, D., & Lai, J. W. M. (2020). Reasons associated with preservice teachers' intention to use immersive virtual reality in education. *British Journal of Educational Research, 51*(6), 2214–2232. https://doi.org/10.1111/bjet.13009

Cheney, A. W., & Terry, K. P. (2018). Immersive learning environments as complex dynamic systems. *International Journal on Teaching and Learning in Higher Education, 30*(2), 277. https://files.eric.ed.gov/fulltext/EJ1185091.pdf

Cheng, K.-H., & Tsai, C.-C. (2019, June 8). A case study of immersive virtual field trips in an elementary classroom: Students' learning experience and teacher-student interaction behaviours. *Computers & Education, 140*. https://doi.org/10.1016/j.compedu.2019.103600.

De Freitas, S., Rebolledo-Mendez, G., Liarokapis, F., Magoulas, G., & Poulovassilis, A. (2010). Learning as immersive experiences: Using the four-dimensional framework for designing and evaluating immersive learning experiences in a virtual work. *British Journal of Educational Technology, 41*(1), 69–85. https://doi.org/10.1111/j.1467-8535.2009.01024.x

Di Natale, A. F., Repetto, C., Riva, G., & Villani, D. (2020). Immersive virtual reality in K–12 and higher education: A 10-year systematic review of empirical research. *British Journal of Educational Technology, 51*(6), 2006–2033. https://doi.org/10.1111/bjet.13030

Dias, L. B., & Atkinson, S. (2001). Technology integration: Best practices—Where do teachers stand? *International Electronic Journal for Leadership in Learning, 5*(10).

Dick, E. (2021, August 30). The promise of immersive learning: Augmented and virtual reality's potential in education. *Information Technology & Innovation Foundation.* https://itif.org/publications/2021/08/30/promise-immersive-learning-augmented-and-virtual-reality-potential

Donally, J. (2021). The immersive classroom: Create customized learning experiences with AR/VR.. International Society for Technology in Education.

Dunleavy, M. (2014). Design principles for augmented reality learning. *TechTrends, 58*(1), 28–34. https://doi.org/10.1007/s11528-013-0717-2

EDUCAUSE Learning Initiative. (2005). *7 things you should know about augmented reality.* https://library.educause.edu/-/media/files/library/2005/10/eli7007-pdf

Flynn, C. & Frost, P. (2021, April 16). Making VR a reality in the classroom. *EDUCAUSE Review.* https://er.educause.edu/articles/2021/4/making-vr-a-reality-in-the-classroom

Fowler, C. (2014). Virtual reality and learning: Where is the pedagogy? *British Journal of Educational Technology, 46*(2), 412–422. https://doi.org/10.1111/bjet.12135

Grajek, S. and the 20221-2022 EDUCAUSE IT Issue Panel. (2021, November 1). Top 10 IT Issues, 2022: The higher education we deserve. *EDUCAUSE Review.* https://er.educause.edu/articles/2021/11/top-10-it-issues-2022-the-higher-education-we-deserve

Hinther, M. (2021, April 9). Education professor enhances virtual campus. *Campus News,* University of Saskatchewan. https://news.usask.ca/articles/colleges/2021/education-professor-enhances-virtual-campus.php

Jacobsen, M., Lock, J., & Friesen, S. (2013, January). Strategies for engagement: Knowledge building and intellectual engagement in participatory learning environments. *Education Canada, 53*(1), 14–18. https://www.edcan.ca/articles/strategies-for-engagement/

Makransky, G., & Mayer, R. E. (2022, April 22). Benefits of taking a virtual field trip in immersive virtual reality: Evidence for the immersion principle in multimedia learning. *Educational Psychology Review, 34*, 1771–1798. https://doi.org/10.1007/s10648-022-09675-4

Mulders, M., Buchner, J., & Kerres, M. (2020). A framework for the use of immersive virtual reality in learning environments. *International Journal of Emerging Technologies in Learning (iJET), 15*(24), 208–224. https://doi.org/10.3991/ijet.v15i24.16615

Pomerantz, J., & Rode, R. (2020, June 29). Exploring the future of extended reality in higher education. *EDUCAUSE Review*. https://er.educause.edu/articles/2020/6/exploring-the-future-of-extended-reality-in-higher-education

Slater, M. (1999). Measuring presence: A response to the Witmer and Singer presence questionnaire. *Presence: Teleoperators and Virtual Environments, 8*(5), 560–565. https://doi.org/10.1162/105474699566477

Southgate, E. (2020). *Virtual reality in curriculum and pedagogy: Evidence from secondary classrooms*. Routledge. https://doi.org/10.4324/9780429291982

Vergara, D., Extremera, J., Pablo Rubio, M., & Dávila, L. P. (2019). Meaningful learning through virtual reality learning environments: A case study in materials engineering. *Applied Sciences, 9*(21), 4625. https://doi.org/10.3390/app9214625

Willms, J. D., Friesen, S. & Milton, P. (2009, May). *What did you do in school today? Transforming classrooms through social, academic, and intellectual engagement*. Canadian Education Association. https://www.edcan.ca/wp-content/uploads/cea-2009-wdydist.pdf

Witmer, B. G., & Singer, M. J. (1998). Measuring presence in virtual environments: A presence questionnaire. *Presence: Teleoperators & Virtual Environments, 7*(3), 225–240. https://doi.org/10.1162/105474698565686

Jennifer Lock, PhD, is a Professor and Vice Dean in the Werklund School of Education, University of Calgary. Her area of specialization is in the Learning Sciences. Dr. Lock's research interests are e-learning, change and innovation in education, scholarship of teaching and learning in higher education, and learning in makerspaces.

Paula MacDowell, PhD, is an Assistant Professor in the College of Education, University of Saskatchewan. Her area of specialization is Educational Technology and Design (ETAD) with research interests in immersive education, emerging technologies, instructional design, and education for social and environmental change. Paula serves as the Practitioner Chair for the Immersive Learning Research Network (iLRN).

Part I
Designing Immersive Learning in K–12 Education

Designing an Interactive Science Exhibit: Using Augmented Reality to Increase Visitor Engagement and Achieve Learning Outcomes

Quincy Q. Wang

Abstract This chapter describes the collaborative design and development of an augmented reality (AR) science exhibition to spark learners' curiosity about science. Learners engage in an immersive experience in which science content is augmented with an interactive-digital experience. Analysis and evaluation results are used to suggest effective strategies for implementing AR immersive designs.

Keywords Augmented reality · Augmented reality learning environments · Augmented reality technology · Educational technology · Immersive learning · Immersive learning design · Learner engagement · Museum education

Introduction

Increasing students' engagement in the learning process motivates them to develop critical thinking skills, solve problems, and attain higher achievement (Carroll et al., 2021; Ito & Kawazoe, 2015; McCormick et al., 2015). An emerging technology that opens additional opportunities to engage students more fully, augmented reality (AR) has been widely explored and studied by educators worldwide. AR refers to layering computer-generated digital content with the physical real world; this digital layer synchronizes with the subject to augment physical environments (Akçayır & Akçayır, 2017; Azuma, 1997).

Research has revealed many ways in which AR contributes to students' engagement. Delivering digital content side by side with real-world objects generates positive attitudes and greater satisfaction during the learning process; highlights emotional qualities through sense of presence; creates an enjoyable experience through digital entertainment elements, hands-on activities, and interface style; and

Q. Q. Wang (✉)
Simon Fraser University, Burnaby, Canada
e-mail: quincy_wang@sfu.ca

© The Author(s), under exclusive license to Springer Nature Switzerland AG 2022
P. MacDowell, J. Lock (eds.), *Immersive Education*,
https://doi.org/10.1007/978-3-031-18138-2_2

promotes intrinsic motivation (Akçayır & Akçayır, 2017; Challenor & Ma, 2019; Cheng & Tsai, 2013; Wojciechowski & Cellary, 2013).

This chapter focuses on the design and development process for a specific AR application project—a beehive exhibit in a science centre—and on the interdisciplinary collaboration among researchers, instructional designers, and science centre curators who created an engaging learning environment to promote students' curiosity about science. The aim of this study is to contribute to the identification of effective immersive design principles and strategies and to provide recommendations for educators and instructional designers, thus allowing them to easily adopt and use AR technology to engage learners more effectively.

The chapter is divided into six parts. First is a vignette that illustrates how static objects in exhibit spaces neglect visitors' interests and their opportunities to engage in learning content. Second is an overview of engaged learning assisted by AR. Third is a contextual description of the object of study, an AR-integrated beehive exhibit at a science centre (an informal educational site on Canada's west coast), and a discussion of how AR is useful as a digital tool to deliver a novel learning experience that motivates learning. Fourth are detailed steps for applying an analysis, design, development, implementation, and evaluation model (ADDIE)—an instructional systems design framework adopted for the development of the AR-integrated beehive exhibit used in this study. Fifth are results from visitor feedback, provided to further improve the AR application. Sixth are immersive design strategies and principles of a theoretical approach for how AR technology can effectively connect content, learners, and exhibition space to create an engaging, interactive learning environment.

A note on the terminology: In the chapter, I use the word "learners" primarily to refer to visitors attending the science centre and interacting with the AR exhibit. Although many of the learners were students visiting the science centre, the AR exhibit was designed to engage all visitors (children, teachers, and adults) in the learning experience.

Vignette

Eric is an elementary science teacher. One of his science lessons is to teach his seven-year-old students about the life cycle of a honeybee. In order to help his students build the connection between knowledge learned in class and real-world experiences, he took them to the observation beehive in a science centre (Fig. 1) to give students first-hand experience and spark their curiosity about science. Although the beehive display in the centre was a state-of-the-art design, there were no live bees in the hive, and the vertical-stacked combs were covered by a black window for safety. Posters in the exhibit offered no content different than what can be found in a textbook. As a result, students spent only a few minutes at the beehive exhibit before moving on to other exhibits. Eric approached the science centre curator and asked if he could help design an AR app to make the honeybee life cycle content interesting and accessible, with the aim of motivating students to explore a bee's life beyond the display.

Fig. 1 The observation beehive exhibit

Overview: Engaged Learning Assisted by AR

In museum education, the inaccessibility of many exhibits can decrease visitors' interest in learning (Hall & Bannon, 2006). Artifacts are frequently inaccessible due to their fragile nature or for safety reasons; even when visitors are allowed to have a close look or, in exceptional cases, touch the exhibits, this is usually done with caution and has limitations. The resulting barrier between displays and learners in an exhibit space decreases learners' overall levels of engagement—including their attention, curiosity, interest, optimism, and passion for learning subjects. In the field of education, engagement refers to the vitality between learner and learning activities (Appleton et al., 2006). Types of engagements can include "intellectual engagement, emotional engagement, behavioural engagement, physical engagement, social engagement, and cultural engagement" (Glossary, 2016).

Museum exhibits with computer assisted technology can enhance engagement by generating new forms of social interactivity, models of behaviour, intelligibility of activities, and physical interactions to produce mutual engagement and improved appreciation of the exhibit (Heath & vom Lehn, 2008). Wang and Hsu's (2008) study also confirmed that learners' curiosity and engagement can be increased by creating a digital simulation learning environment. AR's capability to synchronize a person's physical environment with digital virtual content—to access, reveal, and augment the content beyond the object displayed—is attracting attention from museum educators. In Dunleavy's (2014) study, AR went beyond just a technology interface to acting as a way to visualize invisible phenomena. Enabling "authentic observation and interaction" (p. 32) promoted intellectual engagement by delivering knowledge through personal experiences in authentic simulated environments, allowing visitors to interact with digital content easily and naturally as if they were interacting with objects in the real world.

In addition, the learning content generated by AR is visible, dynamic, and entertaining, inviting learners to pay attention to important information. As a result, AR scaffolds knowledge through interactive learning experiences (Yoon et al., 2018). Compared to static learning content such as 2D text or image displays, interactive elements such as animations, 3D graphics, audio, video, and motion detection delivered by AR create an immersive and enjoyable learning environment. As Yoon and Wang (2014) point out, dynamic digital communication represented by AR helps the learning experience become authentic and informative, which presumably improves learners' understanding, performance, and engagement. Lee et al.'s (2021) museum education research also indicates that AR learning tools enhance educational activities in museums by "providing rich and realistic 3D images that activate the senses" (p. 475). Further, "AR technology creates a blend between the real world and the digital, bringing the digital 3D objects literally in our hands" (Kyriakou & Hermon, 2019, p. 1).

Context

Science centres and museums are informal learning places for students and the broader public to develop an understanding of science. Their purpose is to spark curiosity and extend scientific knowledge and appreciation of science to the community. Heath and vom Lehn's (2008) study indicates that science education sites continuously explore the use of new technologies to engage their audiences and enhance public understanding of science, often in informal and interpersonal ways. Conversations with the science centre staff in this study identified AR as an on-site, real-time digital facilitator of children's sense of curiosity and wonder in learning about science. The AR intervention for the beehive exhibit used in this study was intended to enhance the learning experience with a contextual connection, thereby enabling the learners' emotional and behavioural engagement.

The success of delivering such a project relies on multiple factors. First, from a technology development perspective, it is necessary to include pedagogical expertise, immersive technology design skills, and museum education knowledge. Therefore, the research team members included a researcher in educational technology and multimedia design, a graduate student in scientific literacy research, and two computer science undergraduate students experienced in game design. Second, from the learners' perspective, having their own handheld devices improves safety (especially in the context of the COVID-19 pandemic) and provides easier access to the digital experience. Finally, funding is crucial to accelerate and support research into how AR contributes to the community learning environment.

The research team, together with the science centre curators, chose the beehive exhibit because it could demonstrate the profound potential of AR contribution for informal science education. First, the learning challenge posed by the exhibit was the learners' inability to take a closer look or even touch the bees. Touching bees is not possible in the real world, but could AR make it possible? Second, day-to-day activities within the beehive occur only from May to August. Could AR make the learning content more accessible without those time constraints? Third, learners observe the hive through a glass window on one side (Fig. 2) and a glass tube connecting the window with the outside. This limited observation makes it challenging for learners to have a thorough understanding of bees' natural activity, including social interactions among the types of bees in the colony.

AR has potential as a value-added tool to improve a disengaged learning situation by (a) allowing learners to get closer to observe different bees through interacting and touching 3D digital bees, (b) seeing details inside the beehive by scrolling through a panoramic 360 degree image, (c) discovering aspects of bee behaviour and bees' relation to the natural world through hearing a soundscape in the hive and stories of the roles of worker, queen, and drone bees, and (d) increasing curiosity about the life cycle of bees and their vital role in the earth's biodiversity. Thus, intervention with AR to deliver a novel interaction with bees would help create curiosity about science, motivating visitors to learn more about the bee exhibit while enjoying the experience (Fig. 3).

Fig. 2 The viewing window of the observation beehive

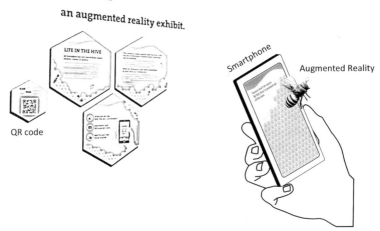

Fig. 3 Visitors use their own smartphone camera to scan a QR code and see a 3D bee live

ADDIE Employed in the AR Design and Development Process

The guiding principle of this study is to increase engagement through digital inter-activity via an AR application that can overcome constraints such as time, space, safety, and access limitations. The outcomes are furthering scientific knowledge development, facilitating knowledge acquisition, stimulating interest in the display, and making learning content relevant to individuals. For those reasons, this exhibit is defined as an intentional learning environment. Branch (2009) indicates that the ADDIE instructional design model is a proven and efficient framework with which to guide product development for an intentional learning environment. Studies from Wang and Hsu (2008) and Yu et al. (2021) have shown the promise of this frame-work for developing immersive interactive learning environments. Hence, the research team chose ADDIE as a framework for the AR app development. It needs to be emphasized that the ADDIE's five development phases are not discrete; instead, they overlap with each other to guide the development process with the ultimate goal of making the learning experience entertaining, interactive, and pleasant.

Analysis Phase

A needs analysis was the first step to identify stakeholder (learners') needs and the learning gap. The research team undertook an extensive literature review to under-stand the reasons for disengagement in museum and science centre learning environments. Often, visitors to these sites have limited access to artifacts due to their uniqueness, value, or a lack of physical space for exhibiting the objects (Kyriakou & Hermon, 2019). Further, Jahreie et al. (2011) found that students need to explore and play with exhibits to understand the meaning of objects in science museums. Otherwise, the artifacts are often treated as passive as in traditional museums, which set limitations on motivating children to learn and explore new knowledge (Lee et al., 2021). AR on the other hand stimulates learners' active exploration and generates curiosity about the artifacts, which makes the learning relevant to individuals' interests. AR also creates the potential, as Morey and Tinnell (2016) have pointed out, for "enhancing one's perceptual and cognitive experience of the spatiotemporal *here and now* ... precisely the ideal that orients AR" (p. 7).

In this phase, the researchers applied interactive learning theory: a pedagogical approach that incorporates technology into learning content delivery. Reeves and Hedberg's (2003) study reveals that digital interactive learning environments escalate authentic interactivity and create a new perspective of interactive learning systems. Learning science through implementing 3D simulations is effective and promises to promote science learning, the development of process skills, and the facilitation of conceptual change during interactive learning (Jacobson et al., 2016). The needs analysis deepened the researchers' theoretical understanding of how best to use AR to increase curiosity about scientific knowledge. It also informed the design principles for AR's pedagogical implementation, thus clarifying the role of AR as an interactive vehicle for providing scientific narratives that motivate and engage learners beyond passive learning. AR was envisioned as a magnifying glass to enhance meaning, thus bringing topics to life and making science exhibits more accessible, exciting, and innovative. It was expected that the AR experience would enhance learners' perception of, and interaction with, the beehive. It was also expected to help users understand more about what goes on in a beehive and about honeybee colony behaviours, including the different types of bees and their role in the colony, thus igniting learners' interest in ecology at large. Most importantly, the needs analysis phase also helped the researchers analyze the intersections of interactive learning theory and educational practices associated with AR, to build and appreciate physical places beyond time and space and reduce communication barriers for learners.

Design Phase

This phase focused on creating and developing the learning activities. The main affordance of AR is the delivery of embodied activities, thus combining hands-on experimentation with a novel experience to extend and stimulate learning and visualize otherwise invisible concepts. In alignment with desired pedagogical approaches and learning content, the researchers and science centre curators listed ways in which AR could be most effective for enhancing learners' engagement and appreciation for the beehive exhibit: (a) increase accessibility to the beehive by allowing learners to explore the combs covered by the darkened part of the glass (Fig. 2) through the AR interface by adding a motion control feature or scrolling on the AR application directly; (b) create hands-on *play* opportunities for learners by putting digital 3D bees literally in their hands to touch, observe, and rotate; and (c) avoid passive learning by combining visual elements, audio, and animation presentations to stimulate learners' interest and give learners agency by letting them pick the activity topic.

Also planned was a design that balances the physical exhibit space with the AR content. As such, learners would not only focus on the novelty of the technology but also enjoy the exhibit, thus gaining more meaning from and more appreciation of the physical displays in the exhibition. For example, the AR code was placed close to the exhibit artifact to scaffold interactions with real and virtual objects, and colourful graphic signage was placed in the centre of the exhibit to attract attention by introducing the AR learning content and explaining how to access the AR experience.

Development Phase

During the development phase, design concepts were applied to AR application development. This phase involved three activities. The first was to create the user interface (UI) and user experience (UX) flows. Designing for AR requires completely new ways of thinking about UI and UX. For envisioning how users will interact with the learning content, a user flow chart was created (Appendix A) to assist with and establish the structure of content delivery with learner-centred design thinking. The chart informed developers that the core of the app is representing different types of bees in real life by using 3D bees to guide the learning journey.

The second development activity was to choose an AR platform. There are many on the market, so a team consisting of a curriculum designer, a pedagogy researcher, and two computing science students listed, reviewed, and compared the pros and cons of different AR application platforms. The following list of considerations guided the final choice:

- Licence fee: the platform needed to be open-sourced because the funding was for one year only.
- User-end consideration: users would not need to download an app; that would distract from their learning experience, and they could lose enthusiasm.
- Access to free Wi-Fi connection to visitors: the AR app must be able to connect to the cloud server space without consuming memory on users' own devices.
- Multimedia file formats: must support real-time 3D development.
- Ease for developer: ability to efficiently create, manipulate, and update AR user flow.
- Scalability: allow customization and future expansion.

After considering the comparisons, the team decided to combine an open-source platform (*Unity*) and an AR toolkit (*ZapWorks* Universal AR SDK) to create the application. This choice also allowed the researchers to work within the funding mandate received for this project, which is to advocate and encourage research collaboration with local communities and to mobilize the research to benefit diverse stakeholders.

The third activity was to list key development features. To foster an inclusive design culture and promote the value of learner-centred design and digital accessibility within the open community space, the researchers envisioned features such as using a QR code to activate the AR experience, using 3D animated bees to apply interactive learning theory for engagement, applying responsive design so that content can be adjusted for differing screen sizes of various handheld devices, ensuring a consistent user experience across operating systems such as Android and iOS, and saving and continuing the learning activities at school or home.

Implementation Phase

The purpose of the implementation phase was to shift the work from the AR development stage to the exhibition where visitors would interact with the AR. The QR code was disseminated to science centre curators, teachers, and educational researchers for critique before printing the QR code and on-the-wall signage (Fig. 4). Curators and graphic designers created a visual atmosphere through signage and posters for attracting visitors to experience AR. During the pandemic, fewer staff were able to assist visitors; therefore, the AR app became the primary facilitator in the beehive exhibit to engage visitors. We learned that well-designed signage encourages observation and sparks visitors' conversation about the display as well as promoting the AR exhibit. Such visual cues are also an easy way to build a connection among visitors, the exhibit, and AR technology. This implementation phase was also a transition to prepare the evaluation activities and place the actual product into action for the visitor engagement process.

Evaluation Phase

The evaluation phase had two parts: internal and on-site evaluation. First, the researchers conducted rapid user testing internally with science centre staff to evaluate whether desired results were achieved. Second, the researchers moved to a quantitative on-site evaluation to review the beta version of the AR by conducting surveys with a small number of visitors. The survey questions (see Appendix B) focused on user experiences to understand whether the AR was easy to use and added meaningful value to their experience.

Fig. 4 Signage for beehive exhibit

Twenty beehive exhibit visitors (14 families and six individuals) were asked to fill out a brief survey immediately after their interaction with the AR exhibit. The target audience for the exhibit is children aged 7 and older, so most visitors were parents accompanied by their children (parents used their own devices to assist children in exploring the wonders of the beehive). Six questions were asked, focusing on the functionality of the AR app on various visitors' own handheld devices, the ease of using the app, any confusion about the app, and any comments. Analysis of the responses indicated that the AR app functioned successfully. As seen in Fig. 5, visitors' responses were mostly positive. Visitors were satisfied and understood how to use AR in the beehive exhibit.

In the final open-ended question (not included in Fig. 5), users responded that this was a cool idea for the exhibit and that they were motivated to visit the hive when live bees came back. Though this is a very small data set (a beta-version to inform further development), responses to the last question suggested there was more confusion than satisfaction. Most comments among the 11 visitor groups indicated they did not know how to interact with the AR bees (although, because the digital bees are very cute, they were motivated to interact and play with them more). Another outstanding issue is that on some visitors' phones, the bees disappeared from the phone screen if the position of the phone was changed too quickly.

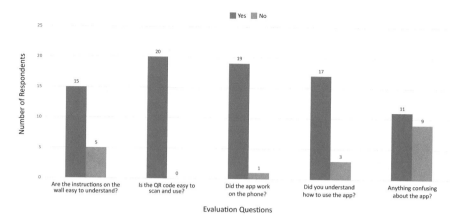

Fig. 5 Visitor responses from the onsite evaluation of the AR app (beta version)

Improving the AR Application

Challenor and Ma's (2019) research showed there are learning curves for users experiencing AR because of the potential for cognitive overload. Their research result is consistent with our evaluation results. To address visitors' confusion about how to play with 3D digital bees, an updated version was created that included a short tutorial on how to interact with 3D bees on users' own phones (Fig. 6). This improvement increased users' confidence using the AR app. Additionally, transcripts were added to the animation videos to address disability needs, and changes were made to some of the English vocabulary in the story to allow English-as-an-additional-language learners to acquire content more easily.

Strategies for Implementing AR Immersive Design

To begin the immersive design process, having a clear sense of the learning goal provides focus and guidance for each step of the design development so it is manageable. The learning goal when designing AR activities can be seen as an inquiry intersecting storytelling with meaning-making. A clear goal serves as the backbone of the AR instructional design structure.

- **Creating effective UX assets.** "UX assets" in this study refers to user flows, storyboards, multimedia, and visual elements. In this case, "effective" means two things: UX assets spark users' interest, desire, and motivation to participate in AR activities, and the AR activities achieve the learning outcomes. Therefore, designers need to be creative in ensuring that UX assets—such as colours, shapes, animations, audio, and video—interrelate with learning content to connect with target audiences and achieve learning goals. Preparing and working on

Fig. 6 Graphic tutorial on how to play with the 3D bees

UX assets is an essential step before programming in an AR platform. Effective UX assets also motivate AR application developers to enjoy the development process and can stimulate more innovative ideas.

- **Having learners in mind.** The design and development of AR immersive learning environments should have a target audience in mind. Developers need to consider the audience's knowledge and technology skill level. For example, the primary age range of this study's target learners is 7 to 12 years. Therefore, an age-appropriate short tutorial embedded in the app, and a text and infographic explanation in the physical space, can facilitate use of the app. Also, developers need to be aware of learners' tolerance for the length of content delivery so that this additional layer of interpretation is not overwhelming. While designing educational programs, it is helpful for educators, designers, and developers to remember that AR technology is not meant to replace face-to-face learning, but to complement and facilitate it.

- **Developing narrative structure.** Through storytelling and stories, AR becomes a learning tool that "penetrates the heart of the student" (Donally, 2018). Integrating an engaging narrative structure with an AR app can help enhance learners' understanding and inspire their imagination. Narrative structure frames the story. Unlike traditional modes of storytelling, stories in AR are superimposed onto the learner's existing real-world context. As Kumpulainen et al. (2020) note, "augmented storying enabled the children to enact living and imaginative inquiries into themselves as well as other human and non-human beings through playful, affective, sensuous, identity, cultural, and critical literacies" (p. 3). With this suggestion in mind, stories in AR should be developed with compelling narratives that have clear plot lines for emotional engagement, intersecting with conceptual learning. Interactive storytelling in AR design invites learners to be inquirers who explore and navigate embedded stories while reflecting on their own learning background and lived experience.

- **Encouraging interdisciplinary collaboration with STEM.** Implementing AR technology highlights the interdisciplinary nature of this work. The definition of *interdisciplinary* in this project is a collaborative team approach involving people with diverse skills and expertise. Thus, interdisciplinary collaboration is key to the success of an AR design in an informal learning setting. In this project, as stated above, the team consisted of a graduate student with extensive backgrounds in science education and curriculum theory, a researcher with expertise in educational technology and multimedia design, and undergraduate students from a computing science program who were enthusiastic about coding and game design. Science centre staff and volunteers offered extensive knowledge of museum education and usage of space; they curated the learning content and provided the logistics to enact the AR technology. Interdisciplinary collaboration allowed the researchers to work with experts from educational psychology, science education, learning design, and educational technology. Through this collaborative process, participants learned much from each other and thus leveraged their knowledge for innovation.

Conclusion

The AR platform in the science centre beehive exhibit provided teachers with an opportunity to extend their science curricula and lessons, enabled visitors to increase their sense of wonder and curiosity, delivered a complex science topic more efficiently, and cultivated a culture of active learning, which ultimately contributed another informal learning space in the community. As one elementary school teacher commented while providing informal feedback, "this is a great inquiry learning tool for elementary students to become curious and want to engage more with learning bee ecology. It provides a close-up experience to observe bees that may be impossible in real life."

This AR development project for a science centre highlights the potential of AR immersive technology for educators, instructional designers, and AR immersive application developers. The experiment of designing and implementing an AR app encouraged the researchers to be more creative in developing immersive technology pedagogies in a consistent manner. For learners, the project enhanced the experience of the beehive, which has now been transformed into a more engaging, entertaining, and interesting educational experience that also helps learners retain scientific knowledge longer. For educators, appropriate development of AR experiences reduces barriers created by limited resources such as funding, skills, and time to adapt emerging technology into teaching practice.

As of today, although AR contributes to education by creating high-context forms of learning situated within real world environments, it has not fully reached its potential to enrich learning because of a lack of consistent research on its effectiveness. In addition, there are still challenges arising from technological limitations. For example, there are no sufficient "off the shelf" platforms for teachers to easily adopt for their classrooms. The design and development solutions proposed in this chapter shed light on applying AR in education with a limited budget; the design model is affordable, scalable, and achievable for most educators if people with expertise are willing to work together. Utilizing the affordances of AR to engage learning and develop curiosity about science subjects, the design principles offered in this chapter make specific pedagogical contexts *live* and thus leverage contemporary digital experience to benefit informal educational spaces like science centres, community centres, and museums. Educators should not fear incorporating emerging technology into curricula. Rather, we need to be open to and share new discoveries, resources, and creative pedagogical strategies to bravely move into new dimensions of teaching and learning.

Acknowledgments This chapter is the result of collaborative work with a science centre on Canada's west coast. The author would like to express gratitude to all who generously contributed their museum education knowledge to this project. The community-based research funding was supported by a Community Engagement Initiative (CEI) grant from Simon Fraser University, Canada.

Appendices

Appendix A: Flowchart

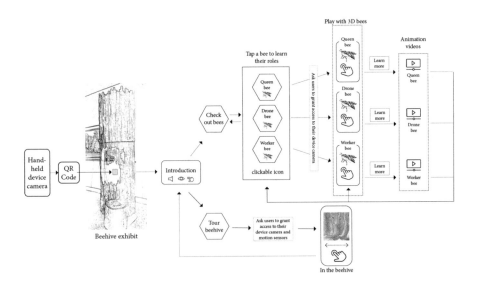

Appendix B: Onsite Survey Questions

1. Are the instructions on the wall easy to understand?
2. Is the QR code easy to scan and use?
3. Did the AR app work on your phone? If not, what phone do you have?
4. Did you understand how to use the AR app?
5. Was there anything that was confusing about the app? Can you explain what was confusing?
6. Are there any other comments that you would like to share?

References

Akçayır, M., & Akçayır, G. (2017). Advantages and challenges associated with augmented reality for education: A systematic review of the literature. *Educational Research Review, 20,* 1–11. https://doi.org/10.1016/j.edurev.2016.11.002

Appleton, J. J., Christenson, S. L., Kim, D., & Reschly, A. L. (2006). Measuring cognitive and psychological engagement: Validation of the student engagement instrument. *Journal of School Psychology, 44*(5), 427–445. https://doi.org/10.1016/j.jsp.2006.04.002

Azuma, R. T. (1997). A survey of augmented reality. *Presence: Teleoperators and Virtual Environments, 6*(4), 355–385.

Branch, R. M. (2009). *Instructional design: The ADDIE approach.* Springer Science & Business Media.

Carroll, M., Lindsey, S., Chaparro, M., & Winslow, B. (2021). An applied model of learner engagement and strategies for increasing learner engagement in the modern educational environment. *Interactive Learning Environments, 29*(5), 757–771. https://doi.org/10.1080/1049482 0.2019.1636083

Challenor, J., & Ma, M. (2019). A review of augmented reality applications for history education and heritage visualisation. *Multimodal Technologies and Interaction, 3*(2), 39. https://doi.org/10.3390/mti3020039

Cheng, K.-H., & Tsai, C.-C. (2013). Affordances of augmented reality in science learning: Suggestions for future research. *Journal of Science Education and Technology, 22*(4), 449–462. https://doi.org/10.1007/s10956-012-9405-9

Donally, J. (2018, April 4). Unleash the power of storytelling with these new AR and VR tools. *EdSurge.* https://www.edsurge.com/news/2018-04-04-unleash-the-power-of-storytelling-with-these-new-ar-and-vr-tools

Dunleavy, M. (2014). Design principles for augmented reality learning. *TechTrends, 58*(1), 28–34. https://doi.org/10.1007/s11528-013-0717-2

Glossary of Education Reform. (2016, February 18). *Student Engagement Definition.* https://www.edglossary.org/student-engagement/

Hall, T., & Bannon, L. (2006). Designing ubiquitous computing to enhance children's learning in museums. *Journal of Computer Assisted Learning, 22*(4), 231–243. https://doi.org/10.1111/j.1365-2729.2006.00177.x

Heath, C., & vom Lehn, D. (2008). Configuring "interactivity": Enhancing engagement in science centres and museums. *Social Studies of Science, 38*(1), 63–91. https://doi.org/10.1177/0306312707084152

Ito, H., & Kawazoe, N. (2015). Active learning for creating innovators: Employability skills beyond industrial needs. *International Journal of Higher Education, 4*(2), 81–91. http://dx.doi.org/https://doi.org/10.5430/ijhe.v4n2p81

Jacobson, M. J., Taylor, C. E., & Richards, D. (2016). Computational scientific inquiry with virtual worlds and agent-based models: New ways of doing science to learn science. *Interactive Learning Environments, 24*(8), 2080–2108. https://doi.org/10.1080/10494820.2015.1079723

Jahreie, C. F., Arnseth, H. C., Krange, I., Smørdal, O., & Kluge, A. (2011). Designing for play-based learning of scientific concepts: Digital tools for bridging school and science museum contexts. *Children, Youth and Environments, 21*(2), 236–255.

Kumpulainen, K., Burke, A., & Ntelioglou, B. Y. (2020). Young children, maker literacies and social change. *Education Sciences, 10*(10), 1–5. https://doi.org/10.3390/educsci10100265

Kyriakou, P., & Hermon, S. (2019). Can I touch this? Using natural interaction in a museum augmented reality system. *Digital Applications in Archaeology and Cultural Heritage, 12*, 1–9. https://doi.org/10.1016/j.daach.2018.e00088

Lee, J., Lee, H.-K., Jeong, D., Lee, J., Kim, T., & Lee, J. (2021). Developing museum education content: AR blended learning. *The International Journal of Art & Design Education, 40*(3), 473–491. https://doi.org/10.1111/jade.12352

McCormick, N. J., Clark, L. M., & Raines, J. M. (2015). Engaging students in critical thinking and problem solving: A brief review of the literature. *Journal of Studies in Education, 5*(4), 100–113. https://doi.org/10.5296/jse.v5i4.8249

Morey, S., & Tinnell, J. (Eds.). (2016). *Augmented reality: Innovative perspectives across art, industry, and academia.* Parlor Press LLC..

Reeves, T. C., & Hedberg, J. G. (2003). *Interactive learning systems evaluation. Educational Technology.* Publications.

Wang, S.-K., & Hsu, H.-Y. (2008, November 17). Using the ADDIE model to design Second Life activities for online learners. In C. Bonk, M. Lee, & T. Reynolds (Eds.), *Proceedings of E-Learn 2008—world conference on E-learning in corporate, government, healthcare, and higher education* (pp. 2045–2050). Association for the Advancement of Computing in Education (AACE).

Wojciechowski, R., & Cellary, W. (2013). Evaluation of learners' attitude toward learning in ARIES augmented reality environments. *Computers and Education, 68*, 570–585. https://doi.org/10.1016/j.compedu.2013.02.014

Yoon, S. A., & Wang, J. (2014). Making the invisible visible in science museums through augmented reality devices. *TechTrends, 58*(1), 49–55. https://doi.org/10.1007/s11528-013-0720-7

Yoon, S. A., Anderson, E., Park, M., Elinich, K., & Lin, J. (2018). How augmented reality, textual, and collaborative scaffolds work synergistically to improve learning in a science museum. *Research in Science & Technological Education, 36*(3), 261–281. https://doi.org/10.1080/02635143.2017.1386645

Yu, S.-J., Hsueh, Y.-L., Sun, J. C.-Y., & Liu, H.-Z. (2021). Developing an intelligent virtual reality interactive system based on the ADDIE model for learning pour-over coffee brewing. *Computers and Education: Artificial Intelligence, 2*(100), 030. https://doi.org/10.1016/j.caeai.2021.100030

Quincy Q. Wang is a doctoral student in Educational Technology and Learning Design at the Faculty of Education, Simon Fraser University, Canada. Her research interests include immersive learning experiences with augmented reality and virtual reality, simulation-based learning, learning sciences, and web technology for knowledge co-creation and dissemination. She currently works at the Faculty of Education, Simon Fraser University.

Augmented and Virtual Reality in the Classroom: Adding a Postdigital Perspective to Backward Design Lesson Planning

Annie Beaumier and Marguerite Koole

Abstract This chapter is written for current educators who are interested in integrating augmented (AR) and virtual reality (VR) into their current lesson-development and teaching practice. This chapter offers the reader an opportunity to consider these technologies from a new philosophical perspective: the postdigital.

Keywords Analog · Augmented reality · Backward design framework · Constructivist · Conceptualization · Digital · Postdigital · Virtual reality

Introduction

In our day-to-day lives, humans are surrounded by living and non-living things. As we go about our regular activities, we forget about the tight interrelationships amongst all that surrounds us. These interrelationships are complex. Colloquially, we often refer to computers as digital; however, as we will argue in this chapter, computers may be analog or digital. That is, some computers offer continuous, analog measures/experiences (such as a thermometer or a movie) and others provide discrete, countable measures (such as bits or the individual cells of a 35 mm film). The digital and analog nature of our computing tools is so ubiquitous and seamless that their characteristics are often rendered invisible to us. In other words, these tools no longer seem novel or noteworthy; they have become *postdigital*. Postdigital is a philosophical perspective in which old and new media form hybrids, old media are used like new media, or old media become repurposed (Cramer, 2015; Jandrić & Hayes, 2020).

A. Beaumier (✉)
Saskatchewan Polytechnic, Saskatoon, SK, Canada
e-mail: beaumiera@saskpolytech.ca

M. Koole
University of Saskatchewan, Saskatoon, SK, Canada
e-mail: m.koole@usask.ca

© The Author(s), under exclusive license to Springer Nature Switzerland AG 2022
P. MacDowell, J. Lock (eds.), *Immersive Education*,
https://doi.org/10.1007/978-3-031-18138-2_3

A postdigital analysis reveals that augmented reality (AR) and virtual reality (VR) are phenomena with *both* digital (discrete values such as numbers or bits) *and* analog (continuous variability such as an oil painting) characteristics (Cramer, 2015). In practice, this seemingly confounding nature of analog-digital phenomena may render it difficult to develop or choose pedagogical approaches since teachers and students are generally not trained to notice or differentiate between digital and analog. Both AR and VR can add a different kind of reality in which the learner senses *being there,* potentially impacting their sense of relationality with the environment. We suggest that a major benefit of designing AR and VR lessons with a postdigital sensitivity is to increase learners' appreciation for the interrelation of all living (i.e., animals, plants, and insects) and non-living things (i.e., machines and computers) within the environment. We propose that a better understanding of digital and analog characteristics can help teachers envision creative possibilities for integrating AR, VR, and other technologies in the classroom. For example, a typical class can discuss the impact of humans on the environment by referring to examples, showing pictures, and playing videos. On the other hand, through a mobile AR application, learners can aim their cameras at an environment and read information bubbles, listen to audio, or watch videos about people and objects in their surrounding environment. Alternatively, using a VR application, students can virtually walk on, fly over, or swim through environments and choose actions that stimulate changes in waterways, air temperature, or other environmental elements.

Starting from a social constructivist lens (Jonassen, 1998; Vygotsky, 1978) familiar to most teachers, this chapter is organized in the following way. We begin with a vignette to set the context and tone of the chapter, followed by a discussion of AR and VR in education. We then introduce the postdigital perspective, providing history and origins of this perspective and how it is defined. Next, we discuss the *analog* and *digital* characteristics of AR and VR as well as the freedom and constraints they afford. Having examined these philosophical and conceptual aspects, we present a sample AR lesson using the *World Wildlife Federation (WWF) Free-Flowing Rivers* app. The lesson is designed using a practical and well-established lesson development framework called *backward design* (Wiggins & McTighe, 2005). The sample lesson offers commentary that illustrates how a postdigital perspective can inform the lesson design. We speculate how the lesson might be altered by and questioned through the shifting of postdigital attributes. We conclude by offering a checklist of practical design considerations for including postdigital perspectives into AR and VR lessons, using the backward design framework.

In this chapter, we start with familiar concepts such as social constructivism and backward design and expand towards less familiar concepts (i.e., the postdigital) and technologies (i.e., AR and VR). We aim to show how a postdigital sensitivity might assist educators in more deeply interrogating *and* inspiring their use of AR and VR in the classroom as well as helping learners to better comprehend their interrelationship with social and material environments.

Vignette

The Grade 8 classroom was abuzz as the kids were anticipating the AR lesson on waterways. As the lesson began, Robby started daydreaming about the marshy swale near his house. The last time he rode his bike through there, he saw a sign which said that the nearby South Saskatchewan River used to flow through this area years ago, leaving behind this old riverbed pathway. He wondered, "What had caused the river to change its course?" Suddenly, Robby's reveries were interrupted as the class began talking, shifting around, and picking up their phones. Using the WWF Free-Flowing Rivers AR app, Robby's group decided to add a virtual dam in a particular spot on a river to see what would happen. Sure enough, the virtual water started collecting above the dam while the flow lessened downstream (Fig. 1). However, the group realized that's not what happened here with the South Saskatchewan. They began discussing how they could create their own simulation in relation to the swale. They could get some silly putty and create a scene with trees, rocks, water, and other discrete things (digital elements) and create a video (a continuous, analog product). The teacher was amazed at how easily the students shifted between digital and analog in their thinking. After the teacher made the group aware of their 'shifting', the group considered how they could shift even more. Someone suggested using stop motion animation (digital) to create a video (analog) … Another group member suggested repurposing the videos to create their own AR activity! The ideas began ricocheting from person to person. Robby could hardly get a word in edgewise! The excitement and creativity were palpable.

Fig. 1 Screenshot of the Build-a-Dam feature of the WWF app

AR and VR in Education

AR and VR technologies have already begun to take on a prominent role in our society. VR has been used by the military in Western countries in the Army, Air Force, and Navy for flight as well as for battlefield simulations and treating post-traumatic stress disorder (Sokhanych, 2018). AR and VR are gradually spreading across many areas of education: K–12, higher education, and informal learning contexts. Dick (2021) provides a lengthy list of AR and VR resources for K–12, special education, science, technology, engineering, and math (STEM) education, medical training, arts and humanities, soft skills and careers development, technical education, and teacher training. AR and VR technologies have the potential to expand learning environments "by reducing barriers from physical space, enhancing collaboration and hands-on learning, and providing individualized learning approaches that can help students at all levels thrive" (Dick, 2021, p. 1).

AR and VR in education can facilitate a move away from the traditional *chalk and talk* teaching methods and towards experiential adventures that foster a greater sense of learner presence and embodiment. Learning through 3D modeling can make abstract concepts seem more concrete and manipulable. In 2005, Cline wrote that

> the adoption and integration of virtual reality in education will also signal a much-needed shift away from learning that is too abstract and disconnected from practice and experience and empower students by offering a more experiential mode of learning and promoting the need for conceptual understanding. (p. 154).

Drawing upon the work of Krokos et al. (2019), Dick (2021) notes,

> immersive experiences have been shown to reduce cognitive load and distance, encourage higher engagement, and improve memory recall for complex or abstract topics, such as STEM (science, technology, engineering, and mathematics) subjects that often rely on two-dimensional representations of otherwise intangible concepts. (p. 2).

AR and VR may help students not only to grasp abstract concepts but also foster critical thinking. Elmqaddem (2019) argues that "the value of adopting virtual reality in education and learning is related in part to the fact that this technology can improve and facilitate learning, increase memory capacity and make better decisions while working in entertaining and stimulating conditions" (p. 237). Sotiriou and Bogner (2008) add that AR and VR can help learners develop better investigation skills and gain more accurate knowledge on a given topic.

In addition to supporting active learning and cognitive development, AR and VR can have positive effects on motivation and engagement while also decreasing risk (Dick, 2021). Eastman et al. (2011) report in their study that with the implementation of AR in classes, 87% of students reported they would be more likely to attend class, and 72% said they were more likely to actively participate (p. 32). Similarly, Fatih Özcan et al. (2017) observe that "the use of augmented reality in education and training environments has positive contributions to student success and satisfaction" (p. 27). On a practical level, AR and VR may offer a safe way to learn skills for high-risk situations: "an obvious advantage of virtual reality is that this technology allows a learner to experience environments, which cannot be experienced in the real world due to the cost and/or risk factors" (Chen, 2009, p. 75). For example, in the vignette the *WWF AR* app allows the students to explore activities outside the realm of possibility in a classroom, such as building dams.

From Constructivism to Postdigital

Ertmer and Newby (2013) argue that humans not only create meaning from experience, but that it is important for learners to "elaborate on and interpret information" (p. 56). They add that to achieve this higher-level thinking, learners should be provided with "the means to create novel and situation-specific understandings" (p. 56). For example, in the vignette for this chapter, Robby's group engages in elaboration and interpretation as they imagine what strategies, materials, and media they can use to better understand the swale on the outskirts of their city. The vignette shows how Robbie connects his prior experiences with the new, unfamiliar technology as he actively attempts to understand the swale situation. This is what we mean by constructivist pedagogy: a learning approach in which learners are encouraged to negotiate meaning and build upon their prior knowledge. As Chen (2009) notes, "constructivist philosophy holds that knowledge is constructed through an individual's interaction with the environment" (p. 73). AR and VR both offer opportunities for learning through immersion in an exploratory environment as well as personal and social negotiation of meaning.

An important goal in a constructivist classroom is to create a collaborative problem-solving environment where students become active rather than passive participants in their learning. Active learning can occur when learners manipulate objects or affect the environment in some way (Jonassen, 1998). By using virtual technologies in a constructivist approach, teachers can orchestrate a student-centred learning experience and "manipulation space" (Chen, 2009, p. 75) where students can actively control what they want to explore. Mixed reality has been shown to support collaborative learning modalities in adaptive and creative environments in which people may blend aspects of the physical world and the virtual world (Martín-Gutiérrez et al., 2017). Combined with good pedagogical approaches, AR and VR can offer meaningful social interaction with opportunities for inquiry learning. Driscoll (2005) lists five constructivist conditions for learning that would, hypothetically, lead to good pedagogical practices:

1. Embed learning in complex, realistic, and relevant environments.
2. Provide for social negotiation as an integral part of learning.
3. Support multiple perspectives and the use of multiple modes of representation.
4. Encourage ownership in learning.
5. Nurture self-awareness of the knowledge construction process. (pp. 393–394)

In the vignette, when Robby shares his thoughts about the swale, the group starts negotiating their strategy for creating their own environmental simulation. The situation is complex and realistic: the learners negotiate, they share their perspectives, and they start to show signs of awareness, moving in the direction of postdigital sensitivity as described in the next section. Constructivist pedagogical approaches can be complemented with a postdigital perspective in which teachers can ask the learners to envision technology in different ways while at the same time negotiating meaning, elaborating, strategizing, and blending aspects of the physical and virtual world.

What Is Postdigital?

A postdigital sensitivity can help educators raise awareness of how technology, such as VR and AR, is "already embedded in, and entangled with, existing social practices and economic and political systems" (Knox, 2019, p. 358). Without such an awareness, learners may not realize how they, as human beings, affect and are affected by the environment or—for that matter—other living things (i.e., animals, plants, and insects) and non-living things (i.e., machines and computers) (Jandrić & Hayes, 2020). The lack of awareness may result in poor decisions such as over-use or uncritical use of resources, possibly impacting local or global poverty, climate change, economic conditions, and other important socio-political-economic issues. For this reason, we have turned to the postdigital approach to complement constructivist pedagogy.

The postdigital movement had its beginnings in art, music, and aesthetics (Andrews, 2000; Cascone, 2000; Metzinger, 2018). Rather than representing a rejection of computer technology, it is more so characterized by *pervasiveness*; that is, the digital has become such a prevalent aspect of social-material interactions that it is no longer regarded as something external or other (Knox, 2019). By this account, all education is *blended* in that digital and analog elements are entangled, socially, materially, and temporally—so much so that it is easy to forget how they co-construct our world. The *post* prefix may also suggest *after* digitization in which the disruption has already occurred; postdigital is the aftermath when technologies and associated processes are repurposed. Old media become used in new ways or with new sensibilities. For some theorists, "the term 'post-digital' usefully describes 'new media'-cultural approaches to working with so-called 'old media'" (Cramer, 2015, p. 21). There is a subtle movement from the illusory *perfection of the digital* back to analog, from post-modern to modern (Andrews, 2000; cited in Cramer, 2015)—or to illustrate, "vinyl as anti-CD, cassette tapes as anti-MP3, analog film as anti-video" (Cramer, 2015, p. 21). In education, AR and VR can permit this type of *shifting* between forms such as analog and digital, described in detail in the next section. Teachers' awareness of such *shiftings* may result in creative ideas and enhancement of pedagogical practices.

Analog Versus Digital

At a colloquial level, the word *digital* has come to refer to anything pertaining to computers or electronic devices (Cramer, 2015). In fact, this is not the original meaning. Rather, an etymological analysis of *digital* shows us that it originally referred to fingers (the digits of one's hand). It later came to mean "signals or information represented by discrete values of a physical quantity such as voltage" (Stevenson, 2010a). The *Oxford English Dictionary* defines analog as "relating to or using signals or information represented by a continuously variable physical quantity" (Stevenson, 2010b). Time displayed using hour and minute hands is analog, while time displayed with discrete numbers is digital. An ancient Roman mosaic is digital because it comprises individual pieces to make up the whole (Cramer, 2015). It is also important not to construe analog as the opposite of computational (Cramer, 2015). An analog computer processes continuous data while a digital computer processes binary code (discrete units of input become 1 s and 0 s) (Satayabrata, 2020). A thermometer (temperature) and a barometer (pressure) are examples of analog computers. "The structure of an analog signal is determined entirely by its correspondence (analogy) with the original physical phenomenon which it mimics" (Cramer, 2015, p. 18). A barometer indicates in real-time the atmospheric pressure; as pressure changes, the barometric instrument simultaneously indicates change. Table 1 summarizes the ontological and epistemological characteristics of analog and digital.

Postdigital Conceptualizations of AR and VR

It may be easy for people to conceptualize AR and VR; indeed, some philosophers suggest that it is not much different from our current experiences of everyday consciousness: "the conscious experience produced by biological nervous systems *is* a virtual model of the world—a dynamic simulation" (Metzinger, 2018, p. 3). In other words, our experience of the world is mediated through our sensory-motor capabilities and interpreted through our brains, outside of which we cannot achieve ontological certainty.

At a psychological level, Metzinger (2018) suggests VR is a form of hallucination, similar to a dreamlike state in which our sensory organs and our brains are constantly creating representations of the world. To explain, the human brain

Table 1 Ontology and epistemology of analog and digital

	Ontology	Epistemology
Analog	Correspondence to physical phenomenon/a	Observed through continuity; continuous variability, such as a naturalistic painting
Digital	Perfect (seemingly) representation and reproduction	Observed through discrete values such as numbers, bits, pieces such as a mosaic or pointillism

interacts with visual and auditory stimuli (whether in real life [IRL] or computer-generated) to create an "integrated ontology" experienced in a given "lived moment" (Metzinger, 2018, p. 4). As with how we experience presence or situatedness in our day-to-day world, we can experience presence in virtual worlds. People can interact with and act upon that which is perceived. The difference between our experience of presence in IRL or VR can be difficult to ascertain. As Metzinger (2018) suggests, some VR applications aim at creating realistic experiences that provide a strong sense of embodiment in time and space, while others aim to create more dream-like experiences.

According to Chalmers (2017), "a virtual reality environment is an immersive, interactive, computer-generated environment" (p. 312). Because it is computer-generated, it is labelled as virtual, yet because humans can perceive it and interact with it, it is also considered a form of reality (Chalmers, 2017). "Most 'digital media' devices are in fact analog-to-digital-to-analog converters" (Cramer, 2015, p. 23): for example, AR and VR rely on coding, decoding, and recoding, and both rely heavily on visual display. Although pixels (and light particles if seen through the appropriate apparatus) are digital in nature, the experience of light waves (as seen with the naked eye) is analog.

Table 2 provides a summary of Chalmers' (2017) categories of VR as well as examples related to the vignette and examples for classroom implementation.

Arguably, since AR is a form of semi-immersive or non-immersive reality (Greenwald, 2021), it can be referred to as "mixed reality" (Chalmers, 2017, p. 314). AR "adds an environmental layer that is invisible for others, superimposing a new and additional set of priors onto the conscious subject's model of reality" (Metzinger, 2018, p. 14). AR allows the blending of IRL and VR. In VR, people can violate the physical laws of IRL (ontological freedom). AR, however, tethers activity to physical laws (ontological constraints) yet, like VR, extends epistemological possibilities. Table 3 compares the ontology and epistemology of AR and VR.

While it is beyond the scope of this chapter to determine the underlying ontological (*real*) nature of AR and VR environments, we can safely suggest that these technologies can have an impact at an epistemological level (*how we come to know*). To illustrate the concepts in Table 3, consider how a learner interacts with AR: the learner is immersed in a physical environment; the environment is analog with a correspondence of 100%; upon this environment, various analog and digital elements can be overlaid such as text annotations and labels, video, and audio; the overlays provide additional information about the physical environment. In a VR environment, the learner can navigate freely and manipulate objects within a 3D environment constrained only by the rules programmed into the environment.

Table 2 Types of VR

Type	Description	Examples for the classroom
Immersive	An environment in which one has a sense of being present in a three-dimensional space that can be explored with visual, auditory, and possibly tactile senses. Sensory tools are required, such as headsets, speakers, and visual displays	The students in the vignette could create and/or view a 360° video of the swale to see if it captures any informative details to help them build their simulation
Non-immersive	"Computer-generated interactive environments displayed on a desktop computer or television screens" (p. 313). Involve virtual worlds but may not be a type of VR. Some suggest that AR fits into this category (Greenwald, 2021)	Video games such as *Endling* (critique of habitat construction), *Temtem* (a pre-man-made-climate change world emphasizing coexistence and eco-friendliness) or *Bee Simulator* (raising awareness of the issues of bee survival) can be played on desktop computers in a classroom (Maher, 2020)
Interactive	An environment in which someone's actions can affect, direct, or change objects or environmental characteristics. Input devices are needed to track head and body movements as well as controllers, keyboards, and mice to permit interaction	Wii video games, flight simulators; a remote-controlled robot with a desktop display. *Second Life* could allow learners to create a simulation of the swale which their avatars could walk through and explore
Non-interactive	Passive simulations: Sensory tools are required, such as headsets, speakers, and visual displays	Computer-generated movies. In the vignette, Robby and the group could create an AR application that simply allows the user to project text, image, or video overlays but lacks any button clicking or other actions (i.e., view only)
Non-computer generated	"Immersive and interactive camera-generated environments" (p. 313)	In our vignette case, Robby and the group could attempt to combine robotics with AR, thereby allowing a remote-controlled vehicle or a drone to move around the swale and, at the same time, capture video, which could later be used in a VR or AR application

Table 3 Ontological and epistemological characteristics of AR and VR

	Ontological characteristics	Epistemological Characteristics
AR	Activities are overlaid upon and **constrained** by physical environments and objects. (Example: the user cannot fly.) Physical space and locale play an important role (Klopfer & Squire, 2008)	Virtual features can be superimposed upon the physical. Freedom to alter one's perception of the environment (yet experience remains tethered to a physical environment)
VR	Activities occur within digitally rendered environments. **Freedom** to alter the environment (example: The user can fly). Space and locale are virtual	Virtual features can be superimposed and added to the environment. **Freedom** to alter perception of the environment (neither tethered to a physical environment nor laws of physics)

Design Framework and Sample AR Lesson

Having established the importance of a postdigital approach and the current uses of AR and VR in education, this section will demonstrate how postdigital and constructivist approaches can be integrated into an actual lesson using the backward design framework. The mini-sample lesson we provide in Appendix A was prepared using backward design (Fig. 2) as conceptualized by Wiggins and McTighe (2005). According to Frey (2018), "backward design is largely grounded in constructivist learning theory" (p. 24) with a focus on creating and negotiating understanding while working towards achieving specified learning outcomes.

In Wiggins and McTighe's framework, teachers first consider what they wish the student to know, understand, or be able to do at the end of a lesson or unit of learning. Second, having established the end goals of the lesson, the teacher can then envision what evidence they wish to see for assessment purposes; in other words, how can a teacher determine if the student has acquired the understanding or abilities targeted in the lesson? Teachers can examine whether the learner can (1) explain concepts, principles, and processes in their own words, (2) interpret the lesson content, (3) apply the new knowledge in different contexts, (4) recognize different points of view, (5) show empathy for others and their experiences, and (5) demonstrate self-knowledge and meta-cognitive awareness (Wiggins & McTighe, 2005, p. 5). Third, once these first two stages have been conceptualized, the teacher can then consider how the lesson will unfold in terms of instructional strategies and learning activities. Some important considerations for planning activities include determining the knowledge and skills the learners will need to achieve the lesson goal(s), activities that support acquiring the desired knowledge and skills, how the knowledge and skills should be presented or acquired, and which materials and resources will be useful (Wiggins & McTighe, 2005).

In Fig. 3 we have added the postdigital and constructivist perspectives to illustrate how they complement each other. On the left-hand side, we have provided

Fig. 2 Backward design (Wiggins & McTighe, 2005)

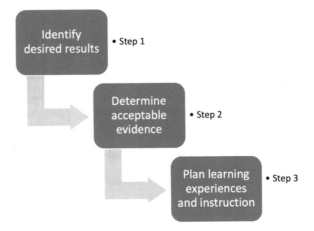

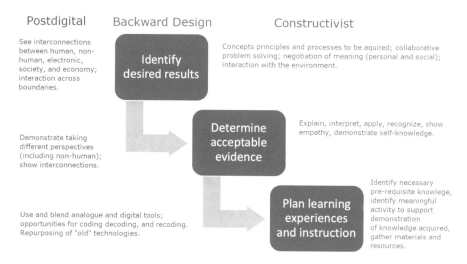

Postdigital

See interconnections between human, non-human, electronic, society, and economy; interaction across boundaries.

Demonstrate taking different perspectives (including non-human); show interconnections.

Use and blend analogue and digital tools; opportunities for coding decoding, and recoding. Repurposing of "old" technologies.

Backward Design

Identify desired results

Determine acceptable evidence

Plan learning experiences and instruction

Constructivist

Concepts principles and processes to be aquired; collaborative problem solving; negotiation of meaning (personal and social); interaction with the environment.

Explain, interpret, apply, recognize, show empathy, demonstrate self-knowledge.

Identify necessary pre-requisite knowlege, identify meaningful activity to support demonstration of knowledge acquired, gather materials and resources.

Fig. 3 Backward design with postdigital and constructivist goals

postdigital nuances a teacher can integrate. To illustrate how a postdigital mindset would alter a constructivist lesson, we provide a sample based on the *WWF Free-Flowing Rivers* app mentioned in the vignette (see Appendix A).

Appendix A provides a sample lesson prepared at Saskatchewan Polytechnic in Canada for a grade 8 class. The layout of the lesson and components follow the backward design framework using the table layout (Figs. 2 and 3) recommended by Wiggins and McTighe (2005). The column on the right provides commentary and suggestions for teachers considering a postdigital aspect to their lessons. The post-digital commentary in Appendix A provides additional ways of considering the lesson activities. The commentary weaves throughout four levels of focus: (1) on technology (analog, digital, manipulation of technology, what technology means/offers), (2) on context (i.e., on how the classroom and participants are grouped and re-grouped like tiles in a mosaic), (3) on content (rivers, water systems, and how they are related to human activity), and (4) on socio-political considerations (such as who benefits from decisions or what the underlying motivations are for various stakeholders). Important to keep in mind is that the postdigital perspective expands learners' awareness of and ability to work beyond a human-centred mindset toward one in which analog, digital, human, and non-human are interconnected.

Asking learners to shift their activities between analog and digital encourages them to explore representations and ontological aspects of learning about the social, the content, the context, and associated technologies. Many of the activities in the lesson sequence are analog: e.g., discussion, video/film. Classroom interactions can also be viewed metaphorically from a postdigital perspective. For example, teachers can consider how they might sequence lessons to move between analog and digital technologies: whole class discussion (analog) followed by discrete group work (digital) in which they try the application (metaphorically, "classroom as mosaic" in which individuals work separately but are still connected to each other). Students can also try the activity individually (digital), and their individual discoveries can be reported back to the class as a whole (analog). Students gather their comments into a model or mosaic in which each person's conceptions form a part. Submitting individual paper exit slips shifts the activities back to digital (piece by piece submissions; one from each student) once again. Applying the postdigital as a way of viewing classroom activity provides a mindful way for teachers to consider how learners can interact.

An important aspect of a postdigital learning activity is for learners to interrogate the technology itself and bring potentially hidden social, political, and economic interrelationships to the surface. The postdigital is especially useful in expanding awareness of interrelationships. Questions such as who made the technology become important vehicles for discussions on social justice, for example, and may contribute to deepening learners' critical thinking skills for the immediate learning activity and beyond. To illustrate, learners may discuss social justice issues of technological accessibility: does the use of some technologies exclude people who face different socio-economic issues? Or learners may explore if some tools have built-in biases that might affect users' perspectives. For example, how might an app sponsored by a pro-environmental company affect learners differently from an app sponsored by a pro-fossil fuel company? While the constructivist aspects of the lesson succeed in creating a learning experience in which learners negotiate meaning for themselves and in collaboration with classmates, the postdigital pushes the learners to interrogate the social, material, *and* digital to better understand the relationality of the phenomena under discussion.

To assist educators in integrating a postdigital approach with backward design, we have created a checklist (Appendix B). Not all the elements are required; however, the checklist may serve as a heuristic or suggestion list for what may be considered in postdigital-backward design.

Strategies for Implementation of Design

- **Focus on using the backward design framework to integrate AR and VR technologies into lessons (Appendix B).** Using backward design to create effective lessons plans, teachers start with the outcome in mind and then plan activities that contribute to achieving the outcomes. Incorporating a postdigital approach can guide teachers in developing lessons that better emphasize the human-environment-technology interrelationship.
- **Develop activities that are interchangeable between analog and digital.** By understanding the difference between analog and digital, teachers can conceptualize how a class can constantly move from one aspect to the other. Awareness of this *shifting* between analog and digital can foster creativity and innovation as learners attempt to apply physical and digital technologies in unusual ways.

- **Consider how constructivism can blend with a postdigital approach to shape students' learning experiences.** Drawing upon (1) their previous technological knowledge and (2) negotiation of meaning (individually or in groups), students can increase their awareness of the ways digital technologies are co-shaping the world. Such awareness can and should stimulate reflection about their own lives and their use of technology both in the classroom and beyond.
- **Establish a classroom culture that respects and acknowledges learners, the environment, and technology.** The embeddedness of information communication technology (ICT) in our socio-cultural world is making it increasingly important for teachers to better understand the inherent interrelationship of the human, environmental, technological world. Not only is a personal relationship between teachers and students important, but so is interaction within the classroom as well as with society and the physical and digital world. The hope is to provide a platform for discussions of social and environmental justice issues.

Conclusion

AR and VR are useful tools for asking learners to think about the interrelationships of people and technology. AR and VR make the human-technology relationship perceptible; they are visible and tangible examples of ways to integrate the virtual and physical as well as the analog and digital. A postdigital approach can provide much-needed sensitivities and inspiration for the integration of technology. For An and Oliver (2021), technology is "an intervening factor in human activities and our understanding of the world" (p. 11). Technology has become such an integral and pervasive part of the social-material world that we may not even notice it. But if we neglect this aspect of our world, we may miss important opportunities to recognize the misuse and/or abuse of the environment and technology. Or, more optimistically, we may miss opportunities to conceptualize better ways to apply, manage, and/or bring technology into harmony with our environments. Rather than technology being viewed as external or secondary to the teaching and learning process, technology is more helpfully viewed as an inherent aspect of human activity and worthy of overt discussion about our socially, materially, and technologically interdependent world. As Knox (2019) suggests, "education has tended to be understood in terms of 'pure' human relationships between teachers and their students, or amongst constructivist social groupings" (p. 358). We argue that *relevant and engaging* educational experiences can, indeed, benefit learners when they are confronted by new and challenging perspectives that reveal our complex intertwining with the physical, digital, and social environment from which we are inseparable.

Appendix A: Sample Lesson

Topic: Free-Flowing Rivers and Water Sustainability
Subjects: Grade 8 Science (Saskatchewan, Canada)

ESTABLISHED GOALS	*Transfer*	*Postdigital analysis and suggestions*
Learning outcomes: **Science** **Earth and space science: Water systems on earth** WS8.1 Analyze the impact of natural and human-induced changes on the characteristics and distribution of water in local, regional, and national ecosystems. **Ways of knowing:** *(WS8.1)* examine the significance of water to first nations and Métis people of Saskatchewan, including water as an essential element of life, transportation, water quality, fishing practices, and treaty rights regarding fishing	*Students will be able to independently use their learning to …* Use diverse augmented reality (AR) applications as an educational, recreational, professional purpose. *(note: This sample lesson uses AR only, not VR.)* Independently modify their behaviours to protect waterways by understanding the impact of water damage on the planet. Independently reflect on Truth and Reconciliation Calls to Action (2015) by understanding the inherited rights of hunting and fishing of Indigenous people in Canada.	Content considerations: Lesson goals.

Meaning

UNDERSTANDINGS	ESSENTIAL QUESTIONS	Socio-political considerations: Learners could think about how their understanding might be different if they played a different role (including roles played by non-humans)
Students will understand …	What are two ways that humans modify the path that water travels?	
What AR is	What are some energy sources that can be used to reduce the impact of water damage on the planet?	Technological considerations: AR can be discussed from a physical, social, and personal perspective. It is possible to examine the technology's advantages and limitations: What can it offer? Is there anything they cannot do or know with AR?
The cause and effect of using dams to control water		
That first nations have an aboriginal (including Métis) right to hunt and fish in certain territories		Socio-political considerations: Who developed the *WWF Free-Flowing Rivers* application? What motivates them? What inspired them to create the AR application? (students interrogate the technology to surface potentially hidden social, political, and economic interrelationships.)
Ways of knowing:		
Water is very important according to first nations and Métis nations rights; how can dams affect hunting and fishing rights for first nations communities?		

(continued)

Appendix A (continued)

Topic: Free-Flowing Rivers and Water Sustainability
Subjects: Grade 8 Science (Saskatchewan, Canada)

	Acquisition	Technological and contextual considerations:
	Students will know …	AR applied to environmental context
	How to use AR – WWF (Free-Flowing Rivers) to enhance what they learned on rivers and the importance of preserving water as sustainable energy	Socio-political considerations: people's rights
	Students will be skilled at …	
	Explaining what AR is	
	Knowing how to manipulate content on an AR application	
	Explaining how waterways are important to all living things for survival	
	Explaining how the fishing and the hunting of indigenous communities can be affected by the construction of dams on waterways	

Stage 2 – Evidence and assessment

Evaluative criteria	Assessment evidence	
Analytic rubric on a 1–4 scale	**PERFORMANCE TASK(S):** Each student will create a paper prototype to simulate and critically think about how the construction of an AR dam can affect communities that are in proximity. Then using a program like *CoSpaces Edu*, each student will learn how to create their prototype (basic information)	Technological considerations: The learners can create something that shifts between analog and digital by using old analog technologies such as paper prototype or overhead projector transparency sheets. For example, the students could use such technologies to create stop-motion (digital) animation from drawings (analog). The media can become repurposed or new
	OTHER EVIDENCE: Observations of students collaborating and discussing together while working in their groups Students complete a "1-2-3 exit slip" answering two questions and asking one burning question Demonstration of basic skills in the use and integration of technology in an educational context	Socio-political considerations: The social aspects here not only support constructivist activity, but also set the stage for community-generated or community-manipulated media through collaborative activities

Stage 3 – Learning plan

Summary of key Learning events and instruction

1. Learning new vocabulary words on watershed from brainstorming with students and a predetermined list
2. Watching a video on YouTube explaining AR and VR and discussing their differences
3. Buzz session by having students come together in a larger group to discuss what waterways are and their importance to the survival of all living things
4. Experimenting with AR using the application *WWF Free-Flowing Rivers*
5. Picking the winner: Problem-solving a prototype on the creation of an AR application linked to the construction of a dam. Informal evaluation through peers
6. Completing a 1-2-3 exit slip before leaving class

Technological considerations: Students can choose ways of representing their work (analog and/or digital)

Appendix B: Backward Design Checklist

	Identify Desired Results	Determine Acceptable Evidence	Plan learning experiences
Constructivist	Identify what the students are to ☐ understand ☐ describe ☐ be able to do	Construct assessment tools in which learners ☐ explain ☐ interpret ☐ apply ☐ recognize ☐ show empathy ☐ demonstrate self-knowledge ☐ Other: _____	Identify ☐ pre-requisite knowledge ☐ activities to support trial and demonstration of knowledge and skills ☐ scaffolding lessons that will prepare students for successful completion of the assessment ☐ materials to support activities
Postdigital	Identify factors ☐ contextual ☐ technological ☐ social ☐ interconnections	Show evidence of perspective taking for ☐ other people ☐ non-human entities Show inter-connections between ☐ the social ☐ the material ☐ the technological	Consider activities that allow sequencing between ☐ digital materials ☐ analog materials ☐ classroom as a mosaic (i.e., individual students comprising a class; a group project in which individual contributions are identifiable) ☐ classroom as a continuous group (i.e., group project in which individual contributions are not identifiable) Provide opportunities for ☐ coding ☐ decoding ☐ recoding ☐ repurposing ☐ reconfiguring

References

An, T., & Oliver, M. (2021). What in the world is educational technology? Rethinking the field from the perspective of the philosophy of technology. *Learning, Media and Technology, 46*(1), 6–19. https://doi.org/10.1080/17439884.2020.1810066

Andrews, I. (2000). Post-digital aesthetics and the return to modernism. *Ian Andrews*. https://ian-andrews.org/texts/postdig.pdf

Cascone, K. (2000). The aesthetics of failure: "Post-digital" tendencies in contemporary computer music. *Computer Music Journal, 24*(4), 12–18. https://doi.org/10.1162/014892600559489

Chalmers, D. J. (2017). The virtual and the real. *Disputatio, 9*(46), 309–352. https://doi.org/10.1515/disp-2017-0009

Chen, C. J. (2009). Theoretical basis for using virtual reality in education. *Themes in Science and Technology Education, 2*(1–2), 71–90. http://earthlab.uoi.gr/theste/index.php/theste/article/view/23

Cline, M. S. (2005). Power, madness, and immortality: The future of virtual reality. University Village Press. https://books.google.ca/books?id=7OxbJWzIaVEC&printsec=frontcover&source=gbs_ge_summary_r&cad=0#v=onepage&q&f=false

Cramer, F. (2015). What is 'post-digital'? In D. M. Berry & M. Dieter (Eds.), *Postdigital aesthetics* (pp. 12–26). Palgrave Macmillan. https://doi.org/10.1057/9781137437204_2

Dick, E. (2021, August 30). The promise of immersive learning: Augmented and virtual reality's potential in education. *Information Technology and Innovation Foundation.* https://itif.org/publications/2021/08/30/promise-immersive-learning-augmented-and-virtual-reality-potential

Driscoll, M. P. (2005). Psychology of learning for instruction (3rd ed.). Pearson Education Inc.

Eastman, J. K., Iyer, R., & Eastman, K. L. (2011). Interactive technology in the classroom: An exploratory look at its use and effectiveness. *Contemporary Issues in Education Research (CIER), 2*(3), 31–38. https://doi.org/10.19030/cier.v2i3.1084

Elmqaddem, N. (2019). Augmented reality and virtual reality in education. Myth or reality? *International Journal of Emerging Technologies in Learning (IJET), 14*(03), 234–242. https://doi.org/10.3991/ijet.v14i03.9289

Ertmer, P., & Newby, T. J. (2013). Behaviourism, cognitivism, constructivism: Comparing critical features from an instructional design perspectives. *Performance Improvement Quarterly, 26*(2), 43–71. https://doi.org/10.1002/piq.21143

Fatih Özcan, M., Özkan, Â., & Şahin, N. (2017). The influence of the augmented reality application on students' performances in ottoman Turkish readings. *Universal Journal of Educational Research, 5*(12B), 27–33. https://doi.org/10.13189/ujer.2017.051403

Frey, B. B. (2018). Backward design. In B. B. Frey (Ed.), *The SAGE encyclopedia of educational research, measurement, and evaluation* (Vol. 1–4). SAGE Publications. https://doi.org/10.4135/9781506326139.n71

Greenwald, W. (2021, March 31). Augmented reality (AR) vs. virtual reality (VR): What's the difference? PC Magazine. https://www.pcmag.com/news/augmented-reality-ar-vs-virtual-reality-vr-whats-the-difference

Jandrić, P., & Hayes, S. (2020). Postdigital we-learn. *Studies in Philosophy and Education, 39*(3), 285–297. https://doi.org/10.1007/s11217-020-09711-2

Jonassen, D. (1998). Designing constructivist learning environments. In C. M. Reigeluth (Ed.), *Instructional design theories and models* (2nd ed., pp. 215–239). Lawrence Erlbaum Associates.

Klopfer, E., & Squire, K. (2008). Environmental detectives—The development of an augmented reality platform for environmental simulations. *Educational Technology Research and Development, 56*(2), 203–228. https://doi.org/10.1007/s11423-007-9037-6

Knox, J. (2019). What does the 'postdigital' mean for education? Three critical perspectives on the digital, with implications for educational research and practice. *Postdigital Science and Education, 1*(2), 357–370. https://doi.org/10.1007/s42438-019-00045-y

Krokos, E., Plaisant, C., & Varshney, A. (2019). Virtual memory palaces: Immersion aids recall. *Virtual Reality, 23*(1), 1–15. https://doi.org/10.1007/s10055-018-0346-3

Maher, C. (2020, February 13). *A new wave of indies are using games to explore climate change: Interactive education.* The Verge. https://www.theverge.com/2020/2/13/21135321/video-games-climate-change-beyond-blue-bee-simulator-temtem-endling

Martín-Gutiérrez, J., Mora, C. E., Añorbe-Díaz, B., & González-Marrero, A. (2017). Virtual technologies trends in education. *EURASIA Journal of Mathematics, Science and Technology Education, 13*(2), 469–486. https://doi.org/10.12973/eurasia.2017.00626a

Metzinger, T. K. (2018). Why is virtual reality interesting for philosophers? *Frontiers in Robotics and AI, 5.* https://doi.org/10.3389/frobt.2018.00101

Satayabrata, J. (2020). Difference between analog computer and digital computer. *GeeksforGeeks.* https://www.geeksforgeeks.org/difference-between-analog-computer-and-digital-computer/.

Sokhanych, A. (2018, March). Virtual reality in the military. *ThinkMobiles.* https://thinkmobiles.com/blog/virtual-reality-military/

Sotiriou, S., & Bogner, F. X. (2008). Visualizing the invisible: Augmented reality as an innovative science education scheme. *Advanced Science Letters, 1*(1), 114–122(9). https://doi.org/10.1166/asl.2008.012

Stevenson, A. (2010a). *Analogue. Oxford dictionary of English* (3rd ed.). Oxford University Press.

Stevenson, A. (2010b). *Digital. Oxford dictionary of English* (3rd ed.). Oxford University Press.

Truth and Reconciliation Commission of Canada. (2015). *Truth and reconciliation: Calls to action.* https://ehprnh2mwo3.exactdn.com/wp-content/uploads/2021/01/Calls_to_Action_English2.pdf

Vygotsky, L. S. (1978). Mind in society: The development of higher psychological processes. Harvard University Press.

Wiggins, G., & McTighe, J. (2005). *Understanding by design* (2nd ed.). Association for Supervision & Curriculum Development. https://www.ascd.org/books/understanding-by-design-expanded-2nd-edition

Annie Beaumier is a Bilingual Online Curriculum Developer at the Saskatchewan Polytechnic School of Continuing Education. She has a Master of Education in Educational Technology and Design from the University of Saskatchewan. She previously worked as a teacher for 20 years in the K–12 educational system, specializing in STEM Education.

Marguerite Koole is an Associate Professor in Educational Technology and Design at the University of Saskatchewan. She has a PhD in E-Research and Technology-Enhanced Learning from Lancaster University, UK and a Master of Education from Athabasca University, Canada. Dr. Koole has worked in educational technology for over 15 years.

Student Emotions in Virtual Reality: The Concept of Psychopedagogy by Design

Géraldine Perriguey

Abstract Virtual reality (VR) impacts students' emotions in learning situations. Psychopedagogy is an integrative approach to emotions and learning that could help protect students' emotions in VR. Based on the challenges of developing VR experiences for natural disaster preparedness that remain emotionally healthy, this chapter introduces the concept of Psychopedagogy by Design.

Keywords Designing virtual environments · Educational virtual reality · Emotions · Pedagogy · Psychopedagogy · Virtual reality learning environments

Introduction

When educators design a virtual environment (VE), one aspect often forgotten is the student's emotional state induced in virtual reality (VR). Unfortunately, it is challenging to consider the emotions of all students in a traditional classroom context. Students experience a range of emotions in learning situations, such as joy, excitement, or frustration when discovering the results of a scientific experiment (Hascher, 2010). Students bring a rich array of emotional states into the classroom, which may mean experiencing different emotions in the same learning situation. Research has shown that emotions influence cognitive processes, including perception, attention, learning, memory, reasoning, problem-solving (Tyng et al., 2017), motivation, engagement, and learning strategy choices (Pekrun, 2014; Zhang, 2021). Therefore, learning processes and students' emotions must be viewed in an integrated way, particularly in learning situations that stimulate emotions.

G. Perriguey (✉)
XR PEDAGOGY, Paris, France
e-mail: contact@xrpedagogy.com

© The Author(s), under exclusive license to Springer Nature Switzerland AG 2022
P. MacDowell, J. Lock (eds.), *Immersive Education*,
https://doi.org/10.1007/978-3-031-18138-2_4

VR is a new technology that triggers numerous emotions in a learning situation. VR involves the sensory system in learning by providing students with visual, auditory, olfactory, and haptic sensations (Seth et al., 2011). This technology enables a sense of presence and immersion which can foster emotionally engaging learning situations. The emotional impact of a VR experience may involve real challenges for educators. Educators need to anticipate and avoid the possibility that some students may physiologically feel or remember that a VE was unpleasant or frightening (McCall et al., 2015; Vesisenaho et al., 2019). An approach inspired by psychopedagogy may help teachers address students' emotional states in VR learning situations.

In this chapter, I draw on our work at XR PEDAGOGY to design VEs that simulate dangerous situations while remaining emotionally healthy for students. I introduce different strategies for creating a reassuring and positive VE that is emotionally safe. The first section defines the crucial role of emotions in VR and why VR may benefit from psychopedagogy. In the second section, I discuss the concept of Psychopedagogy by Design and the practical ways it can be harnessed to design emotionally healthy VEs favourable to learning.

Vignette

Our client is the team in charge of seismic risk preparedness in Guadeloupe (French West Indies, France). When we first met, they told us that the VR scenarios must raise awareness among high school students that an earthquake can occur in various situations (at home, in the classroom, and at the beach). VR is the best technology to simulate an earthquake in various situations and thus increase the population's perception of risk. Direct experience of an earthquake directly impacts risk perception, and people with high-risk perception are more likely to undertake preparedness measures and take personal action. We wondered: how can we use VR to effectively impact students' emotions without leading to an unpleasant or frightening experience? When designing the VEs, we aimed to balance raising awareness without leading to trauma. Our mission was to ensure an emotionally healthy virtual experience that can increase seismic risk perception. Emotions felt by the user immersed in the earthquake simulation were at the center of the VE design.

Psychopedagogy and Emotions in VR

Psychopedagogy is a European term that embraces theoretical principles from psychology and the practical application of those principles in teaching. The aim of psychopedagogy is to resolve to resolve learning difficulties considering the child's affective context (Stones, 1978). Experts in psychopedagogy analyze learning difficulties and propose solutions that aim for a global psychological approach to the child's difficulties (Boimare, 2010). Psychopedagogy can be used in a preventive way: according to Moura et al., (2019), providing various strategies to deal with psychological problems that may interfere during the learning process. Practitioners in Psychopedagogy analyze, among other aspects, the emotions felt by the students that interfere with the learning process (Moura et al., 2019). The goal is to address any existing learning difficulties or anticipate learning difficulties.

The word *emotion* implies dynamism: motion concerning movement, whose Latin root *emovere* means "to set in motion." However, as explained by Claudon and Weber (2009), there is no consensus on the definition of emotion. Emotion is a complex state of consciousness intimately linked to physiological reactions. Emotions are essential in rational decision-making, perception, learning, and other functions that affect human physiological and psychological states (Marín-Morales et al., 2020). According to Rosalind Picard (1997), who introduced affective computing, if we want computers to be as intelligent as we are and to interact with us more naturally, we must give them the ability to recognize, understand, and even have or express emotions.

It is not difficult to hypothesize that emotions play a crucial role in VR. Attesting to this hypothesis is the increased number of research publications each year that include topics of VR and emotion analysis (Marín-Morales et al., 2020). VR is a human-computer interface that provides users with various physical sensations (e.g., visual, haptic, auditory) (Seth et al., 2011), enabling the student's immersion in the VE. Involving the sensory system, VR can activate emotions (Diemer et al., 2015). The sensory system can stimulate various positive or negative emotions in VR. McCall et al. (2015) recorded physiological reactions (skin conductance and heart rate) during VR experiences involving threatening content. Their research team demonstrated that the user's memorized reports of the arousal levels reliably followed the physiological changes recorded during the VR experience. These results imply that memory encodes physiological information during emotional episodes in VR.

In addition to sensation, the VR setup can affect students' emotions, such as the stress of being equipped with the VR headset, the loss of visual and audio connection with reality, and the immersion alone into an unfamiliar new VE full of various parameters inducing emotions (Riva et al., 2007). One of the unique psychological features of a VR learning experience is the sense of presence. Presence is dependent on the individual's ability to experience VR: it is the feeling of *being there* physically in the VE. It is a psychological state where users perceive the environment around them as real, forgetting the role of technology in the experience (Jerald, 2015). Although the link between presence and the emotional reaction to a VE is a subject of debate (Felnhofer et al., 2015; Slater, 2004), presence is thought to be a precondition for an emotion to occur in a VE (Felnhofer et al., 2015). If an environment elicits anxiety, so will a corresponding VE if the user experiences presence in it (Slater, 2004).

Avatar agents (computer-animated characters) can also impact emotions in a virtual classroom. For example, Ling et al. (2015) studied the impact of a spectator avatar (or virtual spectator) on the students' beliefs, self-efficacy, and anxiety in a virtual classroom. They demonstrated that a virtual spectator's positive attitude towards the participants led them to have a more positive attitude about their self-efficacy and behave more engagingly (e.g., showing less avoidance behavior, interpreted as a manifestation of decreased anxiety). Virtual appearance can also impact students' emotions in VR. Students can take on different appearances or embodiments in VR, impacting emotions, behaviors, and cognitive abilities. For example, the embodiment can induce what is commonly referred to as the Proteus Effect, the effect of an altered representation of self on behavior (Yee & Bailenson, 2007). The embodiment also impacts cognitive abilities, as in the original experiment by Banakou et al. (2018) where 15 male participants were embodied in a virtual body signifying super-intelligence, called *Einstein*. Participants in the *Einstein* body, particularly those with low self-esteem, performed better on a cognitive task. Dressing up in a carnival costume when embodying an avatar suggests that the students could step back from their emotions while embodying an avatar character. Although the effect can be positive for teenagers, helping with self-reconstruction without putting oneself at risk (Vlachopoulou et al., 2018) and showing positive effects on creativity and episodic memory performance in young adults (Guegan et al., 2016; Tuena et al., 2019), such embodiment can foster an array of emotions in students that must be anticipated.

Psychopedagogy and the Emotional Maturity of Students in VR

During early childhood, the distinction between what is real and what is not is gradually established according to children's psychological and cognitive development (Piaget, 1929). Before age 10, the child progressively learns to recognize and manage various emotions. While some children might have a completely fulfilling virtual experience, others might experience strong or traumatic emotions without the educators noticing. Some children may even develop false memories: confusion between the elements experienced in VR and those in reality.

Today, the official recommendations for the minimum age to experience VR are controversial, but headset manufacturers (including Meta) indicate not to use the headset before 13 years old. Differences in psychological maturity may be enough to justify waiting until at least early adolescence (11–12 years old) to start testing VR for a short period. Depending on the design of the environment, VR could alter the students' emotional reality. On the one hand, simulating reality can be traumatic; on the other departing from it can be bewildering. Therefore, educators must consider the students' maturity and their psychological development.

Psychopedagogy and the World of Affectivity in VR

In Psychopedagogy, the global approach helps anticipate students' emotions activated by the learning situation (Moura et al., 2019). The affective life explored in psychopedagogy refers to a medium composed of emotions, personality, and maturity. Various theories based on psychopedagogy suggest that the student's affective life is inseparable from learning (Chevallier-Gaté, 2014). As Delory-Momberger (2021) underlines, if we are asked about our school memories long after we have left school, are not we emphasizing memories with an emotional dimension rather than the memories of the knowledge we have learned? Learning is an interaction that is richer and more complex than a simple circulation of information. Investigating emotions in educational activity are challenging (Schutz et al., 2006). Subject are in contact with the world of affectivity, the world of objects, and the world of others (Gaté, 2009). In VR, the world of affectivity is exposed to a virtual world made of many three-dimensional objects and avatars.

When designing a VE, the educator has tremendous flexibility in combining three-dimensional objects. In this immersive educational world, the types of three-dimensional elements in the VE are unlimited and the possible combinations infinite. For example, elements of the VE can be real or imaginary three-dimensional objects. Characters or embodied agents can take a human or imaginary appearance. Even the player is embodied in an avatar that can be realistic or entirely unreal, fantastic, and even eccentric. Therefore, the emotional signals the virtual elements will trigger in the students' affective life can be numerous and difficult to master. In a pilot study, Vesisenaho et al. (2019) demonstrated that physiological measurements and qualitative data related to an emotional response could be measured simultaneously in university students exposed to different VR experiences. They note that VR in the classroom impacts learning and student well-being through the emotions experienced.

Psychopedagogy by Design

There is a need to help educators design emotionally safe VEs that also consider affectivity and learning in an integrative approach. At XR PEDAGOGY, Psychopedagogy by Design helped us focus on inducing positive emotional states in the VEs we created. There is a direct link between the design of the VE and the emotions induced in VR. Riva et al. (2007) assessed emotions in VR by playing on variables in the VE. They designed three similar virtual parks where the user can move freely: two parks had the same structure but different sounds, music, lights, shadows, and textures, each chosen to induce anxiety or relaxation. The third was a neutral park used as a control. The results confirmed the efficacy of VR as an effective medium: anxiety- and relaxation-inducing VEs induced feelings of anxiety and relaxation. Assessing the impact of virtual forest therapy, Felnhofer et al. (2015) confirmed the ability of VR to induce emotions determined by the design of the VE. They designed five parks with identical structures but different elements according to the expected emotions (e.g., for joy, sunshine and birds; for anger, construction noises and machinery; for boredom, an empty park and dead trees; for anxiety, nighttime with some lanterns, owl noises, and moving silhouettes; for sadness, rain and gloom). The results show that participants felt the expected emotions of joy, anxiety, anger, and boredom. Detection of emotions was possible after five minutes of immersion in the VE. Therefore, educators who want to design a VE must anticipate the emotional impact of their design and ensure that students will feel emotionally comfortable in the VE.

Minimalist Graphic Design

There is a fundamental psychological difference between VR and other non-immersive digital media in education. Non-immersive digital media allows natural emotional protection to students because they are outside the learning medium, whereas in VR, there is a sensory-motor anchoring of the student. Designing VE that helps students feel comfortable and secure is crucial. One way to design an emotionally healthy VE is to is to get inspired by the psychology behind web design (Imitiaz, 2016). Psychopedagogy by Design is applied through a minimalist graphic design approach to avoid feeling emotionally trapped. The term minimalist is often applied to suggest anything stripped to its absolute essentials or a meaningful utilization of elements (Vaneenoo, 2011). The more three-dimensional objects, the more information students get at the sensory, cognitive, and affective levels. Thus, a minimalist graphic design can reduce the emotional impact of the VE.

As the vignette described, I developed a VR experience to prepare young people for the earthquake risks in the French West Indies (Guadeloupe, France). When designing one of the scenes for earthquake preparedness, minimizing emotions was crucial. The earthquake is already highly impacting students' emotions in VR. Graphical minimalism was easier to respect when the design was started using *Unity 3D* software. Different designs were created with geometric blocks during the first prototyping steps to achieve minimalist graphic design (Fig. 1) prototypes helped identify the critical elements students should see falling (Fig. 2). The goal was to prioritize visual information and achieve a visual hierarchy. The number of three-dimensional objects was stripped to its essentials to ensure a meaningful utilization of elements and favor simple interaction levels. As Fig. 3 shows, the minimalist graphic design allows organizing the visual information using Gestalt principles (Imtiaz, 2016). To control the emotional impact. The first element visualized by the player is the avatar: there is a means of escape and the fact that only a few elements will fall.

Level of Realism in the Virtual Environment

If educators anticipate the VE's emotional impact, one design aspect to consider is the level of realism. According to Dalgarno and Lee (2010), three-dimensional VEs rely on two key features: (1) fidelity in representation and (2) interaction with the learner. Fowler (2014) points out that there may be a trade-off between

Fig. 1 Prioritize visual information using minimalist graphic design

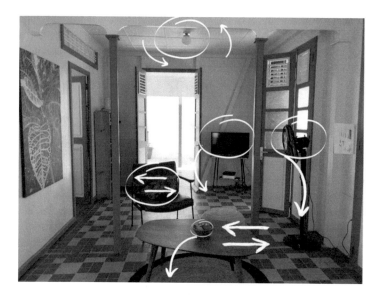

Fig. 2 Visual hierarchy and simple interactions

photorealism and behavioural realism. Indeed, when teenagers become adults, they gradually learn to keep an emotional distance from reality because reality may be traumatic. When designing a learning experience in VR, educators may wonder how much realism they want and limit the quest for a sense of presence and fidelity in representation. A VE with a pedagogical purpose does not need to be emotionally

Fig. 3 Final view of the scene, the first elements viewed by the player

brutal to be educational. A VE that promotes learning and protects students' emotional states should seek to omit the traumatic aspects of reality. For example, in the VR experience for earthquake risk education, a fade to black was added to the timeline of the earthquake experience when it became too violent. The goal is to understand the rise of emotion related to an earthquake and not to show that a roof collapsing can kill a human. After the VR experience, if it is crucial, teachers can introduce the missing realistic elements. In the early design process of the VE, a limitation of the level of realism should be decided in advance according to the student's emotional maturity and their psychological development.

Reassuring by Creating a Framework and Defining Roles

In a traditional classroom, the roles of students and teachers are well-defined. In VR, students may share the learning experience with avatars whose roles are unknown. They may encounter situations where behavior should be defined. If the VE design is like a classroom, students tend to behave similarly in the VR class as in the in-person class (Ling et al., 2015). However, when the VE and the situation of being immersed in VR are new for a student, there may be an increase in anxiety that impacts learning. Students could ask themselves: Are the other avatars also teachers? Am I being assessed in VR? Am I being observed in this situation? Do I get to have fun? It is by placing students in a situation that is safe and stable that we promote learning. VE can include a reassuring framework where the roles are defined in advance. For example, it is possible to integrate short tutorials at the beginning of the experience to help the student understand the behaviour codes. A safe zone can be imagined where a wise person-avatar could explain what is happening in this environment. Educators should not underestimate the need to define the roles and expected behaviour codes of the VE.

An Emotional Adjustment Period

Lev Vygotsky (1997) may be considered a pioneer in psychopedagogy, evoking in his time the link between psychology and pedagogy. His work leads us to review teaching as a practice of external regulation that supports and guides the psychological activities of the student. Vygotsky's work teaches us to consider the means of regulation offered by the social context and the child's capacity to take advantage of the environment that forms his or her sensitivity to instruction. The psychological context is unknown when students are immersed in a dynamic, interactive, new, unreal world. In an educational context, immersion in VR can cause anxiety from the start of the immersion in a VE. A usual first challenge is that of timing. There are usually few VR sessions, and not all students have the luxury of being equipped with a VR headset. Educators may expect students to act quickly in VR because there is insufficient time. However, in VR (just as in the classroom) there are individual variances in behaviour. The student may ask, Can I test this or that, or will I break things? The risk is becoming tied up in emotional knots that may impact creativity, initiative, and self-confidence. It is essential to reassure students about their capacity to interact in the VE. Students should have time to explore, discover, test, destroy, and reconstruct before they can start to learn. Two to three exploration sessions may be needed before they can begin learning in VR. When students begin, it is possible to consider a sandbox scene. This malleable space for experimentation (an adjustment period) will allow students to adapt to the new VE and perhaps establish the sensitivity to instruction that Vygotsky (1997) mentioned.

Taking Advantage of Avatars

It is essential to anticipate the negative emotions of feeling guilty about making a mistake. Using avatar agents is one possible strategy to ensure a student feels comfortable making mistakes. Avatar agents are computer-animated characters, not players equipped with a VR headset, and are an excellent means to give a pedagogical status to mistakes. For example, avatar agents were used in the VR experience for earthquake preparedness. The experience of teenagers in a VR earthquake feeling guilty about making a mistake in a potentially deadly situation could be emotionally and psychologically negative for our young students. The earthquake is a natural risk for which it is difficult to train because it requires learning situation analysis skills. The problem is that understanding the correct reaction requires time for analysis and depends on the situation in which we find ourselves (e.g., at sea, at home, upstairs, downstairs, at school with an adult, or at school alone).

I used a combination of different avatars: one avatar who acts correctly with two avatars who make mistakes (Fig. 4). Three different avatars were added to the same VR scene of our earthquake preparedness experience. The experience starts, and the student can see all three avatars in their field of view (Fig. 4). One avatar (Fig. 5, the

Fig. 4 One avatar who acts correctly with two avatars who make mistakes

Fig. 5 Two avatars will underestimate the seismic risk and the tsunami risk

woman next to the car) makes a mistake; she is taking pictures instead of running as far as possible from the sea to avoid the tsunami risk. The second avatar (Fig. 5, the girl next to the information board) is also making a mistake by staying where she is. The third avatar (Fig. 6, the man in blue) acts appropriately and starts to run up the hill immediately. Students in VR must decide which avatar they want to mimic. Moreover, in another VR scene of the same experience, I exploited the possibility that one avatar can make good decisions but mistakes afterward, as a human person could do. Then, after the VR simulation, students can verbalize their reactions. The goal is for students to understand their reading of the situation and why they chose to act like the avatar or differently. We discussed with them how the avatar's behaviour influences their behaviour. In this approach, it was easier for students to share

Fig. 6 One avatar will run away and show the correct behaviour to adopt

their mistakes. Students felt less guilty about their mistakes because the avatars can also make mistakes. It was easier for students to judge the avatar's mistakes and analyze them than to judge their own, especially in an anxiety-provoking situation like an earthquake.

An Empathy Map Canvas to Focus on Student Emotions

To design an emotionally supportive learning environment, I used a tool with our clients inherited from design thinking methods: the Empathy Map Canvas (EMC) (Fig. 7).

Created by Scott Matthews and Dave Gray, the EMC is a collaborative tool to understand customers better (Gray et al., 2010). The goal is to initiate a degree of empathy for a specific person (Gray et al., 2010). It is a user-centered approach, exposing a person's needs and revealing opportunities on how to connect with that person (Bratsberg, 2012). For example, the EMC can be used to design customer-centric business models and personas (Ferreira et al., 2015; Osterwalder & Pigneur, 2013). The EMC can be used to assist in prototyping a VE. Although creating an empathy map is not a rigorous, research-based process, it is an efficient way for a group to focus on the most critical element: people or in this case, students (Gray et al., 2010). This playful method can help focus on the emotions students might feel in the VE and identify the most crucial elements to design.

There are seven defined areas around and inside a smiley face representing the student in the EMC. Each area is employed to classify ideas about: (1) whom we are empathizing with, (2) what they need to do, (3) what they see, (4) what they say, (5)

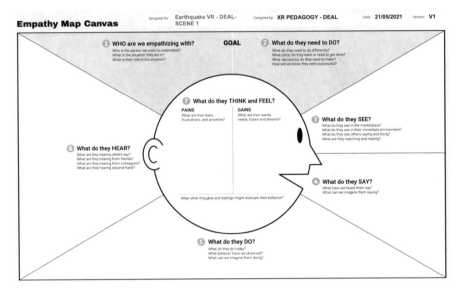

Fig. 7 The EMC by Dave Gray

what they do, (6) what they hear, and (7) think and feel (Fig. 7). When the EMC is used to design a VE, the first area helps teams define what they want students to understand and to clarify their role in the VE. The second area allows classifying ideas about what students need to do in the VE, including possible interactions. The other five areas are dedicated to classifying ideas about what students see in the VE, say, may do, hear, and think and feel in the VE. Therefore, the activity requires using the EMC template (Fig. 7) and preferably a video projector. Remotely, the post-it notes from a presentation tool (e.g., Keynote or PowerPoint) and the screen-share option of the video conference tool may be used as well.

The activity starts by gathering all the people involved in the VE design: teachers, technical assistants, pedagogues, and students, if possible. First, the team must know the goal and the storyboard of the VR scene. Then brainstorming starts, and one person classifies ideas in each area of the EMC, focusing on ideas that are particularly likely to arouse emotions. This tool also appears to help avoid saturating the environment with three-dimensional objects (graphical minimalism) by prioritizing visual information and favouring simple interaction levels.

For example, I organized an EMC activity with XR PEDAGOGY's team to design the prototype of a VE for earthquake preparedness in VR (Fig. 8). The VR scene takes place in a classroom, and when the earthquake starts, the player is seated at a desk facing another student-avatar (Fig. 9) who will hide under the table during the earthquake (Fig. 10). In Fig. 8, the first area helped us initiate a degree of empathy with the student immersed in the VR experience. The student is a 16-year-old alone in an unknown classroom. The second area encouraged the team to manage their expectations regarding what they wanted the student to do in VR: understand why the avatar does not go outside and go under the desk for safety. The third and

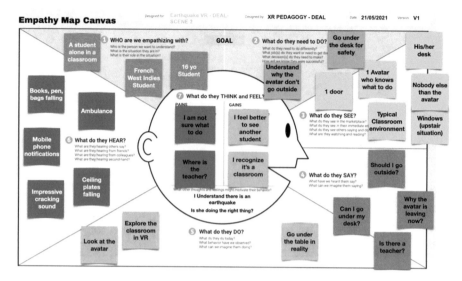

Fig. 8 Example of an EMC used for VE design

Fig. 9 View of the player when the earthquake starts: the reassuring context

sixth areas were crucial in focusing on the student's emotions. What the student sees and hears is highly participating in the emotion-induced in VR. As a result, the team identified that only three-dimensional elements were needed to create an atmosphere encouraging the player to take the initiative. Sounds were preferred over visual effects for a reasonable level of realism to simulate the earthquake. Area four was an exciting part of the brainstorming because it helped the team imagine what the student could say if they were in the VE. For example, the note "Is there a teacher?" illustrated the potential emotions of students trained to follow the

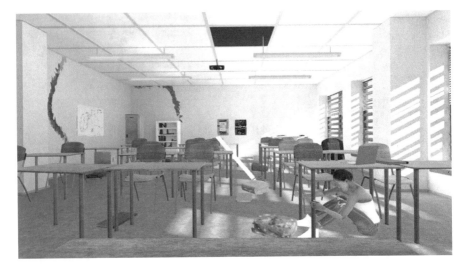

Fig. 10 The behaviour of the avatar when the earthquake intensifies

teacher's instructions in case of an emergency in the classroom. Likewise, area seven—dedicated to what student thinks and feels—highlighted the same emotion with the note "Where is the teacher?"

Overall, the EMC activity efficiently helped us empathize with the student and led to valuable discussions. For example, the indication "I recognize it is a classroom" (Fig. 8) in area seven resulted in a discussion about cultural sensitivity and the sense of cultural belonging to the VE (Fowler, 2014). Considering the VE is designed for students from the French West Indies (Fig. 8, area 1), the team chose to include architectural elements typical of the Creole culture, sounds characteristic of tropical islands (birds and typical sound effects), and a Caribbean brightness. These graphical aspects, combined with avatars whose ethnic background reflects that of the Caribbean islands, are all elements that can promote a reassuring immersion and a positive emotional context for learning (Figs. 9 and 10).

Strategies for Implementation of Design

Educators and designers may consider the following five strategies when creating or implementing VR for an immersive learning experience that considers students' emotions

- **Psychopedagogy by design**. From the start of designing VR, drawing on practices from the field of psychopedagorgy should be considered to ensure a focus on students' emotions. Various practical tools suggested in this chapter can help educators anticipate students' emotions in VR. For example, the EMC can help designers develop empathy with students by mapping the expected emotions according to the different elements of the VE. When both psychology and peda-gogy are stakeholders in the design process, emotional states beneficial to learn-ing in VR are more likely to be induced. The VE design should consider the students' affectivity, their maturity, and their need for an emotional adjust-ment period.

- **The teacher's role, before, during, and after VR sessions.** The VR session should be integrated into a pedagogical continuity and not be the only session. Educators play a critical central role before, during, and after the VR experience. Perhaps there is a metaphor to be made with educators and the Oculus Guardian. In a Meta Quest VR headset, the Oculus Guardian is a built-in safety feature to set up boundaries in VR that appear when a player gets too close to the edge of the play area. In this sense, the teacher is the true guardian of the psychology and pedagogy of the student immersed in VR. The teacher should also ensure that learning in VR should be on a continuum between virtual and real. The VR learn-ing experience can be designed so that educators can initiate questions at the end of the session. For example, in the VR experience for natural risk preparedness, the phase after the VR experience allows the instructor to highlight the learner's choices. This phase encourages students to analyze decisions made in a stressful, emotional context and to consider after the earthquake what their decision might have been in a relaxed emotional context. Educators are a binding agent for the educational learning experience, even in VR experiences where students are autonomous and interact on their own in the environment.
- **A reassuring atmosphere.** A VE should elicit a reassuring atmosphere. For example, the VE may address cultural sensitivities through choices of three-dimensional objects, sounds, lights, and avatars' ethnic origins. In addition, the behaviours of realistic elements should be consistent; for example, the different physical states of water should change according to the temperature (Fowler, 2014). Promoting a reassuring atmosphere can be achieved by including a sym-bolic construction identified as a safe place to retreat, or by adding reassuring characters such as an adult, a teacher, a pet, or a protective figure (e.g., a tree). A reassuring VE is also one that facilitates a feeling of freedom—an essential ele-ment of an emotionally supportive VE for learning, as is the case in design-based learning (Zhang, 2021). Facilitating the feeling of freedom can enhance curios-ity. Students should feel they are actors in the VE and have freedom of choice in their interactions.
- **Graphic design minimalism.** The VE should utilize graphic design minimalism and avoid saturating the student with information. This strategy could also be called Feng shui VR because the aim is to arrange the elements to create balance with the natural/real world and establish harmony between students and the VE, as in the philosophy of Feng shui (Kryžanowski, 2021). A minimalist graphic design approach prevents students from feeling emotionally trapped in the VE. It may be tempting to embellish the environment with many elements to make it more realistic and ensure students will understand the educational activity. However, this is not because the environment is more realistic that the sense of presence is better (Sungchul & Lindeman, 2021). The fewer three-dimensional

objects in a scene, the more fluid will be the experience. The fluidity is especially crucial when the VE is experienced with a standalone VR headset such as the Meta Quest 2.

- **Visual hierarchy and simple interactions.** Some objects in the environment are more important than others. One way to achieve visual hierarchy is by using the EMC (Fig. 7) and circling the elements that need to stand out. A visual hierarchy can be established and affordance improved; for example, it is important to introduce the essential element in the player's field of vision from the beginning of the experience (Fig. 3). VR is also visually dynamic. As an avatar moves, the computer calculates lights and shadows, so students can focus on detail but may also miss the point. As well, when the VE is too big, students tend to explore everything. However, a few simple interactions from the beginning can make the experience convenient and reassuring. These interactions can replicate the interactions the student experiences in real life with natural objects. In VR, the aim is to create an environment that creates an atmosphere of well-being by using a simple and uncluttered graphic design and natural interactions.

Conclusion

In this chapter, I highlighted the need to anticipate the emotional impact of VR on students more carefully. VR uniquely elicits emotions and rumination due to its ability to stimulate levels of emotional arousal that are almost identical to those in real life (Lavoie et al., 2021; Slater et al., 2006). VR can foster various emotions; the more students feel they are physically in the VE, the more emotions they will experience. Recent advances in neuroscience show that most of the brain processes that regulate our emotions, attitudes, and behaviours are not conscious. In contrast to explicit processes, students cannot verbalize these implicit processes (Barsade et al., 2009; Marín-Morales et al., 2020). Therefore, negative emotional responses in VR could be harmful to students if not appropriately managed (Lavoie et al., 2021).

Educators must seek to immerse students in an emotionally healthy, pleasant, and constructive medium for their cognitive and psychological development. The concept of Psychopedagogy by Design is one approach to overcome the challenges associated with designing an emotionally healthy VR environment. Because VR can awaken the emotional reality of students, their age and maturity must be considered from the beginning of the project. It is also crucial to set limits for the level of realism. In addition, numerous emotions are intimately linked to the design of the VE (Felnhofer et al., 2015; Riva et al., 2007). An Empathy Map Canvas (Gray et al., 2010) can be used to chart the VE design elements and their emotional impact. Further, the use of minimalist graphic design and an emotional adjustment period can reduce the emotional impact of the VE.

VR represents an opportunity to approach learning and the student's affectivity in a more integrative way. The goal is to encourage spontaneity in the VE to better guide the learner in the real world. In VR, educators become designers involved in the emotional journey of their students. They accompany their students in their cognitive and psychological development.

References

Banakou, D., Kishore, S., & Slater, M. (2018). Virtually being Einstein results in an improvement in cognitive task performance and a decrease in age bias. *Frontiers in Psychology, 9*. https://doi.org/10.3389/fpsyg.2018.00917

Barsade, S., Ramarajan, L., & Westen, D. (2009). Implicit affect in organizations. *Research in Organizational Behavior, 29*, 135–162. https://doi.org/10.1016/j.riob.2009.06.008

Boimare, S. (2010). *Pratiquer la psychopédagogie: Médiation, groupes et apprentissage*. Dunod.

Bratsberg, H. M. (2012). Empathy maps of the FourSight preferences. *Creative studies graduate student Master's projects* (paper 176). https://digitalcommons.buffalostate.edu/cgi/viewcontent.cgi?referer=&https redir=1&article=1180&context=creativeprojects.

Chevallier-Gaté, C. (2014). La place des émotions dans l'apprentissage: Vers le plaisir d'apprendre. *Education, 3*. http://revue-educatio.eu/wp/

Claudon, P., & Weber, M. (2009). L'émotion: Contribution à l'étude psychodynamique du développement de la pensée de l'enfant sans langage en interaction. [emotion. Contribution to the psychodynamic study of the development of the infant's thought during affective interaction]. *Devenir, 21*(1), 61–99. https://doi.org/10.3917/dev.091.0061

Dalgarno, B., & Lee, M. J. W. (2010). What are the learning affordances of 3-D virtual environments? *British Journal of Educational Technology, 41*(1), 10–32. https://doi.org/10.1111/j.1467-8535.2009.01038.x

Delory-Momberger, C. (2021). La recherche biographique en éducation : émergence, projet et enjeux [Biographical research in education: Emergence, project and issues]. *Le sujet dans la cité, 12*, 27–37. https://doi.org/10.3917/lsdlc.012.0027

Diemer, J., Alpers, G. W., Peperkorn, H. M., Shiban, Y., & Mühlberger, A. (2015, January 30). The impact of perception and presence on emotional reactions: A review of research in virtual reality. *Frontiers in Psychology*. https://doi.org/10.3389/fpsyg.2015.00026.

Felnhofer, A., Kothgassner, O., Schmidt, M., Heinzle, A., Beutl, L., Hlavacs, H., & Krypsin-Exner, I. (2015). Is virtual reality emotionally arousing? Investigating five emotion inducing virtual park scenarios. *International Journal of Human Computer Studies, 82*, 48–56. https://doi.org/10.1016/j.ijhcs.2015.05.004

Ferreira, B. M., Silva, W. A. F., Oliveira, E., & Conte, T. (2015). *Designing personas with empathy map*. USES Research Group, Instituto de Computação - IComp Universidade Federal do Amazonas (UFAM). http://ksiresearchorg.ipage.com/seke/seke15paper/seke15paper_152.pdf.

Fowler, C. (2014). Virtual reality and learning: Where is the pedagogy? [special issue]. *British Journal of Educational Technology, 46*(2), 412–422. https://doi.org/10.1111/bjet.12135

Gaté, J. (2009). Apprentissage. In J.-P. Boutinet (Ed.), *L'ABC de la VAE* (pp. 79–80). Érès. https://doi.org/10.3917/eres.bouti.2009.01.0079

Gray, D., Brown, S., & Macanufo, J. (2010). *Gamestorming: A playbook for innovators, rulebreakers and changemakers*. O'Reilly Media, Inc.

Guegan, J., Buisine, S., Mantelet, S., Maranzana, N., & Segonds, F. (2016). Avatar-mediated creativity: When embodying inventors makes engineers more creative. *Computers in Human Behavior, 61*, 165–175. https://doi.org/10.1016/j.chb.2016.03.024

Hascher, T. (2010). Learning and emotion: Perspectives for theory and research. *European Educational Research Journal, 9*(1), 13–28. https://doi.org/10.2304/2Feerj.2010.9.1.13

Imtiaz, S. (2016). The psychology behind web design. http://dx.doi.org/10.13140/RG.2.2.17394.56001

Jerald, J. (2015). *The VR book: Human-centered design for virtual reality*. Association for Computing Machinery and Morgan & Claypool. https://doi.org/10.1145/2792790

Kryžanowski, Š. (2021). Feng shui: A comprehensive review of its effectiveness based on evaluation studies. *Indian Journal of Scientific Research, 7*(11), 61–71. https://ijasre.net/index.php/ijasre/article/view/1383.

Lavoie, R., Main, K., King, C., & King, D. (2021). Virtual experience, real consequences: The potential negative emotional consequences of virtual reality gameplay. *Virtual Reality, 25,* 69–81. https://doi.org/10.1007/s10055-020-00440-y

Ling, Y., Qu, C., Heynderickx, I., & Brinkman, W.-P. (2015). Virtual bystanders in a language lesson: Examining the effect of social evaluation, vicarious experience, cognitive consistency, and praising on students' beliefs, self-efficacy, and anxiety in a virtual reality environment. *PLoS One, 10*(4). https://doi.org/10.1371/journal.pone.0125279

Marín-Morales, J., Llinares, C., Guixeres, J., & Alcañiz, M. (2020). Emotion recognition in immersive virtual reality: From statistics to affective computing. *Sensors, 20*(18), 5163. https://doi.org/10.3390/s20185163

McCall, C., Hildebrandt, L., Bornemann, B., & Singer, T. (2015). Physiophenomenology in retrospect: Memory reliably reflects physiological arousal during a prior threatening experience. *Consciousness and Cognition, 38*, 60–70. https://doi.org/10.1016/j.concog.2015.09.011

Moura, A. A. D., Martins, E. D., Moura, V. A. D., & Martins, A. P. (2019). Psychopedagogy and its facilitating strategies in the learning process. *Revista on line de Política e Gestão Educacional, 23*(2), 479–493. https://doi.org/10.22633/rpge.v23i2.12654

Osterwalder, A., & Pigneur, Y. (2013). *Business model generation*. Alta Books.

Pekrun, R. (2014). *Emotions and learning*. UNESCO International Bureau of Education. http://www.ibe.unesco.org/en/document/emotions-and-learning-educational-practices-24

Piaget, J. (1929). *The child's conception of the world*. Routledge & Kegan Paul.

Picard, R. W. (1997). *Affective computing*. MIT Press.

Riva, G., Mantovani, F., Capideville, C. S., Preziosa, A., Morganti, F., Villani, D., Gaggioli, A., Botella, C., & Alcañiz, M. (2007). Affective interactions using virtual reality: the link between presence and emotions. *Cyberpsychology & Behavior, 10*(1), 45–56. https://doi.org/10.1089/cpb.2006.9993

Schutz, P. A., Hong, J. Y., Cross, D. I., & Osbon, J. N. (2006). Reflections on investigating emotion in educational activity settings. *Educational Psychology Review, 18*(4), 343–360. https://doi.org/10.1007/S10648-006-9030-3

Seth, A., Vance, J. M., & Oliver, J. H. (2011). Virtual reality for assembly methods prototyping: A review. *Virtual Reality, 15*(1), 5–20. https://doi.org/10.1007/s10055-009-0153-y

Slater, M. (2004). Presence and emotions. *Cyberpsychology & Behavior, 7*(1), 121. https://doi.org/10.1089/109493104322820200

Slater, M., Antley, A., Davison, A., Swapp, D., Guger, C., Barker, C., & Sanchez-Vives, M. V. (2006). A virtual reprise of the Stanley Milgram obedience experiments. *Plos One, 1*(1), e39. https://doi.org/10.1371/journal.pone.0000039

Stones, E. (1978). Psychopedagogy: Theory and practice in teaching. *British Educational Research Journal, 4*(2), 1–19. http://www.jstor.org/stable/1501117

Sungchul, J., & Lindeman, R.W. (2021, July 15). Perspective: Does realism improve presence in VR? Suggesting a model and metric for VR experience evaluation. *Frontiers in Virtual Reality*. https://www.frontiersin.org/article/10.3389/frvir.2021.693327

Tuena, C., Serino, S., Dutriaux, L., Riva, G., & Piolino, P. (2019). Virtual enactment effect on memory in young and aged populations: A systematic review. *Journal of Clinical Medicine, 8*(5), 620. https://doi.org/10.3390/jcm8050620

Tyng, C. M., Amin, H. U., Saad, M. N. M., & Malik, A. S. (2017). The influences of emotion on learning and memory. *Frontiers in Psychology, 8*, 1454. https://doi.org/10.3389/fpsyg.2017.01454

Vaneenoo, C. (2011). Minimalism in Art and Design: Concept, influences, implications, and perspectives. *Journal of Fine and Studio Art, 2*, 7–12. https://academicjournals.org/journal/JFSA/article-full-text-pdf/3A668BC60 40

Vesisenaho, M., Juntunen, M., Paivi, H., Pöysä-Tarhonen, J., Fagerlund, J., Miakush, I., & Parviainen, T. (2019). Virtual reality in education: Focus on the role of emotions and physiological reactivity. *Journal For Virtual Worlds Research, 12*(1), 7–12. https://doi.org/10.4101/jvwr.v12i1.7329

Vlachopoulou, X., Missonnier, S., Houssier, F., & Marty, F. (2018). Un adolescent dans la peau d'un avatar: enjeux de la rencontre entre le processus adolescent et les mondes virtuels [A teenager in the skin of an avatar: Issues of the meeting between the adolescent process and virtual worlds]. *Revue québécoise de psychologie, 39*(2), 207–221. https://doi.org/10.7202/1051228ar

Vygotsky, L. (1997). *Pensée et langage*. La Dispute.

Yee, N., & Bailenson, J. (2007). The Proteus effect: the effect of transformed self-representation on behavior. *Human Communication Research, 33*(3), 271–290. https://doi.org/10.1111/j.1468-2958.2007.00299.x

Zhang, F. (2021). *Emotions in design-based learning.*[Doctoral dissertation]. Eindhoven University of Technology. https://doi.org/10.13140/RG.2.2.11388.05767

Géraldine Perriguey is a practitioner in Immersive Psychopedagogy©, author, speaker, and CEO/co-Founder of XR Pedagogy. She graduated from the Paris-Cité University in VR & Psychology and obtained the highest distinction for her VR project: *Study of the Denial of the Hurricane Risk in Teenagers*. Today, she develops meaningful VR experiences for institutions and schools, and trains teachers/parents to use immersive technologies.

Immersive Intercultural Language Learning at the Crossroads of Virtual Reality and Game-Based Learning

Stephanie Wössner

Abstract Virtual reality and game-based learning offer many opportunities to put the future at the centre of learning. This article describes three projects based on educational, psychological, and game-design frameworks, as well as a vision of teachers and learners becoming learning partners on a shared path toward a better future.

Keywords Europe · Exponential future · Extended reality · Future oriented learning · Game-based learning · Immersive learning · Virtual reality

Introduction

Since the turn of the millennium, early pioneers of twenty-first century learning (also called *contemporary education*) have been trying to make policy and decision makers aware of the fact that schools need to catch up with the social and cultural changes driven by digital transformation. In most European countries, these early advocates for change have spent the last 15 to 20 years as members of a tiny educational community, either ignored or gently mocked for believing a paradigm shift from teaching to learning is long overdue. Little did they know that COVID-19 would, in less than a year, reveal the malaise of educational systems throughout the world. Not only has the pandemic shown that antiquated teaching methods of the twentieth century are incompatible with a world where it is no longer a given that learners go to school on a daily basis, but it has also made clear that the future transcends national borders: we can survive the many challenges of the twenty-first century only by working together as an international community. Adapting our

S. Wössner (✉)
Landesmedienzentrum Baden-Württemberg, Karlsruhe, Germany
e-mail: steffi@steffi-woessner.de

© The Author(s), under exclusive license to Springer Nature Switzerland AG 2022
P. MacDowell, J. Lock (eds.), *Immersive Education*,
https://doi.org/10.1007/978-3-031-18138-2_5

educational practices has become mandatory. This adaptation includes moving from the idea of contemporary education—which usually focuses on technology as a facilitator for motivation and teacher-led learning integrating the 4Cs (communication, collaboration, creativity, critical thinking)—to future-oriented learning. We need to move away from digitalization and towards digital transformation by adding character and citizenship to the 4Cs, following the concept of the 6Cs of Deep Learning (Fullan & Scott, 2014). For we must be concerned less with the present than with the future.

In this chapter, I will show how virtual reality (VR) and game-based learning (GBL) can be integrated into a future-oriented learning process enhanced by immersive experiences, thus replacing the paradigm of teaching with a paradigm of active learning. After a brief discussion of the current state of education, the chapter points toward the greatest problem education faces and suggest an easy-to-implement solution using VR and GBL based on educational, psychological, and design frameworks. I will contribute concrete examples of how immersive learning adventures can be implemented.

Vignette

When Kassandra was trained to be a teacher at the beginning of the millennium in Germany, she was evaluated based on how well she was able to plan a lesson within a unit of the manual the school was using, how well she did when implementing that lesson, and how much the students learned according to the evaluators in this specific lesson. After graduating from the teacher training academy and starting her first job, she soon realized her uneasiness about a school system firmly anchored in outdated educational practices from the Industrial Revolution and an intellectual paradigm dating as far back as the Enlightenment. She knew the digital transformation had changed the core of society and altered the needs that contemporary educational systems must address. Digitizing or digitalizing education (Academia, 2021) was simply not enough. She shifted her pedagogical focus towards the transformation of learning through personalized projects that challenged learners to be creative and solve problems collaboratively, across geographical boundaries. Solving problems together included language learning leading to mutual understanding and effective problem-solving skills.

What Is Wrong with Education and How Can It Be Rectified?

During the Enlightenment, education for the masses flourished; intellectual exchange became important for the elite in striving for individual happiness and reason. During the Industrial Age, a time that saw many inventions like the automobile, workers needed to acquire new knowledge and those in charge needed compliant workers. Teacher-centered instruction in an educational system resembling an assembly line was necessary to achieve this goal: once students became part of this system, they were educated in a linear manner until their graduation, when they would move on to work in the factories. What they learned were hard facts, and academic excellence paved the way towards being a successful member of society and contributing to its future. So back then, all that mattered was the learning outcome, and the focus of schooling was on teachers who disseminated knowledge to their students (Robinson, 2010).

The ideal of academic excellence is still present in the twenty-first century; being a straight A-student is still considered a sign of success. Today, though, we live in the Digital Age. This does not simply mean that we are surrounded by technology or that technology has had a tremendous impact on our work and daily lives. A cultural change has taken place that we can no longer ignore. The world has become complex and intertwined. New knowledge must be constructed daily to solve current problems. Today is about continuous innovation that requires people to be flexible and creative members of an international community. To achieve that, they need to build on their individual strengths. Education in the Digital Age is about learning and learners taking responsibility for their learning (Chasse et al., 2017). Teachers can create opportunities and accompany learners in their individual learning journey and help them excel at life, not just in the world of academia.

When we look at the lives of young people outside of school, we realize that for them the physical and virtual worlds are inextricably linked and that they roam freely between them in their free time. These worlds also impact each other. The virtual world offers a means of expression they rarely have in the physical world: a place they go to define their identity and sort out sometimes very personal issues with defining where they belong. Therefore, we need to not only acknowledge the virtual world but integrate it into our practices: for instance, by taking advantage of the pedagogical potential that lies in games and VR.

In their process of life-long learning, teachers need guidelines and frameworks that allow them to redefine their practices in the context of the Digital Age. Contrary to what many people think, we do not necessarily have to wait for new frameworks to be developed, but we can use already existing ones and combine them in a new way because frameworks are easily adaptable to new conditions. The complexity we are dealing with brings with it a great number of design frameworks for educational activities, some of which stress the importance of feedback and learning design (Hattie, 2017). Others highlight the potential for integrating technology into the learning process (Puentedura, 2014), refer to older frameworks like Bloom's taxonomy (Anderson et al., 2001; Churches, 2008) or insist on the value of task- and project-based learning (Levine, 2004).

Design Frameworks for Future-Oriented Learning

Immersive learning assumes that personal experiences are conducive to learning in various ways: for instance, they motivate, evoke emotions, help visualize abstract concepts, and make interaction possible, turning the learner into an explorer. Immersive learning can be implemented by using VR and GBL, for instance. However, no unique magical solution can be applied to all situations and learners. The multitude of educational design frameworks available offers a variety of options we can combine as needed. For the world is neither black nor white, and there are a lot of variables to consider when preparing younger generations for the future. We must also not forget that no generation is homogeneous but that we are dealing with individuals.

From observations I have made over the past 15 years as a teacher and based on my cultural experiences from living in different countries (see https://www.steffi-woessner.de), learning in the twenty-first century is a fusion of several interconnected concepts. I call it *future-oriented learning*. A few months after first using the term in German, I discovered that the English equivalent of the term had been coined by a group of researchers from New Zealand almost 10 years ago (Bolstad et al., 2012). Their main goal was to bring education and future-thinking together. For them, "future(−oriented) learning" meant a wide array of ideas, convictions, knowledge, theories, and practices. However, while for various reasons Bolstad et al. used the term as a synonym for twenty-first century education back in 2012, now it is time to reconsider this notion and differentiate twenty-first century education from future-oriented learning. This may not be the case for all countries in the world, but for most. While in 2012, looking at changing practices and evaluating new ideas with the potential to change the system may have been promising, the much-needed paradigm shift has still not arrived. The system is stuck, and we need new inclusive language to speak about learning (Wössner, 2021, 2022).

Future-oriented learning is based on Bloom's Revised Taxonomy (Bloom et al., 2001; Churches, 2008) and the SAMR model of technology integration (Puentedura, 2014). They are complemented by the 6Cs of Deep Learning (Fullan & Scott, 2014) as well as the pillars of good game design by Jane McGonigal (2011). They all contribute their fair share to making learning successful. Based on my experience, learning is successful when the following aspects are present in a learning situation: motivation, emotion, interaction, visualization, discovery, play, as well as positive relationships and feedback.

Bloom's Revised Taxonomy stresses the importance of learner autonomy and creation in the learning process. The flipped version of the pyramid (as seen in Mohan, 2018) highlights that creation is much more important than just remembering facts. Visualizing the concept using circles (McNulty, 2020) is useful for showing that the taxonomy isn't hierarchical in nature but allows for natural transitions from one level to another and back (Fig. 1).

The SAMR model for technology integration is helpful to understand how technology can enable us to achieve a pedagogical objective. The enhancement section

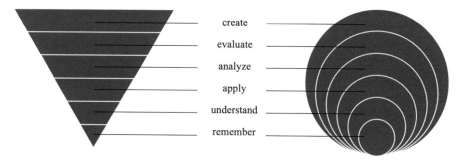

Fig. 1 Bloom's revised taxonomy according to Mohan (2018) and McNulty (2020)

of this framework refers to teacher-led scenarios that see technology merely as a tool, whereas the transformation portion of the framework refers to redesigning and redefining learning. Its purpose is not to justify the use of technology per se, but to show how integrating technology can make learning more purposeful by opening a whole new universe for expression and creation. However, the SAMR model is no longer completely appropriate, for it claims the transformation of learning can be facilitated by modifying tasks and creating new tasks previously inconceivable, thanks to technology. Modification is directly linked to contemporary education: technology enables us to redesign tasks so learners reach the pedagogical objective better than they would have had the task not been redesigned. This generally means using the creative potential of technology, that the 4Cs (communication, collaboration, creativity, critical thinking) (Battelle for Kids, 2019) are considered in the learning design and that deep learning (Hattie, 2017) is in place. Nevertheless, these alone do not constitute a transformation of learning, but rather a transitory space leading up to it. Therefore, I suggest modifying the SAMR model as shown in Fig. 2.

Future-oriented learning is not primarily defined by the many possibilities new technologies inject into our practices but by the nature of the tasks at hand. Most of all, it paves the way for a shift in perspective: teachers and learners become equals on a lifelong common learning journey. Future-oriented learning also redefines the purpose of education in that it not only integrates the 4Cs but also stresses two more Cs we can't do without anymore: character and citizenship (Fullan & Scott, 2014). For our character—including our relationships, empathy, and understanding of the fact that we are citizens of the world—helps us embrace the challenges of today so we can create a better future for humankind.

Creating a better future requires a creative space in which ideas can grow. One such space is play. It is important that we recognize the importance of play in our lives and make it accessible again to learners of all ages. When designing new learning adventures, we must consider the pillars of good game design (McGonigal, 2011): clear rules, (personal) challenges, feedback, and self-determination. Only when we face meaningful challenges that make us grow can we reach the state of flow that leads to happiness (Csikszentmihalyi, 2010). Once we have overcome a

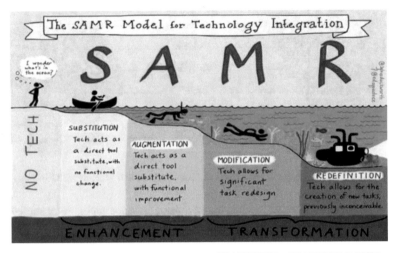

Fig. 2 The modified SAMR model for technology integration by Sylvia Duckworth & edappadvice
Note: Puentedura's (2014) original model, depicted by Duckworth and edappadvice, has been modified to include teaching and learning (contemporary and future-oriented)

challenge in a game, we are rewarded. The reward itself can be social (e.g., badges or XP as used in gamification), it can be the reward of the hunt (usually found in educational games where scores may become more important than the actual learning outcome such as memorizing facts), or it can be our individual success. If the latter is the case, our actions become meaningful, and we are intrinsically motivated to reinvest time and effort to face new, harder challenges without extrinsic motivation (Eyal & Hoover, 2014). This is when self-determination comes into play because no one else defines our challenges for us; we do it ourselves, happily anticipating more individual success (Deci & Ryan, 2008). It can of course be argued that the educational system and games share several features of good game design, but one is missing, self-determination. Game challenges are not determined by a third party, and rules and feedback seem to make more sense than they do at school. Also, we may learn from our mistakes instead of being punished for them. Integrating the pillars of good game design into learning and turning learning into a creative experience is, therefore, one way of making sure we will be ready for the future.

Newer games often also come with a motivating and clear story designed to immerse the player. This is not true for casual games like Candy Crush, where the narrative is often ornamental, while the story in sandbox games like Minecraft might be carefully hidden. Sandbox games thus open the opportunity to introduce an interesting narrative that makes learning meaningful.

Defining VR and GBL

Since different people understand different things when speaking about new technologies and educational practices, it is necessary to define certain terms before addressing examples of how future-oriented learning can be implemented using VR and GBL.

Augmented reality (AR) superimposes a virtual image on the physical world with limited interaction, usually via a device like a smartphone or tablet. AR in its present form is mostly about visualization. Mixed Reality is like AR in that virtual content is superimposed on the physical world, but it allows for greater as well as haptic interaction, through gestures with the HoloLens or more recently the Meta Quest, or with an object like the Merge Cube. This interaction adds some functionality to the physical world.

VR is part of the Extended Reality (XR) spectrum (Fig. 3). It is about immersion in and varying degrees of interaction with a computer-generated reality in which the user feels physically present and has agency. This can happen with or without a head-mounted display (HMD), so VR can be a video game as well as a virtual world in the broader sense, even though the feeling of presence might vary. Immersive 360° content is a kind of VR that limits interaction to gazing or allows simple interactions by clicking on hotspots. Whereas 360° content provides only three degrees of freedom (3DOF), so you are limited to looking all around but cannot move away from that point of view, VR provides six degrees of freedom (6DOF), so you can walk around in the virtual space. Judging from developments in recent years, in my opinion AR will most likely influence our daily lives in the near future, but the immersive and interactive qualities of MR and VR are much more interesting for education.

When speaking of games, three terms that come to mind: gamification, educational games (sometimes called *serious games*), and game-based learning. Gamification occurs when elements of games (points, badges, etc.) are integrated into the physical world such as a classroom. Consequently, students are socially

PHYSICAL WORLD	XR: EXTENDED REALITY		
	AR: AUGMENTED REALITY	MR: MIXED REALITY	VR: VIRTUAL REALITY INCLUDING 360°
	virtual image superimposed on user's view of the physical world		computer-generated world
	no immersion: physical world + virtual elements		immersion (with/without VR headset)
	limited interaction usually by touching a screen	haptic interaction A Windows Mixed Reality → gestures, controller B Merge Cube → object with virtual elements C Meta Quest → passthrough & hand tracking	various kinds of interaction via keyboard, controllers, hands various degrees of interaction from looking at something to manipulation, creating and getting feedback
	→ visualization	→ added functionality	→ feeling of presence in the virtual world

Fig. 3 The Extended Reality spectrum by Stephanie Wössner

rewarded for behaving a certain way, which follows a behaviouristic approach to learning. Educational games look like video games at first, but a closer look reveals that the pillars of good game design (McGonigal, 2011) have usually been neglected because the games were designed by educational professionals without the help of game designers, in general due to lack of funds. Educational games are usually made with the intention to teach facts to learners while removing the important aspect of self-determination. The reward learners get from overcoming a challenge they might not even have chosen themselves is usually that they score points and then compare themselves to others. So, they play more for the hunt (e.g., chunks of information) than for personal success related to what they learned.

Game-based learning means that real (digital) games are integrated into the learning process. Usually, this means that the pillars of good game design are present because commercial games are designed to become popular. Players choose their path and their own challenges and are rewarded for their personal success when they complete a challenge on their own or in collaboration with others. In many popular games, in order to solve problems, players have to communicate, collaborate, and be creative and critical thinkers; they experience first-hand what it means to be part of a community (citizenship) while they grow individually as a person (character).

In the following paragraphs, I focus on digital game-based learning and consider digital games as part of VR. According to the *Handbook of Game-Based Learning*, digital games can have a variety of purposes: from preparing for future learning and learning new knowledge and skills to practising and reinforcing existing knowledge and skills, as well as developing skills for learning and innovation (Plass et al., 2019).

Immersive Learning Adventures

This section presents three VR activities in which learners (and more traditionally oriented teachers) are gradually immersed in a future-oriented learning process, a project leading to creating a bilingual 360° rap video about Franco-German friendship, and a (digital) game-based learning scenario in which learners create their own virtual worlds. All three projects are set in a Franco-German environment and use one or more languages as a *lingua franca* in an authentic communication situation, leading to a shared European identity through negotiating one's own national identity and shared values. The focus of all these activities is on oral communication, both synchronous and asynchronous. They include reflective feedback loops to make learners aware of the learning process. However, they are not dependent on learners being in the same place all the time. This opens new possibilities, including learning anytime, anywhere, and in hybrid contexts as well as in intercultural settings.

These learning adventures can be adapted to any age and language proficiency level by adjusting language requirements and tailoring the tasks to a specific group of learners. They can also be implemented in any context where two or more countries collaborate by using other languages and/or modifying the geographical setting. The importance of immersion is two-fold: to create virtual spaces, the learners are immersed in the learning process and express their ideas in a foreign language in a virtual environment they can shape according to their ideas and without the limitations of the physical world. When visiting the spaces created by their peers or when being immersed in virtual spaces during live communication, the multisensory experiences are linked to emotions and self-efficacy (Immordino-Yang, 2016).

VR Learning Activities

This series of activities is designed to immerse learners gradually in a new way of learning while collaborating with partners from another country. Their *lingua franca* is English. Both the technological and the linguistic challenges increase while they work on projects that become more and more abstract. From a technological point of view, they start out with creating a 360° (3DOF) space, move on to creating a VR (6DOF) space, then create their own avatars to meet up in a virtual world. From a linguistic and collaborative point of view, they start with a simple monologue and create the digital space within their own group of learners, receiving feedback from another national group only at the end. The next step combines a monological task with an asynchronous dialogue while working in binational groups. The culmination point is a synchronous dialogue in real-time. In terms of content, they start by speaking about their immediate surroundings, combining a collective and an individual point of view. They then move to a personal viewpoint about people who have changed the world and then establish a relationship between themselves, the world, and the future. Finally, as a group, they agree on a topic that is important to them and start a real-time conversation about it. Depending on their language proficiency, they can (but do not necessarily have to) prepare these conversations, and the conversations can either be made up of a short monologue followed by a dialogue or be a true debate.

The first VR activity, "Welcome to our school," is a 360° school tour that each group of learners creates collaboratively for their partners in the other country. This is a personalized experience created by one group of learners for another that considers intercultural differences (e.g., a French school usually has a full-time school nurse on call, whereas German schools do not), thus making learners acutely aware of their common European identity as opposed to their national identities. The digital skills addressed are taking 360° photos, recording MP3 files, taking photos and videos, and integrating all these media into a virtual tour. All six Cs are addressed, and the task can be adapted to accommodate any language proficiency level. The project can be done in approximately six to nine hours covering pre-tasks, production, and feedback for the partners. A full description can be found online: https://www.petiteprof79.eu/welcome-to-our-school-vr-360.

The second VR activity, "Europe United," is about heroes. The learners choose their personal heroes from past and present before coming up with a cause that is important to them and that might turn them into a hero in the future. They create a virtual museum with all kinds of media they can legally use and audio recordings in English that explain their choices. This time, the learners share their individual projects with partners from both countries and receive feedback in the form of questions they answer asynchronously. Potential topics include changing the world, being a world/European citizen, human and civil rights, current and future problems, or trends. Digital skills include media literacy (e.g., research, copyright, Creative Commons), recording MP3 files, and creating interactive presentations, as well as coding skills. All six Cs are addressed, and language proficiency may vary. The project requires approximately six to nine hours including pre-tasks, production, and feedback. Scaffolding may be used with heterogeneous groups of learners. A full description can be found online:
https://www.petiteprof79.eu/europe-united.

The third VR activity, "Let's talk," places learners from both countries in a virtual environment, where they discuss a topic relevant to them and that they have previously prepared. Topics may range from friendship, video games, or smartphone use to inventions or discoveries from their respective countries to the workplace. The digital skills include media literacy (research, finding photos to use), presenting a topic and one's opinion in a virtual setting, and taking part in an online discussion. All six Cs can be addressed depending on the topic chosen and the language proficiency requirements. The project requires between three and six hours to complete. A full description can be found online:
https://www.petiteprof79.eu/lets-talk-vr

All three activities have in common that the creation process is followed by or linked to experience and emotion through immersion and interaction in the virtual world. This turns two individual groups of learners from two different countries into one big European group of learners facing the future together.

360° Rap Videos

For groups of learners who meet during an exchange and who like music, there is a possibility of creating music together while preparing for the exchange and to produce a 360° music video when they meet in person. The project requires several workshops that can be done online. During these workshops, learners learn about the elements of rap, practice rhyming, and create their own song about a topic of their choice related to the relationship between their two countries. For instance, depending on the age and language proficiency, they can compare their school days, reflect on their interest in the other country, look at similarities and differences between the two nations, or integrate more abstract topics like politics, immigration, or literature. Once they have finished their song, they discuss where they want to film the video using a 360° camera and how they want to film it, taking into account all aspects of 360°, such as the fact that it means there are no borders, there are different creative perspectives (e.g., looking at the singers, looking in the same direction they do) and that the song encompasses all their different points of view.

This project focuses on a creation process that makes the learners aware of their European identity, but it also ends with having them live through an immersive experience while watching the video. The emotional state stimulated by this experience changes their perspective while reminding them of the fact that none of them could have created the video alone. Just as they did with the video, they will create their future together by considering their respective differences as well as their common European identity.

Both an example video and a project description (in German) can be found here: https://www.petiteprof79.eu/ein-360-rapvideo-zur-deutsch-franzoesischen-freundschaft/

Game-Based Learning

This game-based learning adventure is set in the Franco-German quarter of a fictional European Youth Village in Brussels. It brings together an interesting story that offers various future-oriented learning opportunities and open-world sandbox games like Minecraft, which has been a long-time favorite among teenagers everywhere, including Germany (Medienpädagogischer Forschungsverbund Südwest, 2021, p. 60). The learning adventure is based on the global simulation format (Levine, 2004). In an effort to immerse themselves in the culture of their respective partner country whose language they learn as a foreign language, teenagers from France and Germany reinvent themselves by creating new identities: the Germans become French, and the French become either German, Austrian, or Swiss German. They then apply for a scholarship to move into the European Youth Village, where they live in apartments with roommates from both countries. Over the course of several months, they add their own touches to the Village: for example, by taking into account the 2030 Agenda for Sustainable Development (United Nations Educational, Scientific and Cultural Organization, 2017), they work on projects about cultural aspects of their (assumed) identities, and common European topics and problems to solve. Finally, they create little movies documenting their life in the European Youth Village to share with the larger community. It is also possible to integrate transmedia/immersive storytelling: for instance, creating a collaborative graphic novel about their adventures by using photos taken in the virtual world.

The project can be easily implemented using either Minecraft or Minetest, both of which are creative game engines designed to enable the player to create virtual worlds. Minecraft is a Microsoft product that, in Europe, comes with several privacy concerns, whereas Minetest is an open-source project that needs to be hosted on your own server – or you can use BLOCKALOT (www.blockalot.de) to create your own Minetest world. Since learners are supposed to speak both French and German with each other, another requirement is a voice chat server like Mumble, also open-source software. Both Minecraft and Minetest can mirror the real world with natural disasters or demands for energy, etc. by using mods that can be installed (Figs. 4 and 5).

Fig. 4 Entrance and apartment building of the Franco-German village

Fig. 5 Bird's eye view of the Franco German village

Since Minecraft and Minetest are open world games, there are no limits as to how far the project can go and how many groups of learners can join. It is perfectly possible to create several neighbouring villages whose inhabitants meet on a regular basis. The story can also be appropriated and developed by the players themselves, so they can make it their own. This even includes having other disciplines, such as geography or history, join the project and add new dimensions to it.

In an educational context, these games help players prepare for future learning, acquire new knowledge and skills, practice and reinforce existing knowledge and skills, and continue to develop as learners and innovators. All these functions can be integrated into a scenario because it is completely up to the group of learners to decide on activities and challenges, make their own rules, come up with their own narrative, accomplish tasks together, and reflect on what they learned about themselves, each other, and their group identity by creating their virtual world as a place where everyone feels comfortable.

Strategies for Implementation of Design

The following strategies are suggestions about how to facilitate projects with VR and GBL. These aren't the only way to implement future-oriented learning, but due to the qualities of the technologies involved as well as the proximity to learners' everyday lives, VR and GBL have significant potential waiting to be explored by teachers who feel the need to renew their professional practice. With an understanding of the basic concept of future-oriented learning and a realization that this is not at all about a specific technology, but about the underlying pedagogical objectives they help learners reach, VR and GBL can easily be inspired by the examples provided by this article and be modified for specific purposes and objectives.

- **VR is not defined by technology.** VR is defined by immersion and interaction that lead to a feeling of presence and agency in the virtual world. This feeling of presence and agency is not linked to a specific technology. To understand this, experience virtual worlds first-hand: play a game and explore different virtual worlds without preconceived notions of them being fake. Also, virtual worlds are not limited to games; social media are also part of them. Additionally, take advantage of the unique opportunity to speak with young people for whom there is no clear boundary between the physical and the virtual world. They might teach you about their perception of the world and their place in this world; by speaking with them, you help them reflect on their own identities at the same time.
- **Future-oriented learning requires a new mindset.** Learning requires learners to take responsibility for their learning. You yourself are a learner, too. Learners can teach you as much as you can teach them, and together you can create amazing things. This also means you are not omniscient; there is no shame in not knowing everything if you demonstrate that you know how to learn it. This mindset will cause a shift in your relationship with the students you work with, and you need to remain aware of your impact on their lives as a partner and a role model. Be open-minded and make sure that you help learners become people you trust with your own future. To do this, take every opportunity to speak with learners of all ages. Give up your position as the omniscient teacher, and instead of having learners work for you, work with them on projects as a co-learner.
- **Technology is never the solution, but it can be an asset for the transformation of learning**. If you do not feel comfortable with technology because you think it removes the human connection, think twice. If seen only as a tool to reach a goal that you set as a teacher, technology can isolate learners because they never need others to accomplish a task. However, if you consider the transformative potential of technology when integrated into a larger learning process that takes into account the 6Cs, technology becomes a new means of individual expression, particularly in an intercultural dialogue. You could start by speaking with young people to find out how they use technology to express themselves. Have a look at their YouTube-Videos, TikToks, blogs, and other media and analyze them. What do they tell you about skills and competencies they have learned by using technology to produce these?
- **Learning can happen anywhere and anytime.** Gen Z are the first generation having grown up with technology as an integral part of their daily lives. They do not see the dichotomy between the *real* and the *virtual* world. Gen X and Gen Y (Millennials) are acutely aware of having known a life before the Internet whereas games, media production, and social media are part of the *real* lives of Gen Z and Gen Alpha (Fell, 2022). They navigate between these two different worlds without even realizing it, and they learn in both. We must consider not only their way of life but also the fact learning doesn't happen only in school and that there is a huge untapped source of creativity waiting to be put to good use.

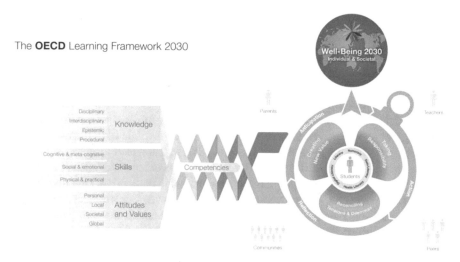

Fig. 6 The OECD learning framework 2030

To challenge learners outside of school, design a project that has them collaborate on presenting their learning beyond the classroom in any form that feels natural to them. While they work, navigate between the groups, and listen. Then apply what you learned to design a project that integrates learners' time outside of school and which they can work on anywhere but in school. Do not put shackles on their creativity but give them a topic and tell them what the learning goal is. Do not tell them exactly how to get there, but make sure they know they can ask for your help any time.

- **Deep learning instead of surface learning.** Even though education still happens in a world where grades and degrees decide our fate, we need to take a step back and reconsider why we became teachers. Surface learning, such as focusing on facts, has long been a big part of schooling. However, in the Digital Age, finding information is easy, but knowing what to do with it and how to use it to solve problems is the difficult part— particularly in an interconnected world. Therefore, we need to focus on the six Cs of deep learning by helping our learning partners learn the skills they need to shape the future for the better. It may not be possible to put a grade on everything, for learning is a life-long process after all, but it will be worth it. Have learners give each other feedback and reflect on their own learning, and do not define learning outcomes for them. Instead, let them be creative. There is no harm in making mistakes when trying out new things. To move from surface learning to deep learning, look at your curricula, assess which skills and competencies they imply, find a sustainable development goal, and put it in a context that is both accessible and relevant for the learners. Design a project that follows the OECD Learning Framework 2030 (OECD, 2018) by combining knowledge, skills, attitudes, and values, and helping learners to develop competencies that can translate into action in the future (Fig. 6).

Conclusion

The future-oriented learning design and learning activities presented have shown how VR and GBL can contribute to meaningful change in educational practices by shifting the focus from teaching to learning. It is not about the technology itself, but about the plethora of opportunities for change that lies dormant in it. The learners who participated in these and similar projects not only took responsibility for their learning but experienced a visible change in attitude towards both themselves and their peers, as well as toward their place in society. They also acquired skills and competencies they could then apply to real-world problems: for instance, implementing a little project to stop others from using plastic bottles, working together on bigger problems, and solving them by combining everyone's talents, or simply going abroad and speaking a foreign language to communicate with people from different backgrounds. The key to change was that, on the one hand, the learners felt valued and had agency, and, on the other hand, they learned in a context that was relevant to them and where they could experience their individual learning journey as a group.

The strategies provided for implementing these changes result in a change in attitude, while the examples and design frameworks provide ideas about how to start changing teaching practices to provide learners with opportunities for future-oriented learning. It is important to acknowledge the power of risk-taking and understand that a potential failure is simply an opportunity to learn and to improve. Being immersed alongside learners in virtual worlds and game-based learning adventures makes it possible to explore important topics, acquire skills and competencies everyone needs to help the world become a better place, and give a voice and agency to the young people into whose hands we place our future: a future that is, above all, exponential and unpredictable.

References

Academia. (2021). Difference between digitization, digitalization, and digital transformation. *Academia ERP*. https://www.academiaerp.com/blog/digitization-digitalization-digital-transformation/

Anderson, L. W. (Ed.), Krathwohl, D. R. (Ed.), Airasian, P. W., Cruikshank, K. A., Mayer, R. E., Pintrich, P. R., Raths, J., & Wittrock, M. C. (2001). *A taxonomy for learning, teaching, and assessing: A revision of Bloom's taxonomy of educational objectives*. Longman.

Battelle for Kids. (2019). *Framework for 21st century learning*. http://static.battelleforkids.org/documents/p21/P21_Framework_Brief.pdf

Bolstad, R., Gilbert, J., & McDowall, S. (2012). *Supporting future-oriented learning and teaching*. New Zealand Government: Ministry of Education.

Chasse, R. P., Auricchio, G., & Liebert, K-H. (2017). *Digital age learning*. https://efmdglobal.org/wp-content/uploads/PoV_Learning_in_the_digital_age_vFINAL.pdf

Churches, A. (2008). *Bloom's digital taxonomy*. https://www.researchgate.net/publication/22838 1038_Bloom's_Digital_Taxonomy

Csikszentmihalyi, M., & Szöllösi, I. (2010). *Flow – Der Weg zum Glück: Der Entdecker des Flow-Prinzips erklärt Seine Lebensphilosophie.*

Deci, E. L., & Ryan, R. M. (2008). Self-determination theory: A macrotheory of human moti-vation, development, and health. *Canadian Psychology/Psychologie Canadienne, 49*(3), 182–185. https://doi.org/10.1037/a0012801

Eyal, N., & Hoover, R. (2014). Hooked: How to build habit-forming products. Portfolio.

Fell, A. (2022, April 20). Understanding generation alpha. *McCrindle.* https://mccrindle.com.au/insights/blog/gen-alpha-defined/

Fullan, M., & Scott, G. (2014). *Education PLUS; the world will be led by people you can count on, including you!* https://www.michaelfullan.ca/wp- content/uploads/2014/09/Education-Plus-A-Whitepaper-July-2014-1.pdf.

Hattie, J. (2017). *LEARNx deep learning through transformative pedagogy* (Module 1: Surface and Deep Learning). [MOOC]. UQx @ edX. https://www.edx.org/course/deep- learning-through-transformative-pedagogy.

Immordino-Yang, M. H. (2016). *Emotions, learning, and the brain: Exploring the educational implications of affective neuroscience.* W. W.

Levine, G. S. (2004). Global simulation: A student-centered, task-based format for intermedi-ate foreign language courses. *Foreign Language Annals, 37*(1), 26–36. http://web.pdx.edu/~fischerw/~fischer/courses/advanced/ methods_docs/pdf_doc/wbf_collection/0151_0200/0172_FLA_2004_Levine.pdf

McGonigal, J. (2011). *Reality is broken: Why games make us better and how they can change the world.* Penguin.

McNulty, N. (2020). Bloom's digital taxonomy: A reference guide for teachers. *HH Books.* https://amzn.eu/85JaxXU

Medienpädagogischer Forschungsverbund Südwest. (2021). *Jim-Studie 2021: Jugend, informa-tion, median.* https://www.mpfs.de/fileadmin/files/Studien/JIM/2021/JIM-Studie_2021_bar-rierefrei.pdf

Mohan, D. (2018). Flipped classroom, flipped teaching and flipped learning in the foreign/sec-ond language post–secondary classroom. *Nouvelle Revue Synergies Canada, 11.* https://doi.org/10.21083/nrsc.v0i11.4016

OECD. (2018). *The future of education and skills: Education 2030 the future we want.* https://www.oecd.org/education/2030/E2030%20Position%20Paper%20(05.04.2018).pdf

Plass, J., Mayer, R., & Homer, B. (Eds.). (2019). *Handbook of game-based learning.* The MIT Press.

Puentedura, R. R. (2014). SAMR: A contextualized introduction. *Hippasus.* http://www.hippasus.com/rrpweblog/archives/2013/08/22/SAMR_ContextualizedIntroduction.pdf

Robinson, K. (2010, October 14) *Changing education paradigms* [Video]. *YouTube.* https://www.youtube.com/watch?v=zDZFcDGpL4U

United Nations Educational, Scientific and Cultural Organization. (2017). Education for sustain-able development goals. Learning objectives. *UNESCO.* https://www.unesco.de/sites/default/files/2018-08/unesco_education_for_sustainable_development_goals.pdf

Wössner, S. (2021). *Zeitgemäßes und zukunftsorientiertes Lernen.* PetiteProf79. https://www.petiteprof79.eu/zeitgemaesses-und-zukunftsorientiertes-lernen/

Wössner, S. (2022). … außer man tut es: Bildung auf dem schwierigen Weg in die Zukunft. *On. Lernen in Der Digitalen Welt, 8*, 4–7.

Stephanie Wössner is is a freelance consultant and speaker for future-oriented learning. She is also team leader for innovation at the Landesmedienzentrum Baden-Württemberg, Germany. Her areas of expertise include extended reality, game-based learning, and artificial intelligence, as well as the Metaverse. She is particularly interested in exploring the potential of digital games that allow for immersive, collaborative learning adventures.

See It and Be It: Designing Immersive Experiences to Build STEM Skills and Identity in Elementary and Middle School

Corinne Brenner, Jessica Ochoa Hendrix, and Mandë Holford

Abstract This chapter describes the process of developing immersive educational science experiences. Three integrated components (virtual or augmented reality, digital science journal website, and an educator dashboard) help students gain STEM knowledge and acquire critical science practice skills aligned with the Next Generation Science Standards in the United States.

Keywords Augmented reality · Design process · STEM education · Virtual reality

Introduction

From climate change to pandemics, global challenges are rooted in science and technology. To face these challenges, students need to develop science, technology, engineering, and mathematics (STEM)-inspired creative and critical thinking skills (Committee on STEM Education, 2018). In the United States, the Next Generation Science Standards (abbreviated as NGSS; Pruitt, 2014) were developed to emphasize skills such as asking questions and defining problems, planning and carrying out investigations, and engaging in argument from evidence.

To address these needs, our educational technology company, Killer Snails LLC, makes games and extended reality experiences inspired by the work of real scientists and engineers. Killer Snails' projects leverage virtual reality (VR) and augmented reality (AR) in curriculum supplements to help students not just learn isolated facts but see themselves as scientists tackling global science and technology challenges.

C. Brenner (✉) · J. O. Hendrix
Killer Snails, LLC, Brooklyn, NY, USA
e-mail: corinne@killersnails.com; jessica@killersnails.com

M. Holford
Hunter College, of The City University of New York, The American Museum of Natural History, Brooklyn, NY, USA
e-mail: mande@killersnails.com

© The Author(s), under exclusive license to Springer Nature Switzerland AG 2022
P. MacDowell, J. Lock (eds.), *Immersive Education*,
https://doi.org/10.1007/978-3-031-18138-2_6

89

Extended reality (XR) technologies like AR and VR serve two important functions: helping students envision what science and scientists look like in the field ("see it"), and giving students a first-person, agentic role in doing scientific tasks ("be it"). In this context, VR refers to technologies that immerse a user in a digital world: for example, by using a head-mounted display. AR refers to technology that puts a digital layer of objects or information over the real world, such as by using an app on a tablet or smartphone. Immersive technologies like VR and AR fill the need for exciting, inquiry-based, student-centred STEM learning that enhances science skills and functions effectively in a classroom setting.

We have used VR to send students on expeditions to explore ocean ecosystems in *BioDive* and travel to faraway planets in *GeoForge*. Using AR in *WaterWays,* students can bring a Mako shark into their classroom to explore shark anatomy and tag it with a GPS transmitter. These experiences serve as anchoring phenomena to ground discussion and further activities that would be impossible or too dangerous, difficult, or expensive for students to have in real life (Bailenson, 2018). We pair immersive experiences with a personalized website called a digital science journal, creating opportunities for students to reflect on their experiences and apply what they have learned in additional activities and questions. This enables students to move beyond memorizing to enacting science and engineering practices and applying them to their own interests and lives. Each product includes an educator dashboard that provides teachers with a real-time summary of the class's progress and access to students' responses from both the XR and digital science journal.

In this chapter, we describe the process we use to develop immersive educational experiences and how the three integrated components (VR/AR, digital science journal website, and educator dashboard) help teachers meet the three-dimensional approach to science instruction envisioned in NGSS. Our approach uses XR to help students gain STEM knowledge and acquire critical science practice skills by seeing the science and being the scientist.

Vignette

After a year and a half outside of formal classrooms, Angela, a sixth grade science teacher, noticed students (ages 11–12) were filled with angst as they returned to school buildings for a summer session in 2021. She needed a safe, budget-friendly, and engaging way for students to explore questions about wildlife and ecosystems without sharing materials due to pandemic restrictions. The prospect of writing a technology-based curriculum a week before the program began was daunting.

At a professional development event, Angela was intrigued by a free trial of BioDive. In BioDive, middle school students acted as marine biologists investigating venomous marine snails' ecosystems. Students used their laptops to learn about Dr. Mandë Holford's work and observed venomous snails capturing prey using phones in a VR viewer. Angela liked the fun NGSS-aligned lessons and how they referred to students as scientists who test and revise their hypotheses to make recommendations.

Angela used BioDive to structure a unit on biodiversity and climate change, mixing in deeper discussions and explorations of topics students were interested in along the way. The educator dashboard showed her each student's progress in real time and automatically graded multiple choice questions, leaving more time for discussions. Angela reflected, "My hope was that it would encourage students to pursue STEM careers and niche areas of research through their experience with this unique scientific narrative, and through meeting a community of diverse scientists through the videos shown on the platform. I do believe it achieved that goal, and I am excited to continue using the platform in the future."

Design Framework: How Killer Snails Integrates XR for STEM Learning

In each learning game, we use three components: (1) a digital science journal (personalized website) to structure the overall experience; (2) an AR or VR activity that puts students in the roles of scientists; and (3) an educator dashboard providing a real-time summary of a whole classroom's activity, which lets educators click into an individual student's work to leave feedback in the form of comments and stickers. This structure has been used to explore Biology topics in *BioDive*, Earth Science in *GeoForge*, and Ecology in *WaterWays*.

Each component serves a function; we have designed them to work together toward such outcomes as improving students' science and engineering practices, increasing student interest in STEM and STEM careers, and improving classroom instruction (Fig. 1). In the following sections, we discuss how these elements address unique science content to achieve our goals of helping students *see it and be it*.

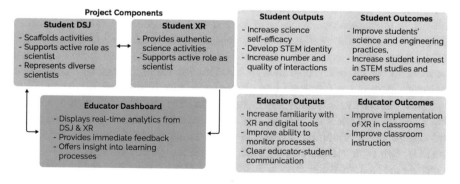

Fig. 1 Killer Snails' XR product components, outputs, and outcomes

The Digital Science Journal: See It

The digital science journal (DSJ) serves two purposes. First, we use digital multimedia—including photos and videos—to introduce students to anchoring phenomena as well as the scientists or experts who study a topic like venomous sea snails or shark migration patterns, allowing students to better understand the context of the unit. Second, web pages in the digital science journal provide a familiar structure for activities that introduce students to new vocabulary or concepts and allow them to process the experiences they have had in VR and AR. This function has its roots in the architecture of human cognition and the cognitive processes that govern learning.

Including examples of diverse scientists and the work they do is intended to strengthen students' feelings that they are represented in the science community. Such examples help build their science identity and reduce feelings that may lead students to become uninterested in science or think they cannot be scientists. Students' interest in science and feelings of self-efficacy, the feeling of being capable of doing the work of science, are high in elementary school but decline over time (Summers & Abd-El-Khalick, 2019). This decline is especially acute for girls, students from low socioeconomic status, and students who belong to Black, Hispanic, Native Hawaiian or Pacific Islander, and American Indian or Alaska Native racial/ethnic categories (National Science Board, 2021). Countering stereotypical beliefs about scientists and exposing students to inquiry-based instruction both help counteract these trends (Nguyen & Riegle-Crumb, 2021; Riegle-Crumb et al., 2019). *BioDive* and *WaterWays* implement these findings by including diverse examples of real scientists and encouraging students, in their game role as scientists, to develop and answer research questions in the DSJ for each experience.

Using immersive technologies in the classroom can bring science to life, but it also comes with challenges. Many researchers and practitioners are cautious about using new technologies because navigating a detailed immersive experience can impose extraneous cognitive load or add information that does not contribute to learning (Moreno & Mayer, 2007; Papanastasiou et al., 2019). Pairing the XR experiences with activities in the DSJ is a powerful way to connect students' experiences with the key information. Activities like comparing observations, transforming observed phenomenon into data in tables, and evaluating whether hypotheses drafted in text are confirmed in a virtual environment take place in the DSJ. Opportunities to actively make sense of information serve to foster generative processing, an important cognitive function, and is recommended as a strategy to help turn incoming information into usable knowledge (Fiorella & Mayer, 2016).

Since *WaterWays* is intended for a younger audience (grades 3–5, ages 8–11), we have paid special attention to sources of cognitive load and how we could manage it throughout the development process. We drew on our experiences creating *BioDive* and *GeoForge* for middle and high school students (grades 6–10, ages 11–16) to leverage the DSJ for *WaterWays* to manage the cognitive load imposed by using new technologies and complex material. The DSJ provides clear, segmented instructions

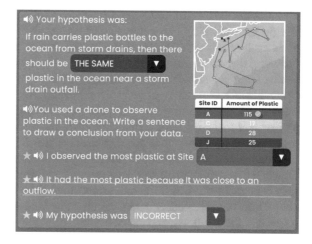

Fig. 2 Evaluating and revising hypotheses in the WaterWays DSJ

to lead students through each part of the experience (Moreno & Mayer, 2007). We designed activities in the DSJ to inspire generative processing without relying too heavily on open-ended text questions, since typing is a skill many students in this age group have not yet mastered and would be an additional source of cognitive load. Eliciting student involvement through drawings was another intentional design element to spark student thinking and share ideas without relying on typing. Multiple choice questions, matching games, and minigames allow students to apply their experiences in AR and demonstrate what they learned without creating extraneous cognitive load.

The DSJ also provides opportunities to provide immediate, contextual feedback. In *WaterWays*, students construct a hypothesis, then evaluate whether their hypothesis was correct and revise it if necessary. A red "x" prompts students to revise their responses while a green check mark confirms that their observations support their initial hypothesis, and students make progress on the task based on their revision, not the initial hypothesis (Fig. 2). This is intended to help students enact processes of science and understand that learning is continual and ongoing.

Using the tenet that connecting experience with cognitive recall fosters learning and retention of new ideas, we intentionally design the DSJ prompts and students' activities to scaffold the AR and VR engagements. These will be discussed in the next section.

Virtual or Augmented Reality: Be It

There's nothing like firsthand experience. Constructivist models of education highlight the importance of students taking an active role in learning; experiences help students connect new information with previously assimilated knowledge. VR can also provide the type of highly interactive, motivating, student-centred experiences that promote learning across domains (Huang et al., 2010).

In each of our experiences, students take on a scientist role to do tasks and see the world through that role. For example, *BioDive* consists of five modules in which students are scientists working through the steps of the scientific process: from observing an ecosystem to experimentation, model building, hypothesis testing, and finally making recommendations based on their findings. Using VR on mobile phones and low-cost, lightweight cardboard headsets, students observe venomous snails hunting for prey, look for organisms occupying different niches in the food web, and use tools to compare water quality at different sites. In one 2-minute experience, VR allows students to shrink in size and travel to the ocean floor to observe how the conoidean "killer" marine snails hunt fish, worms, and other snails as prey (Fig. 3). In another, students use a variety of tools to measure water quality, including its turbidity, salinity, and dissolved oxygen content at sites that may be affected by pollutants.

Having experiences from a first-person perspective and making choices about what to do put students in a scientist's shoes. In a pilot study of *BioDive*, we observed the impacts of these experiences on students (Killer Snails LLC, unpublished internal *BioDive* report, 2020). Educators shared with us that the *BioDive* experience makes a strong impression on students who have never visited the ocean and live in places where it is impractical to visit. Educators specifically mentioned that students were excited for the chance to use VR in class, which motivated a high level of engagement during the session. In surveys of 329 students, 80% reported they would recommend *BioDive* to other students, and 78% reported they enjoyed *BioDive*. We also observed significant learning gains for key vocabulary like *biotic and trophic level*. In a survey of 199 students after using *GeoForge,* 82% of students reported that the experiences helped them see themselves as scientists, as did all 11

Fig. 3 BioDive VR scene: cone snail on the hunt

respondents in a preliminary study of *WaterWays* (Brenner et al., 2021a, b). These responses highlight how XR was an effective tool for engaging students in the classroom, building knowledge, and creating the opportunity for students to see themselves as scientists.

The excitement of taking part in science through XR is unlike the real world in two important ways. First, in a virtual world, students can take a risk and fail the task with minimal consequence. No equipment will be broken, no animals will be harmed, and no time or expense will be wasted because of a mistake. Digital environments invite graceful failure in that students may have to try multiple solutions, revise a strategy, or get more information to succeed (Plass et al., 2020). Instead of being punished for an incorrect response, students are encouraged by the design of the experience to try more than once; since initial incorrect attempts do not have harsh consequences, students are able to explore. Second, and in support of graceful failure, a digital experience allows students to receive immediate, contextual feedback about what went wrong and make a new choice with that in mind. The ability to provide immediate, contextual feedback in a digital environment is extremely helpful for learning gains in a variety of domains (Magalhães et al., 2020; Van der Kleij et al., 2015). VR in products like *BioDive* allows students to get the benefits of a firsthand experience: "being it" without many of the inconveniences of being a novice and with the benefit of immediate, corrective feedback.

Educator Dashboard: Offering Insight While Students See It and Be It

An educator's ability to monitor and respond to student work is also vital to a successful learning experience. *BioDive, GeoForge,* and *WaterWays* all provide educators with a dashboard that allows them to monitor progress and guide instruction for the immersive experience in real time. Educators get an overview page that summarizes the class's progress in each unit. They can immediately spot whether one student is stuck, or if all students are getting stuck on a page of the DSJ. If they click in to see a page, educators see everything a student creates in their DSJ, not just the summarized results of an assessment. Educators can also provide stickers and comments as feedback on student activities in the DSJ to motivate their learning and provide personalized support. Educators reported these features were also helpful for connecting with students during remote learning.

In our first round of user research for *WaterWays,* we received feedback from educators that the dashboard was a particularly appealing tool during user tests with hybrid or remote learning classes. Educators were excited to have the opportunity to monitor student progress and respond to student work in the moment, regardless of whether the students were in the classroom or learning remotely. From monitoring the dashboard, educators could see when a student wasn't progressing through the pages, and called on them or moved them to Zoom (version 5.11, https://zoom.us)

breakout rooms to receive additional support. Based on educator feedback of *WaterWays*, we have also added a chat function to allow for even more tailored conversation. Assisting students in their moment of need is a vital component to teaching and an asset for educators, which digital technologies can provide whether students are in the classroom or working remotely.

Applying Unique Affordances to Build Immersive Learning Games

The previous sections discussed *why* the educational products include specific features and incorporate XR. The following sections detail *how* the design process works to include voices from experts, students, and teachers, as well as technical refinement. We use the Successive Approximations Model (Fig. 4; Allen & Sites, 2012) for designing and developing XR educational experiences. This approach emphasizes incorporating iterative feedback from stakeholders through rapid design and development sprints for every learning game we create. The Killer Snails team includes a Director of Learning, who plans and conducts user research; a Design Director, who crafts the initial visual designs and implements changes; and a Lead Developer, who creates the DSJ and the VR or AR content, and who implements changes. The process also includes feedback from two teachers who are part time employees of Killer Snails LLC as well as full-time teachers in the subject area of the product. We have used this model for the design and development of two VR experiences: *BioDive*, commercially available since Spring 2020, and *GeoForge*, still in development. We are currently using this model to develop the AR-driven experience *WaterWays* during 2021–2022, with some adjustments in our process due to the COVID-19 pandemic.

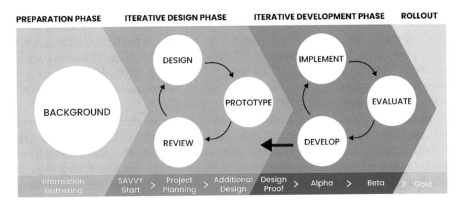

Fig. 4 Successive Approximations Model for designing and developing immersive STEM Experiences. (Adapted from Allen & Sites, 2012)

Preparation Phase

To put students into the role of scientists, we must first define what scientific topics they will investigate. In the Successive Approximations Model, instructional designers first perform a preparation phase to gather information and begin to define learning objectives and goals. Killer Snails interviews teachers and informal educators as well as subject matter experts to better understand a topic (like impacts of plastic pollution on sharks) and reviews recommended resources to understand how the content is currently being taught. We specifically ask educators about common student misconceptions and concepts that are complex to teach and for students to comprehend.

An important feature of our work is using the unique affordances of VR and AR. Reproducing material already available in AR or VR is unhelpful. We look for areas not currently well-addressed by lectures, textbooks, or even 2D digital media, where students would benefit from a 3D or first-person perspective on the issue. We are inspired by unusual science content (like extreme creatures from nature, such as venomous "killer" snails, space travel, or hidden water systems in urban areas) that would not be readily accessible in classrooms. Working with subject matter experts during the preparation phase helps us to learn more about phenomena that align interesting content areas with the affordances of XR, and to implement NGSS standards for disciplinary core ideas and for science and engineering practices.

Iterative Design Phase

Once the concept is clear, we go through an iterative design phase, with cycles of designing, prototyping, and evaluating ideas with our stakeholders, teachers, and content expert advisers. Design prototypes can include low-resolution sketches, slide decks, wireframes, and storyboards. Eventually our designer and developer create prototypes of the DSJ website and VR or AR scene, modelling the patterns of interactions and flow of the experience. Flexible online design technologies allowed us to continue creating and sharing our ideas while working remotely through the COVID-19 pandemic.

Iterative Development Phase

After developing a prototype and evaluating it with educators and content experts, we move into an iterative development phase in which we build a functional prototype and test its implementation in classrooms. We bring each module of an experience (about 40 minutes of class material) to a minimum of three schools for iterative testing, with at least three team members completing an observation tracker that aligns to the content students are seeing. All students and educators are fully informed about what they will be asked to do, and they consent to participate. They know they can ask us questions, decline to answer questions, or stop participating at any time. During development, we pilot with a range of partners including low-income Title I urban schools, well-resourced urban/suburban schools, and rural schools to help assess whether the product will work in a variety of settings (Fig. 5).

The initial school visit provides insight on the product's usability. Are students able to progress all the way through the unit? Did technical challenges prevent completion? After the site visit, our team interviews the teachers to ask for feedback such as the appropriateness of the content, what kind of information teachers would like presented in the educational dashboard, and how teachers could see themselves using the product. The team also reviews the students' responses in the digital science journal to monitor if students were answering the questions correctly, and to discuss any changes needed for a unit to fit into one class period.

The second school visit occurs after improvements are made to the content or technology. Again, three team members monitor the class using the same observation tracker and watch for how students interact with the technology. Generally, the second site visit has far fewer technological issues, and the content pacing is appropriate to complete the task. After the classes have finished, we again interview the teacher to ask about how the teacher could see themselves using the product and what materials would support the teacher in implementing the product in their class. In the past, teachers' responses have included requests for curricular alignment or the ability to download student responses as a spreadsheet. Design changes may still be needed at this point such as changing vocabulary, clarifying instructions, or shifting activities to better fit the class length.

After completing revisions to the content and/or technology, we schedule a third visit for the same unit. The third school visit is for final polishing of the unit before

Fig. 5 Implementation testing in classrooms

moving to start developing the next unit. This visit proceeds in the same pattern, with special attention in the post-visit teacher interview to what data would be most helpful in a dashboard and what supplementary materials might be needed.

Iterative testing with students and educators is vital. When the prototype is being used in an authentic setting with all the limitations, distractions, and less-than-ideal conditions of a classroom, we get to see whether our ideas are being communicated to students, whether the technology is confusing to use, and a host of issues that we never would anticipate on our own. Observing participants work through an educational product reveals things participants might not articulate, either because they do not notice, they do not have access to the inner workings of the experience to identify the problem, or because some may minimize when something is confusing or difficult out of kindness. We intentionally design for diverse school environments to support students across socioeconomic, cultural, and technical backgrounds. In wanting to advance full inclusion of race, genders, and cultures in science and live up to our *see it-be it* credo, we make every effort to design learning games that can be used by any student and educator to foster a love of science.

Preparing for Rollout

Since the experience must work in all types of classrooms, we consider accessibility and equity of the technology. Incorporating a new technology like VR offers students an opportunity to become familiar with new immersive technologies in addition to the science content. The instructional design plans for a 1:4 device-to-student ratio for VR experiences. Our game designs acknowledge the limitations of older generation hardware and limited-bandwidth school Wi-Fi networks and have been optimized for mobile devices. We have also implemented WebVR, where every experience can be completed by navigating through the virtual scenes using a mouse or keyboard on a laptop, tablet, or any web-enabled device students can access. Ensuring our products are compatible with various devices allows us to accommodate as many classrooms as possible. Although WebVR is less visually immersive, it maintains students' agency: a key benefit of VR in our designs.

Once the five units of the learning game are complete, a broader pilot study is conducted throughout the US, in which our team recruits a minimum of 25 teachers to implement the game at their own school. Teachers are provided with free logins, lesson guides, and sets of inexpensive, handheld viewers (Google Cardboard or similar) for VR experiences. In exchange, teachers and students complete pre- and post-surveys on the experience, which we use as a final quality check before officially launching the game.

Note An implementation test of *GeoForge* in a Grade 8 science classroom. Students work in groups, while our staff circulate to make observations and facilitate the lesson. Students in the foreground are using VR to visit planets as a group; students in the background are using the digital science journal to complete other activities.

Strategies for Implementation of Design Using XR in Learning Games

During the COVID-19 pandemic, classrooms changed in profound ways, and we had to change how we conducted user research. It was not possible to observe how students were using our games over Zoom since many students did not have access to devices where they could share their screens or webcam views, and the technology did not support looking at multiple students' screens at the same time. For this reason, we added think-aloud sessions with single student users to our schedule of implementation tests. During these sessions, a student would join a Zoom meeting with our staff and work through a module of *WaterWays* while sharing their screen. Students were asked to "think out loud and say anything that you're noticing, or any questions you have, as it occurs to you." One member of the team facilitated these sessions, asking questions like "What are you noticing right now?" if the participant fell silent. Rather than observing groups of students working on their own, the think-aloud sessions enabled us to closely monitor single individuals as they progressed. This approach offered much deeper user feedback on each page although it could not fully represent classroom use.

The 2020–2021 school year was highly unusual for schools, but we remotely piloted *WaterWays* through eight individual student-user research sessions, and with 170 students (in a mix of in-person, remote, and hybrid classes) and 10 classroom teachers within three schools. Of all the students who completed the post survey, 94% stated they were "interested in playing with *WaterWays* after today" and 83% agreed "*WaterWays* helped me see myself as a scientist."

Based on our grounding in the literature and our experience designing and developing multiple XR products, we recommend the following strategies when designing or using XR in learning games to enhance science education:

- **Pair VR/AR with other resources to take advantage of their respective affordances.** Immersive technologies offer students a chance to have impossible experiences (Bailenson, 2018). Activities that enable students to explore an exotic location, perform activities like taking measurements, and observe differences between sites (just like scientists do) make a big impression on students, and many existing resources can become part of a lesson. A website or other scaffold like the DSJ can be used to complement these first-person experiences and balance demands on learners' cognitive load. Combining these platforms creates opportunities for generative processing. After participating in extended reality, facilitated classroom discussion may also provide additional processing supports for students.
- **Take advantage of opportunities for graceful failure.** In a digital environment, students can try an experience many times; there is no limit on equipment or supplies as there would be in a laboratory. When using XR activities as part of a class, encourage students to make multiple attempts in a VR or AR experience, testing the limits and trying out different actions to observe cause-and-effect relationships.

- **Empower teachers to support students.** Teachers can monitor real-time student progress through the immersive experience, whether students are in-person or remotely learning. An educator dashboard can give teachers an overview of each student's activities in XR—especially helpful during remote learning to tailor instruction as well as keep the class connected and students on task. This observation was confirmed when piloting our games remotely: teachers monitored each student's overall progress and called on them or moved them to breakout rooms to receive additional support when the students weren't progressing. This easy-to-monitor design was also useful when managing a large classroom of students who may progress at different speeds.

Conclusion

Immersive experiences make it possible for students to *see it and be it* in STEM, gaining exposure to new ideas and possibilities. VR/AR encourage students to engage with ideas, take action, and go to places that would be out of reach otherwise. Technology-mediated, first-hand experiences like *BioDive* and *WaterWays* allow students to try out scientific and engineering practices with minimal risk or expense, enabling students to assimilate new material and imagine themselves in the role of a scientist. However, while AR and VR can give students agency and access to thrilling scientific experiences, the excitement of trying something new is not enough of a reason to implement immersive experiences in schools. The first-person experience students have is most compelling when paired with appropriate strategies to reduce cognitive load, connect their background knowledge with those experiences, explore and make mistakes without severe penalties, and receive feedback. For educators, an added benefit is tracking their students' progress as well as the outcomes from any location: whether students are attending school in person or remotely. In sum, each of the three components (DSJ, VR/AR, and educator dashboard) of our learning games is integral to creating, enhancing, and extending the educational experience.

Giving students the opportunity to *see it and be it* better represents the fascinating material and dynamic work of science, helping students to see themselves as scientists. Strengthening feelings that science is accessible and students are part of the science community is key to building STEM-identity through the middle school years, and the affordances of XR offers educational designers new opportunities to incorporate immersive experiences. In turn, building STEM-identity is vital to retaining students' interest and desire to pursue future STEM careers, impact society, and tackle future global science and technology challenges.

Acknowledgements This work was conducted by Killer Snails LLC with support from NSF Grant 1549231, IES Grant 91990019C0025, and NIH Grant 1 R44 GM139577-01. We have no conflicts of interest to disclose. We thank Angela Carcione for sharing her experiences using *BioDive*.

References

Allen, M. W., & Sites, R. (2012). *Leaving ADDIE for SAM: An agile model for developing the best learning experiences.* American Society for Training and Development.

Bailenson, J. (2018). *Experience on demand: What virtual reality is, how it works, and what it can do.* W.W. Norton & Company.

Brenner, C., DesPortes, K., Ochoa Hendrix, J., & Holford, M. (2021a). GeoForge: Investigating integrated virtual reality and personalized websites for collaboration in middle school science. *Information and Learning Sciences, 122*(7/8), 546–564. https://doi.org/10/gmghz2

Brenner, C., Ochoa Hendrix, J., & Holford, M. (2021b). Work-in-progress—Building WaterWays: Investigating AR for environmental education. In D. Economou, A. Peña-Rios, A. Dengel, H. Dodds, M. Mentzelopoulos, A. Klippel, K. Erenli, M. J. W. Lee, & J. Richter (Eds.), *Proceedings of 2021 7th International Conference of the Immersive Learning Research Network (iLRN)* (pp. 1–3). IEEE. https://doi.org/10.23919/iLRN52045.2021.9459372

Committee on STEM Education. (2018). *Charting a course for success: America's strategy for STEM education* (p. 48). National Science and Technology Council.

Fiorella, L., & Mayer, R. E. (2016). Eight ways to promote generative learning. *Educational Psychology Review, 28*(4), 717–741. https://doi.org/10.1007/s10648-015-9348-9

Huang, H. M., Rauch, U., & Liaw, S.-S. (2010). Investigating learners' attitudes toward virtual reality learning environments: Based on a constructivist approach. *Computers & Education, 55*(3), 1171–1182. https://doi.org/10.1016/j.compedu.2010.05.014

Killer Snails LLC. (2020). *BioDive report.* [Unpublished report].

Magalhães, P., Ferreira, D., Cunha, J., & Rosário, P. (2020). Online vs traditional homework: A systematic review on the benefits to students' performance. *Computers & Education, 152,* 103869. https://doi.org/10.1016/j.compedu.2020.103869

Moreno, R., & Mayer, R. (2007). Interactive multimodal learning environments [special issue on interactive learning environments: Contemporary issues and trends]. *Educational Psychology Review, 19*(3), 309–326. https://doi.org/10.1007/s10648-007-9047-2

National Science Board. (2021). *Science & Engineering Indicators 2022: Elementary and Secondary STEM Education* (NSB-2021-1). https://ncses.nsf.gov/pubs/nsb20211/

Nguyen, U., & Riegle-Crumb, C. (2021). Who is a scientist? The relationship between counter-stereotypical beliefs about scientists and the STEM major intentions of Black and Latinx male and female students. *International Journal of STEM Education, 8*(1), 28. https://doi.org/10/gj5pc5

Papanastasiou, G., Drigas, A., Skianis, C., Lytras, M., & Papanastasiou, E. (2019). Virtual and augmented reality effects on K-12, higher and tertiary education students' twenty-first century skills. *Virtual Reality, 23*(4), 425–436. https://doi.org/10/ggm2wd

Plass, J. L., Mayer, R. E., & Homer, B. D. (Eds.). (2020). *Handbook of game-based learning.* MIT Press.

Pruitt, S. L. (2014). The next generation science standards: The features and challenges. *Journal of Science Teacher Education, 25*(2), 145–156. https://doi.org/10.1007/s10972-014-9385-0

Riegle-Crumb, C., Morton, K., Nguyen, U., & Dasgupta, N. (2019). Inquiry-based instruction in science and mathematics in middle school classrooms: Examining its association with students' attitudes by gender and race/ethnicity. *AERA Open, 5*(3). https://doi.org/10.1177/2332858419867653

Summers, R., & Abd-El-Khalick, F. (2019). An exploration of Illinois students' attitudes toward science using multivariate multilevel modeling with a cross-sectional sample of responses from grades 5 through 10. *Journal of Research in Science Teaching, 56*(8), 1106–1134. https://doi.org/10/ghgfcw

Van der Kleij, F. M., Feskens, R. C. W., & Eggen, T. J. H. M. (2015). Effects of feedback in a computer-based learning environment on students' learning outcomes: A meta-analysis. *Review of Educational Research, 85*(4), 475–511. https://doi.org/10.3102/0034654314564881

Corinne Brenner is the Director of Learning for Killer Snails, where she conducts research to drive product innovation using her knowledge of the learning sciences and media design for learning. She is also a PhD candidate in Educational Communication and Technology at NYU, researching educational games and virtual environments.

Jessica Ochoa Hendrix, CEO of Killer Snails, has worked in K–16 education since 2003. Ochoa Hendrix gave a TED talk on incorporating VR into the classroom with 500,000+ views. She serves on the World Economic Forum's Expert Network in Future of Education, Virtual and Augmented Reality, and Entrepreneurship.

Mandë Holford, PhD, cofounder of Killer Snails, examines venomous animals as agents of innovation in evolution and in manipulating cellular physiology in cancer. She is an Associate Professor in Chemistry at Hunter College and CUNY-Graduate Center, with scientific appointments at the American Museum of Natural History and Weill Cornell Medical College.

Part II
Designing Immersive Learning in Higher Education

Levels of Immersive Teaching and Learning: Influences of Challenges in the Everyday Classroom

Andreas Dengel, Josef Buchner, Miriam Mulders, and Johanna Pirker

Abstract This chapter discusses theoretical models for immersive learning and immersive teaching. The subjective and objective factors used in these models are distinguished by levels: micro, meso, and macro. We discuss the terms *immersive teaching* and *immersive learning* and possible strategies for implementing learning experiences in the everyday classroom.

Keywords Augmented reality · Classroom integration · Constructive alignment · Immersive learning · Immersive Media in Schools · Immersive teaching · Virtual reality

Introduction

After recent technological advances in the field of immersive media, teaching and learning with virtual and augmented reality (VR/AR) are closer to everyday classroom integration. Early pilot studies carried out in controlled settings suggest great potential for using such technologies for pedagogical endeavours: particularly, effect on learning (e.g., Krokos et al., 2019; Le et al., 2015), motivation (e.g., Mei & Sheng, 2011), and engagement (e.g., Allcoat & von Mühlenen, 2018; Bressler et al., 2019). Further, literature reviews provide evidence for the use of immersive media in language education (Peixoto et al., 2021), history and cultural heritage

A. Dengel (✉)
Goethy University Frankfurt, Frankfurt, Germany
e-mail: dengel@uni-frankfurt.de

J. Buchner · M. Mulders
University of Duisburg-Essen, Essen, Germany
e-mail: josef.buchner@uni-due.de; miriam.mulders@uni-due.de

J. Pirker
TU Graz, Graz, Austria
e-mail: johanna.pirker@tugraz.at

© The Author(s), under exclusive license to Springer Nature Switzerland AG 2022
P. MacDowell, J. Lock (eds.), *Immersive Education*,
https://doi.org/10.1007/978-3-031-18138-2_7

education (Challenor & Ma, 2019), computer science education (Pirker et al., 2020), teacher education (Billingsley et al., 2019), medicine (Kavanagh et al., 2017), STEM education (Pellas et al., 2020), and various other application areas (Freina & Ott, 2015). However, virtual learning environments face similar conditions, restrictions, and challenges as traditional educational media. The integration of VR and AR in the everyday classroom comes with affordances and constraints that are seldom observed in laboratory settings.

This chapter contributes to research on the challenges of using holistic models to facilitate immersive teaching and learning. First, we present existing theoretical models and frameworks for educational immersive experiences. Second, we categorize these models and frameworks into three pedagogical levels of immersive teaching and learning. The macro level presents general institutional and governmental factors that facilitate or hamper endeavours to integrate immersive media in schools. The meso level describes teacher- and classroom-specific factors. The micro level focuses on learner-specific factors such as individual perceptions and learning activities. Distinguishing between immersive teaching (the process of teaching with immersive technology) and immersive learning (individual learning processes supported by immersive technology) helps clarify internal and external factors related to the educational process, particularly influences and challenges. Third, we outline three pedagogical considerations: the immersive constructive alignment (aligning learning objectives, learning activities, and performance assessment through immersive media), the focus on the learner (keeping in mind the complex interaction of perceptual stimuli with the traits and states of the individual), and the role of the teacher (the need to integrate an immersive experience in an overall teaching sequence rather than as isolated activities).

Vignette

Diane is a primary school teacher with interest in designing technology-enhanced learning environments for her students. In a workshop, she learned about the potential of VR technology. According to the lecturer, VR is now more easily available for schools too: for example, mobile VR based on cardboard glasses and using students' smartphones. However, after looking more deeply into VR technology and the effects studied when used in education, as well as the associated challenges, Diane realized that using VR is more complex than she thought. For example, in her primary school smartphones are not allowed, making it difficult to use the mobile VR approach. Furthermore, during her search for suitable educational VR materials, she came to realize that there are simply no real learning materials available yet that align with the curriculum. The solution usually recommended is to create your own VR content. However, she lacked the skills for this, and neither the school nor the school authorities provide resources for content creation. All of this has left Diane frustrated. In her teacher training, the integration of VR in the classroom had sounded relatively easy and quick to implement. In practice, it didn't turn out that way. Diane decides to tell others about her experience. In doing so, she wants to present a holistic picture on the use of VR. This should then really help other teachers to create effective and engaging learning environments with VR.

Challenges Arising in Classroom Teaching: An Example from Elementary School

To illustrate the complexity of integrating immersive technology in contemporary classroom settings, we present an implementation realized in a German elementary school. In this case study, Buchner and Aretz (2020) describe a mobile immersive VR instructional design based on four critical components. First, an analysis of the circumstances is required. Does the school allow the use of smartphones? Is there a steady WiFi connection? What are the teachers' and parents' attitudes towards using immersive media for learning? Second, the teachers are encouraged to name the learning objectives and to check how these fit the choice of an immersive technology. Third, suitable instructional methods supporting learning with immersive technologies should be specified. Fourth, with a focus on the technology, decisions must be made about what immersive media is appropriate to address the learning objectives or whether there is a need to create new materials.

Considering these components and asking the above questions lead to instructional decisions that guide the development of the instructional design. It is necessary to talk with parents, teachers, school management, and students. As in Buchner and Aretz (2020), mobile VR smartphones and cardboard VR glasses are needed to display the virtual content. In German elementary schools, bringing smartphones to class is not allowed, or these young students do not have a device. Consequently, the parents must be involved, allowing their children to use smartphones. The school management must also be involved, agreeing to the use of smartphones in class for the VR experience. In Buchner and Aretz's (2020) study, other teachers were also involved in the design process. They stated that VR should not be used to separate the students from each other, which directly influenced decisions regarding the instructional method.

The learning objective was to explore the life and habits of past cultures and compare those to our modern way of life. For the instructional method, we considered the concerns mentioned by the other teachers as well as curricular recommendations. For example, in the curriculum for primary education in Germany, teachers are encouraged to design learning environments that engage learners in physical and cognitive collaborative learning activities. In terms of available educational VR applications, it was not possible to find an existing one that covers the described content. Therefore, Buchner and Aretz (2020) designed their own virtual environment, including 360° pictures with hotspots as shown by students exploring in Fig. 1. Considering all these concerns and recommendations led to the instructional design shown in Fig. 2 that was carried out in one morning (4 hours) with one class and three teachers.

Fig. 1 Two learners explore content with cardboard VR glasses and a workbook

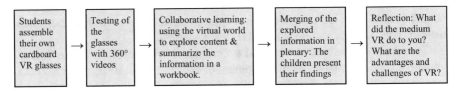

Fig. 2 Instructional design of using mobile VR in the classroom

Implementing VR into a classroom is challenging and needs careful planning and consideration. The results of controlled pilot studies are essential to learn more about what works with VR. As well, to provide practitioners with helpful strategies for implementing VR into the everyday classroom, a more holistic view is needed.

Frameworks and Models for Immersive Education

Endeavours to explore and to explain how people learn in immersive environments have led to the development of various theoretical models. To gather relevant factors influencing immersive education, this section provides a rough overview of existing approaches to structuring predictors, correlates, and outcomes in teaching and learning settings with immersive technologies. One of the most influential theoretical ideas for explaining learning in and with virtual experiences is Dalgarno and Lee's (2010) elaborated model of learning in 3-D virtual learning environments. While the model itself refers to three-dimensional virtual environments in general, the authors note that these influences and relations might apply to highly immersive technologies such as head-mounted-displays, CAVEs, or spherical displays. Dalgarno and Lee (2010) propose representational fidelity, immediacy of control, and presence to describe the relation between immersion and learning. The individual perception comprises the sense of presence (the feeling of *being there*), together with co-presence (*being there together*) and the construction of identity, which is similar to Biocca's (1997) understanding of self-presence. These individual perceptions result from the medium's representational fidelity and the learner interaction. Dalgarno and Lee (2010) present a straightforward conclusion: "[I]t is essentially the fidelity of the representation along with the types of interactivity that are available within the environment that will lead to a high degree of immersion and consequently a strong sense of presence" (p. 12). The different forms of presence will, in turn, lead to greater transfer. Through the afforded learning tasks, three-dimensional virtual environments can benefit learning in five ways: spatial knowledge representation, experiential learning, engagement, contextual learning, and collaborative learning (Dalgarno & Lee, 2010).

This explanation of learning in virtual environments was criticized by Fowler (2015) since higher levels of representational fidelity and interaction might not inevitably lead to better learning. Taking a more pedagogical perspective, Fowler presents three fundamental stages: (1) conceptualization (explaining/describing the context), (2) construction (interacting with the concept), and (3) dialogue (interacting/discussing within a social context). By connecting these stages with the technological, psychological, and pedagogical affordances of virtual learning environments, Fowler (2015) introduces empathy as being able to identify and empathize with concepts; reification, the ability to make the concept more concrete; and identification, the ability to engage in thoughtful and structured arguments and discussions about the concepts.

Quintana and Fernández (2015) present a pedagogical model for creating spaces where pre-service teachers can simulate teaching practices. The model focuses on the construction of scenarios that can help build meaningful learning experiences in VR. Integrating innovative methods in the teaching-learning process supports students in incorporating immersive experiences as teaching resources. According to Quintana and Fernández, future teachers should consider three categories for teaching and learning with immersive media: the scenario, the tools, and the interaction. The scenario comprises the intended learning objectives (depending on class type and setting), the area within VR, the students and their characteristics, the available time for learning activities related to the learning objectives, and the task type. Tools comprise sources or instruments needed for providing a virtual experience in the classroom in the first place, such as tutorials or hardware. The interaction gathers all factors that relate to the exchange of information with other agents (e.g., teachers).

Dengel and Mägdefrau (2018) define immersive learning as learning activities in a media-enriched environment connected to a sense of presence. Their Educational Framework for Immersive Learning (EFiL) localizes the sense of presence as an important predictor of learning outcomes. The framework describes learning in and with immersive experiences as a complex relationship that happens as an interplay of objective and subjective factors. The EFiL proposes objective factors as educational *supply* and subjective factors as the active *use*. The immersive medium, including its technological, didactical/content, and context characteristics, is an objective factor that can be controlled by the teacher. To influence internal factors, such as the individual's motivational, emotional, perceptual, and cognitive states and traits, the immersive medium must be used actively by the learner. Further, the learner's context (e.g., culture, class, peer group, family) influences this relationship between supply and use (Dengel & Mägdefrau, 2018). A recent study connected to the EFiL showed that presence, prior knowledge, and school performance are predictors of learning outcomes in virtual environments (Dengel & Mägdefrau, 2020).

Spiliotopoulos et al. (2019) proposed a framework focusing on game-based learning and the creation of dynamic and interactive virtual tasks, changing the role of the learner from passive observer to active participant. Instructional content blends with game characteristics, leading to a game cycle of judgement, behaviour, and feedback (which leads to judgement again). This cycle of decision, action, and results leads to learning outcomes.

Southgate et al. (2019) give recommendations on the use of VR within educational settings. They name ethical (e.g., touching students) and safety aspects (e.g., barrier-free spaces) concerning the behaviour of teachers and that of and learners when using VR, and organizational difficulties regarding time and space. As well, Southgate et al. (2019) refer to socioeconomic differences among schools. These differences are also evident in the technological equipment. Moreover, the authors claim the need for a carefully designed balance between attending to learning goals and providing fun through immersive technologies.

Popescu et al. (2011) provide a four-dimensional framework synthesizing such factors as mode of representation (e.g., levels of fidelity, immersion, interactivity), context (e.g., learning situation, equipment, technical support), pedagogical considerations (e.g., learning approaches), and learner-specification (e.g., learner profile). The factors of the framework encompass aspects essential for game design, evaluation, and effective adoption in educational processes. The specification of the teaching and learning processes involves investigating the characteristics of the learner population to meet their requirements and optimize outcomes.

Based on Mayer's (2005) Cognitive Theory of Multimedia Learning (CTML), Mulders et al. (2020) propose a meaningful iVR learning (M-iVR-L) framework. Six recommendations for designing iVR learning environments are postulated: 1) reducing extraneous processing by avoiding unnecessary immersion if it is not relevant to achieve the learning objective, 2) providing learning-relevant interactions inside VR (e.g., object manipulation with virtual representations) but avoiding learning-irrelevant nice-to-have interactions, 3) breaking down complex tasks into smaller segments and providing scaffolds to manage essential processing to avoid cognitive overload, 4) providing guidance by highlighting essential material or using pedagogical agents, 5) building on learners' previous experiences and, if necessary, provide pretraining to free working memory capacities for the essential processing within the iVR learning task, and 6) providing constructive learning activities (e.g., summarizing, memory palaces) to apply the knowledge obtained to problem-based tasks inside and outside of iVR.

With their Cognitive Affective Model of Immersive Learning (CAMIL), Makransky and Petersen (2021) combine the technological (e.g., immersion, representation fidelity) and the interrelated psychological (e.g., presence, agency) factors of VR. These psychological factors influence six learning-relevant factors: 1) interest arising from contextual conditions, 2) intrinsic motivation, 3) self-efficacy, 4) embodiment (e.g., presence as the feeling of being in VR and controlling a body), 5) cognitive load, and 6) self-regulation. Therefore, CAMIL offers relevant design criteria for VR application developers and instructional designers.

Emihovich et al. (2021) developed the S.P.E.C.I.A.L. framework. The acronym stands for the following five concepts: situated learning, play, embodied interactive learning, connectivism and social learning, and immersive assessments for learning. For each concept, Emihovich and colleagues offer design, implementation, and evaluation considerations. For example, to support embodied interactive learning, the authors suggest creating embodied interactions that are meaningful and congruent to the learning content. They recommend avoiding embodied interactions that lead to additional cognitive load. The framework synthesizes pedagogical theories, strategies of cognitive development, and innovative assessments that are relevant to immersive learning.

De Freitas et al. (2010) introduce four dimensions regarding the development and evaluation of immersive learning experiences: 1) learner specifics, 2) pedagogy, 3) representation, and 4) context. Learner specifics address the necessary matching of learner characteristics and learning activities with learning objectives. Pedagogy refers to learning theory models, such as whether task-oriented or situated immersive learning opportunities are created. The representation dimension indicates the levels of fidelity (e.g., enabled interactions) and their interplay with immersion and learning. Finally, the context dimension is outlined as an essential factor affecting immersive learning, such as the differences between formal and informal educational contexts.

As the analysis of the theoretical models and frameworks presented in this section shows, there are multiple perspectives on immersive education that are all equally valid. While some of the frameworks take a rather broad view with general, external factors, other models are more concerned with internal, individual learning processes. In the next section, we present a way of distinguishing such approaches into two perspectives.

Defining Immersive Learning and Immersive Teaching

Distinguishing immersive learning and immersive teaching as two different perspectives on immersive education allows the carefully planned use and evaluation of VR and AR in the classroom. We distinguish immersive learning as individual learning processes supported by immersive media (the internal, person-specific side of an educational activity) and immersive teaching as the process of teaching with immersive technology (the external, objective side of education). While immersive teaching describes objective factors together with the learning objectives that can be influenced by teachers and institutions, immersive learning focuses on the subjective, internal processes of the learner as well as the actual learning outcomes. The frameworks and models reported in this chapter offer valuable insights into different factors that are influences and challenges for teaching and learning (summarized in Table 1).

On the immersive teaching side, some factors influencing the beneficial use of immersive media in the classroom can be controlled by the teacher, while others rely on external conditions. The curriculum is a factor of where (for which contents) and when (in terms of the lesson-plan) immersive media can be used (Quintana & Fernández, 2015; Southgate et al., 2019). Most of the time, this is controlled by governmental institutions. The external conditions can be rather restrictive or can give the teacher enough freedom to use various media and methods. The available technological equipment in the classroom or schools in general is one of the most important factors when considering the use of innovative educational media, especially VR and AR (Quintana & Fernández, 2015; Popescu et al., 2011; Southgate et al., 2019). Depending on the school's financial resources, teachers might have a say in what technology will be acquired. It is important to note that this decision process should be driven by considerations about not only costs, but also about the spectrum of application for different classes, age groups, methods, and topics/learning objectives. In light of the COVID-19 pandemic, an interesting aspect might also be how these media could support potential e-learning or blended learning settings. Ethical and safety aspects are also crucial influences (Southgate et al., 2019). Whenever privacy or health concerns (or local/national privacy policies) arise, such considerations come into play. Temporal and spatial conditions as decisive variables

Table 1 Influences and challenges of immersive teaching and immersive learning (Dengel et al., 2021)

	Teaching	Learning
Influences	• Curricula • Technological equipment • Ethical and safety aspects • Temporal and spatial conditions • Interplay between defined learning objectives, learning activities, and learner characteristics	• Physical, social, and self-presence • Representational fidelity and interactivity • Cognitive load and processing • Motivation and interest • Emotional states • Individual contextual circumstances • Ethical and safety aspects
Challenges	• Unequal learning opportunities due to differing perceptions of immersive experiences • Prevalence and use of learning strategies inside/outside of VLEs • Meaningful learning requires integration in the overall teaching sequence • Assessment methods	• User acceptance of game-based approaches is needed before learning can happen • Extraneous processing through overwhelming multi-sensory presentation • Varying previous knowledge regarding the learning objectives and use of the medium • Novelty effect

(Quintana & Fernández, 2015; Southgate et al., 2019) refer to the school's resources in terms of available rooms, including storage for different media. In particular, head-mounted-displays with positional tracking need more space than a traditional classroom setting can provide, and time is required to plan and carry out immersive experiences. While the interplay among the defined learning objectives, learning activities, and learner characteristics (Dengel & Mägdefrau, 2018; de Freitas et al., 2010) happens on the learner's side, it is the teacher's task to select fitting objectives, activities, and assessment methods inside and outside of the virtual experiences to constructively align the teaching and learning processes.

Challenges on the teaching side comprise unequal learning opportunities deriving from differing perceptions, the varying use (or lack) of learning strategies to employ during the learning experience/activity, the need for an efficient integration in an overall teaching sequence, and the integration of assessment methods inside and outside the virtual environments. Regarding the perception of the learning material, varying levels of presence might have an impact on how much the students learn, as presence can be seen as a predictor of learning outcomes (Dalgarno & Lee, 2010; Dengel & Mägdefrau, 2018; Fowler, 2015). The prevalence and active use of learning strategies can benefit the learning process with a given medium (Mulders et al., 2020). This could lead to a strong effect of accumulated advantage, where gifted students—in this case, students who can use efficient learning strategies—will benefit more from learning opportunities (Kempe et al., 2011). To create meaningful learning opportunities, integration in an overall teaching sequence is crucial (Fowler, 2015; Dengel & Mägdefrau, 2018; Mulders et al., 2020; Spiliotopoulos et al., 2019).

While many pilot projects observe the effects of educational immersive media as isolated experiences, integrating such media in the everyday classroom requires careful planning and connections to lessons before and after application of the medium. Considerations about the use of a medium in a particular phase of the learning process (e.g., task definition, fundamentals for solving the task, task solution) can be crucial to learning (Tulodzieckiet al., 2019). Another challenge refers to assessment methods related to the learning objectives and learning activities. Following the approach of constructive alignment, it is necessary to think about the extent to which assessment tasks "embody the target performances of understanding, and how well they lend themselves to evaluating individual student performances" (Biggs, 1996, p. 356). While immersive experiences can help align learning objectives with learning activities through experiential and situated learning (Dalgarno & Lee, 2010), assessment in virtual environments still poses a problem (Emihovich et al., 2021).

In terms of learning influences, various forms of the feeling of presence, technological characteristics, internal cognitive processes, learner traits and states, individual context variables, and ethical and safety aspects affect the learning activities and outcomes. Presence as the perception of non-mediation (Lombard & Ditton, 1997) occurs in the forms of physical presence, social presence, and self-presence (see Biocca, 1997). The theoretical frameworks of Dalgarno and Lee (2010), Fowler (2015), and Dengel and Mägdefrau (2018) emphasize the important role of these different types of presence in the learning process. A higher sense of presence might be connected to better learning outcomes. The importance of technological aspects, such as representational fidelity and interactivity, as influences of learning are mentioned in several models (e.g., Dalgarno & Lee, 2010; Quintana & Fernández, 2015). When taking a deeper look into learning as a subjective process, factors such as cognitive load and even the cognition process itself come into play. Such influences on learning are modeled especially in frameworks based on Mayer's cognitive theory of multimedia learning (Mayer, 2005), such as Mulders et al.'s (2020) M-iVR-L as well as Makransky and Peterson's (2021) CAMIL. Individual characteristics such as motivation and interest are factors closely connected to learning activities (Dengel & Mägdefrau, 2018; Makransky & Peterson, 2021; Spiliotopoulos et al., 2019;). Further, each student has different contextual circumstances regarding culture, religion, family, and peer groups. Together with the student's traits and states (e.g., emotions), these factors influence the learning process (Dengel & Mägdefrau, 2018). In addition, safety and privacy aspects as well as other ethical issues influence the students' experiences with immersive media in educational settings (Southgate et al., 2019).

Challenges on the learning side comprise user acceptance, the possibility of being overwhelmed by multi-sensory stimuli, varying degrees of previous knowledge, and a potential novelty effect. Especially for game-based approaches, a certain level of user acceptance is needed before inducing learning activities (Spiliotopoulos et al., 2019). When taking into account Mayer's (2005) theoretical approaches on internal processing, the dual-channel assumption, the limited capacity assumption, and the active processing assumption, the multi-sensory presentation of immersive media can lead to perceptions of being overwhelmed and to cognitive overload (Mulders et al., 2020). Further, varying previous knowledge regarding the learning objectives and using the technology can make it difficult to provide equal learning experiences for every student (Mulders et al., 2020). Also, while an initial novelty effect can boost students' motivation and interest in using a new medium, it can distract learners from the learning objectives, and the effect can wear off quickly (Southgate et al., 2019).

Pedagogical Levels of Immersive Education

To take a holistic and a more realistic view on the influences and challenges of teaching and learning with immersive media, we assembled aspects of the different theoretical approaches in a comprehensive model. The following three pedagogical levels combine ideas and concepts from educational technology research with a special focus on immersive experiences (see Fig. 3):

- **The Macro-Level:** Every pedagogical effort influenced by several institutional and governmental factors, including ethical and safety regulations; the availability of time, space, and other resources; curricular and general educational

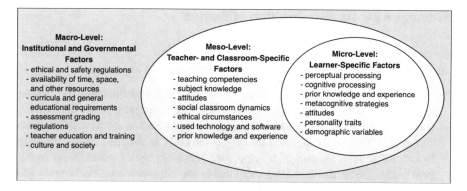

Fig. 3 Macro-, Meso-, and Micro-levels of immersive teaching and learning (Dengel et al., 2021)

requirements; regulations for assessment and grading; characteristics of general and domain-specific teacher education and professional training; and cultural and social factors. One example is the issue of classroom space. A typical classroom is a small space with fixed tables and chairs. For VR experiences, space is also needed to allow learners to use their bodies and physical movements to explore content in the virtual simulation. One solution is to purchase flexible furniture with wheels so that space can be created quickly and easily. Such a task must be initiated and completed by those responsible at the macro-level.

- **The Meso-Level:** This level comprises teacher- and classroom-specific factors such as teaching competencies, technological, pedagogical, and content knowledge, attitudes, social classroom dynamics, ethical circumstances, and technology and software in use as well as prior knowledge and experience with digital media. At this level, teachers can act; for example, they can collaborate in a school development group focusing on VR learning scenarios. Developing the scenarios and designing the materials, as well as testing, evaluating, and reflecting on the implementation process can also be done as a group. Afterwards, the results of these teaching experiments are presented to other colleagues and extended to other subjects.

- **The Micro-Level:** This level addresses learner-specific factors directly related to the learning activities. These comprise perceptual processing (e.g., physical, social, and self-presence), cognitive processing, prior knowledge and experience (on the learner side), metacognitive strategies, attitudes, personality traits, and demographic variables. Teachers should have these aspects of learning in mind when designing VR scenarios. For example, as outlined in Parong and Mayer (2018), VR can be distracting, but in combination with generative learning activities (e.g., summarizing), this problem can be solved and learning with VR improved. As well, adding generative learning activities does not diminish motivational and affective factors when learning with immersive technologies (Buchner, 2021; Parong & Mayer, 2018).

Strategies for Implementation of Design

By separating these perspectives and levels, we can draw out pedagogical considerations for the educational design of immersive educational experiences.

- **Immersive constructive alignment.** More than any other technology, immersive media can support the alignment of learning objectives, hands-on learning activities, and performance assessment by letting students act in a close-to-reality simulation. This was suggested by Biggs' idea of Constructive Alignment long before immersive technologies were foreseen as everyday educational media (see Biggs, 1996). Because immersive technology in everyday classrooms is still a novelty, ground-breaking guidelines for school management are required. Schools as well as governmental institutions should work closely together to publish guidance regarding costs, implementation in existing curricula, and safety concerns (e.g., minimum size for rooms). Ethical aspects, such as how to deal with learners who are not able to wear VR helmets, must be discussed on a governmental level.
- **Focus on the learner.** Separating objective from subjective teaching and learning processes clarifies that immersive media interact with many person-specific states and traits and, thus, affect students differently. Therefore, implementing immersive media into everyday classrooms needs to account for individual pre-experiences and attitudes towards the technology. In advance, the teacher can open a discussion in plenary or ask students individually in writing or verbally. Teachers may also provide incentives and distribute tutorials and further explanations while avoiding false expectations. Moreover, individual attitudes should be tracked continuously during the implementation process. For example, motivation can diminish as the novelty effect wears off or exhaustion increases: both effects are common for immersive media. Observing individual learning processes by using immersive technology is crucial to achieving learning objectives. To that end, assistant teachers may be needed to support learners simultaneously. Next to variable learner-specific factors, stable factors such as age and gender should be considered. For example, younger pupils may need more support to distinguish between reality and VR after using immersive technology.
- **Integration in the teaching sequence.** As with every other medium, VR and AR are educational technologies that must be used efficiently in the learning process. Immersive experiences need to be implemented in an overall teaching sequence carefully planned by the teacher. The teachers can be considered guides who connect all levels: they design and influence the meso-level of the classroom and the instructional medium—given the circumstances of the macro-level—to achieve the potential, activities, effects, and outcomes at the micro-level of the student. Inexperienced teachers may rely on best-practice solutions from colleagues, but comprehensive train-the-trainer concepts are also needed. Therefore, collegial exchange, whether within a discipline (e.g., history) or interdisciplinary, should be established to convey technical skills and share materials.

Conclusion

Integrating immersive media in everyday classrooms requires more than a theoretical exploration of influencing factors. The practical integration of educational technology strongly relies on teachers' self-efficacy and attitudes towards the use and usefulness of media in the classroom. Therefore, future teacher education programs need an open-minded and explorative approach for preservice teachers to try out and experiment with various immersive technologies as part of their courses or practical studies.

We have synthesized existing approaches for learning and teaching with immersive media, including their beneficial and challenging aspects. As our approach was based on theoretical assumptions rather than empirical studies, this assembling of existing frameworks can be considered an overview of the theoretical perspectives on the affordances and constraints of immersive teaching and learning. We created a comprehensive model with three different pedagogical perspectives (micro-, meso- and macro-levels): a holistic approach to immersive learning that comprises institutional and governmental factors, classroom dynamics, and the internal, subjective processes of the individual learner. As such, this model can be used to predict and explain learning in and with immersive experiences. Future studies might investigate specific paths within or between the levels. In doing so, the framework can be used for generating hypotheses to predict certain interactions among factors, which can then be tested in field studies in the everyday classroom. Further research and systematic analyses of published pedagogical frameworks concerning learning and teaching with immersive technology are needed to gather evidence for a desirable yet futuristic goal: integrating immersive educational experiences in the everyday classroom.

References

Allcoat, D., & von Mühlenen, A. (2018). Learning in virtual reality: Effects on performance, emotion and engagement. *Research in Learning Technology, 26*. https://doi.org/10.25304/rlt.v26.2140

Biggs, J. (1996). Enhancing teaching through constructive alignment. *Higher Education, 32*, 347–364. https://doi.org/10.1007/BF00138871

Billingsley, G., Smith, S., Smith, S., & Meritt, J. (2019). A systematic literature review of using immersive virtual reality technology in teacher education. *Journal of Interactive Learning Research, 30*(1), 65–90. https://www.learntechlib.org/primary/p/176261

Biocca, F. (1997). The cyborg's dilemma: Progressive embodiment in virtual environments [1]. *Journal of Computer-Mediated Communication, 3*(2), 113–144. https://doi.org/10.1111/j.1083-6101.1997.tb00070.x

Bressler, D. M., Bodzin, A. M., & Tutwiler, M. S. (2019). Engaging middle school students in scientific practice with a collaborative mobile game. *Journal of Computer Assisted Learning, 35*(2), 197–207. https://doi.org/10.1111/jcal.12008

Buchner, J. (2021). Generative learning strategies do not diminish primary students' attitudes towards augmented reality. *Education and Information Technologies, 27*, 701–717. https://doi.org/10.1007/s10639-021-10445-y

Buchner, J., & Aretz, D. (2020). Lernen mit immersiver virtual reality: didaktisches design und lessonsllLearned [Learning with immersive virtual reality: Instructional design and lessons learned]. *MedienPädagogik: Zeitschrift für Theorie und Praxis der Medienbildung, 17*, 195–216. https://doi.org/10.21240/mpaed/jb17/2020.05.01.X

Challenor, J., & Ma, M. (2019). A review of augmented reality applications for history education and heritage visualisation. *Multimodal Technologies and Interaction, 3*(2), 39. https://doi.org/10.3390/mti3020039

Dalgarno, B., & Lee, M. J. W. (2010). What are the learning affordances of 3-D virtual environments? *British Journal of Educational Technology, 41*(1), 10–32. https://doi.org/10.1111/j.1467-8535.2009.01038.x

De Freitas, S., Rebolledo-Mendez, G., Liarokapis, F., Magoulas, G., & Poulovassilis, A. (2010). Learning as immersive experiences: Using the four-dimensional framework for designing and evaluating immersive learning experiences in a virtual world. *British Journal of Educational Technology, 41*(1), 69–85. https://doi.org/10.1111/j.1467-8535.2009.01024.x

Dengel, A., & Mägdefrau, J. (2018). Immersive learning explored: Subjective and objective factors influencing learning outcomes in immersive educational virtual environments. In M. J. W. Lee (Ed.), *Proceedings of 2018 IEEE international conference on teaching, assessment, and learning for engineering (TALE)* (pp. 608–615). IEEE. https://doi.org/10.1109/TALE.2018.8615281

Dengel, A., & Mägdefrau, J. (2020). Immersive learning predicted: Presence, prior knowledge, and school performance influence learning outcomes in immersive educational virtual environments. In D. Economou, A. Klippel, H. Dodds, A. Peña-Rios, M. J. W. Lee, D. Beck, J. Pirker, A. Dengel, T. M. Peres, & J. Richter (Eds.), *6th international conference of the immersive learning research network (iLRN)* (pp. 163–170). IEEE. https://doi.org/10.23919/iLRN47897.2020.9155084

Dengel, A., Buchner, J., Mulders, M., & Pirker, J. (2021). Beyond the horizon: Integrating immersive learning environments in the everyday classroom. In D. Economou, A. Peña-Rios, A. Dengel, H. Dodds, M. Mentzelopoulos, A. Klippel, K. Erenli, M. J. W. Lee, & J. Richter (Eds.), *Proceedings of 2021 7th international conference of the immersive learning research network (iLRN)* (pp. 1–5). IEEE. https://doi.org/10.23919/iLRN52045.2021.9459368

Emihovich, B., Xu, X., & Arrington, T. L. (2021). S.P.E.C.I.A.L. – A conceptual framework to support learning in immersive environments. *International Journal of Smart Technology and Learning, 2*(2–3), 182–197. https://doi.org/10.1504/IJSMARTTL.2020.112149

Fowler, C. (2015). Virtual reality and learning: Where is the pedagogy? *British Journal of Educational Technology, 46*(2), 412–422. https://doi.org/10.1111/bjet.12135

Freina, L., & Ott, M. (2015, April). *A literature review on immersive virtual reality in education: State of the art and perspectives* [Conference session]. Elearning and Software for Education, Bucharest, Romania. https://www.researchgate.net/publication/280566372_A_Literature_Review_on_Immersive_Virtual_Reality_in_Education_State_Of_The_Art_and_Perspectives

Kavanagh, S., Luxton-Reilly, A., Wuensche, B., & Plimmer, B. (2017). A systematic review of virtual reality in education. *Themes in Science and Technology Education, 10*(2), 85–119. https://doi.org/10.1016/j.compedu.2019.103778

Kempe, C., Eriksson-Gustavsson, A. L., & Samuelsson, S. (2011). Are there any Matthew effects in literacy and cognitive development? *Scandinavian Journal of Educational Research, 55*(2), 181–196. https://doi.org/10.1080/00313831.2011.554699

Krokos, E., Plaisant, C., & Varshney, A. (2019). Correction to: Virtual memory palaces: Immersion aids recall. *Virtual Reality, 23*(1), 17–17. https://doi.org/10.1007/s10055-018-0360-5

Le, Q. T., Pedro, A., & Park, C. S. (2015). A social virtual reality-based construction safety education system for experiential learning. *Journal of Intelligent & Robotic Systems, 79*(3), 487–506. https://doi.org/10.1007/s10846-014-0112-z

Lombard, M., & Ditton, T. (1997). At the heart of it all: The concept of presence. *Journal of Computer-Mediated Communication, 3*(2). https://doi.org/10.1111/j.1083-6101.1997.tb00072.x

Makransky, G., & Petersen, G. B. (2021). The cognitive affective model of immersive learning (CAMIL): A theoretical research-based model of learning in immersive virtual reality. *Educational Psychology Review, 33*, 937–958. https://doi.org/10.1007/s10648-020-09586-2

Mayer, R. E. (2005). Cognitive theory of multimedia learning. In R. E. Mayer (Ed.), *The Cambridge handbook of multimedia learning* (pp. 31–48). Cambridge University Press. https://doi.org/10.1017/CBO9780511816819.004

Mei, H. H., & Sheng, L. S. (2011). Applying situated learning in a virtual reality system to enhance learning motivation. *International Journal of Information and Education Technology, 1*(4), 298–302. https://doi.org/10.7763/IJIET.2011.V1.48

Mulders, M., Buchner, J., & Kerres, M. (2020). A framework for the use of immersive virtual reality in learning environments. *International Journal of Emerging Technologies in Learning (iJET), 15*(24), 208–224. https://doi.org/10.3991/ijet.v15i24.16615

Parong, J., & Mayer, R. E. (2018). Learning science in immersive virtual reality. *Journal of Educational Psychology, 110*(6), 785–797. https://doi.org/10.1037/edu0000241

Peixoto, B., Pinto, R., Melo, M., Cabral, L., & Bessa, M. (2021). Immersive virtual reality for foreign language education: A PRISMA systematic review. *IEEE Access, 9*, 48952–48962. https://doi.org/10.1109/ACCESS.2021.3068858

Pellas, N., Dengel, A., & Christopoulos, A. (2020). A scoping review of immersive virtual reality in STEM education. *IEEE Transactions on Learning Technologies, 13*(4), 748–761. https://doi.org/10.1080/17439884.2018.1504788

Pirker, J., Dengel, A., Holly, M., & Safikhani, S. (2020). Virtual reality in computer science education: A systematic review. In R. J. Teather, C. Joslin, W. Stuerzlinger, P. Figueroa, Y. Hu, A. U. Batmaz, W. Lee, & F. Ortega (Eds.), *Proceedings of the 26th ACM symposium on virtual reality software and technology* (pp. 1–8). Association for Computing Machinery). https://doi.org/10.1145/3385956.3418947

Popescu, M., Arnab, S., Berta, R., Earp, J., de Freitas, S., Romero, M., Stanescu, I., & Usart, M. (2011, October 20–21). *Serious games in formal education: Discussing some critical aspects* [Conference session]. 5th European conference on games based learning, Athens, Greece. https://hal.archives-ouvertes.fr/hal-00985810

Quintana, M., & Fernández, S. M. (2015). A pedagogical model to develop teaching skills. The collaborative learning experience in the immersive virtual world TYMMI. *Computers in Human Behavior, 51*, 594–603. https://doi.org/10.1016/j.chb.2015.03.016

Southgate, E., Smith, S. P., Cividino, C., Saxby, S., Kilham, J., Eather, G., Scevak, J., Summerville, D., Buchanan, R., & Bergin, C. (2019). Embedding immersive virtual reality in classrooms: Ethical, organisational and educational lessons in bridging research and practice. *International Journal of Child-Computer Interaction, 19*, 19–29. https://doi.org/10.1016/j.ijcci.2018.10.002

Spiliotopoulos, D., Margaris, D., Vassilakis, C., Petukhova, V., & Kotis, K. (2019). A mixed-reality interaction-driven game-based learning framework. In *Proceedings of the 11th international conference on Management of Digital EcoSystems, ser. MEDES '19* (pp. 229–236). Association for Computing Machinery. https://doi.org/10.1145/3297662.3365802.

Tulodziecki, G., Grafe, S., & Herzig, B. (2019). *Medienbildung in Schule und Unterricht: Grundlagen und Beispiele.* UTB GmbH. https://doi.org/10.17877/DE290R-5976.

Andreas Dengel is a Professor of computer science education at the Goethe-University of Frankfurt (Main), Germany. His research interests are immersive education, media in computer science classrooms, and computer science unplugged.

Josef Buchner is a researcher in the field of learning, design, and technology. His research focuses on the design of effective technology-enhanced learning environments, learning designs for teacher education, and multimedia learning. He is a member of the board of the Media Education Section of the Austrian Society for Educational Research.

Miriam Mulders is a research assistant at the Learning Lab at the University of Duisburg-Essen in Germany. In her research, she studies virtual reality learning scenarios (e.g., in vocational education) and associated learning processes.

Johanna Pirker is an Assistant Professor at Graz University of Technology (Austria), leading the research group Game Lab Graz, and studies games with a focus on AI, HCI, data analysis, and VR technologies.

The XR ABC Framework: Fostering Immersive Learning Through Augmented and Virtual Realities

Christine Lion-Bailey, Jesse Lubinsky, and Micah Shippee

Abstract This chapter explores how XR technology (augmented reality, virtual reality, and all realities on the mixed reality spectrum) will continue to play a role in influencing education. The XR ABC Framework is explained to provide context on how to adopt these technologies for meaningful teaching and learning experiences.

Keywords Augmented reality · Design framework · Immersive learning · Instruction · Pedagogy · Teaching · Training · Virtual reality

Introduction

We use the term Extended Reality (XR) to describe augmented reality (AR), virtual reality (VR), and all realities on the mixed reality spectrum. XR can be leveraged to provide students with in-the-moment experiences that relate to their immediate surroundings. With XR, we have the ability to deploy interactive museum pieces and models and transport students to locations relevant to our content of study. We can also support student identification of elements and objects around them and throughout the world. These types of learning opportunities allow students to maintain an unprecedented sense of mindfulness toward their learning context, developing meaning at a whole new level (Lion-Bailey et al., 2020).

C. Lion-Bailey (✉)
Ramapo College, Mahwah, NJ, USA
e-mail: christine@readylearner.one

J. Lubinsky
Manhattanville College, Purchase, NY, USA
e-mail: jesse@readylearner.one

M. Shippee
Syracuse University, Syracuse, NY, USA

© The Author(s), under exclusive license to Springer Nature Switzerland AG 2022
P. MacDowell, J. Lock (eds.), *Immersive Education*,
https://doi.org/10.1007/978-3-031-18138-2_8

A pressing issue in education is the rate at which we adopt emergent technologies to achieve our instructional goals and best prepare our students for their future (Shippee, 2019a). Sometimes we need to take a pause to truly understand our goals and objectives for leveraging emergent technologies like XR. Before we move forward and explore XR's potential, we must understand that education and technology have had a long partnership. One of the clearest examples of emergent technology's influence on education is from approximately a hundred years ago, when radio was considered high technology. From that partnership, we can learn lessons that will benefit us all moving forward with XR.

In this chapter, we begin by exploring how XR technology has played a role in influencing education, resulting in an increased need for frameworks to improve the adoption of emergent technologies in the classroom. To that end, we introduce a framework we have developed: XR ABC, which stands for absorb, blend, and create. The framework is designed to help educators understand and adopt VR/AR into their instruction. We then examine the three aspects of the XR ABC Framework—absorb, blend, and create—and the role they can play in designing impactful learning experiences. The chapter concludes with some strategies for the implementation of design.

Vignette

Each year, Micah's students read the Diary of Anne Frank in their English Language Arts (ELA) classes while also studying World War II in his social studies classroom. Micah and his ELA colleague have found a way of designing cross-curricular instruction to amplify content understanding for their students in a way that was previously not possible. After reading the Diary of Anne Frank, *Micah's classes use VR headsets to explore the Anne Frank House VR experience. Students are immediately immersed inside Anne Frank's home in 1942. Micah's students emphasized the power of seeing and feeling the environment as it existed while the Frank family were in hiding. One student stated that the Anne Frank House VR Experience*

> *...showed how cramped the rooms were that Anne Frank was living in. It made it seem like I was actually in the rooms that Anne was in... it showed me why they had to be very cautious of being quiet because the floors were all made out of wood that is very creaky and the only thing that is keeping them hidden is a bookshelf on hinges.*

Radio: An Example of Technology's Influence on Education

In 1895, Guglielmo Marconi carried out the first experimental transmission of wireless signals over 400 metres and then 2000 metres (Blin, 1997). Twenty-five years later, the instructional uses of radio technology began to develop, and radio as a medium for distance learning began to be explored. It is important that we recognize the existence of a 25-year gap between the development of radio and the exploration of radio's instructional uses. In today's world, we have a sense of expediency that can ignore both levels of adoption and actual accessibility.

Historically, cultural forces have favoured an educational perspective that embraces newer trending technology, specifically regarding film, radio, television, and eventually computers. In the 1920s, parents and businesses supplied schools across the United States with radio receivers in an effort to integrate trending technology into their children's educational experience. Parents and community members understood that providing students with access to emergent technology in an educational setting would help prepare children for their future.

However, radio's initial adoption was delayed due to barriers that included poor battery life and poor reception. In addition, educators were unsure about how radio technology could be used to improve learning and learning outcomes. In our imagination, we might visualize classroom closets full of radios not being used; thus, availability of the technology, while very important, does not equate to actual instructional value. (These barriers form a pattern we see even today with new technology: battery, reception (Wi-Fi), and a lack of understanding of how emergent technology can be used to improve learning and learning outcomes.) Yet momentum gained around radio technology even with these barriers in place. In the 1930s, both industry and educational leaders predicted film and radio as the great catalysts of a revolutionary shift in instructional delivery. Benjamin Darrow, Founder of the Ohio School of the Air, believed that

> [t]he central and dominant aim of education by radio is to bring the world to the classroom, to make universally available the services of the finest teachers, the inspiration of the greatest leaders ... and unfolding events which through the radio may come as a vibrant and challenging textbook of the air. (As cited in Cuban, 1986, p. 19)

Radio, it seemed, was going to cause a shift in the instructional paradigm. Within a few decades (as with most technologies over time), radios became more powerful, more reliable, less expensive, and smaller (Traub, 2004; Vardhan, 2002).

The next barrier for educational institutions can be expressed by the question: How can radio be used to improve learning and learning outcomes? Instructors hoping to use radio broadcasts for instruction often had no control over the content. These ground-level decision-makers were hesitant to integrate technology within educational contexts due to a lack of control over content delivery. Using emergent technology simply because it is emergent is not going to lead to a sustainable paradigm shift. For example, in its original form, radio was a one-way communication medium; interaction with listeners was minimal. As a result, a radio program's pace was primarily set by the broadcaster (one-way, information), who found it difficult to gauge the listener's prior knowledge and attitudes, which are critical to learning (Berman, 2008). Over time, with increased scheduling and broadcast regulation, radio was more frequently used for instructional delivery (Romiszowski, 1974).

To develop instructional value when using radio to replace a teacher's lecture, instructors began to include well-designed preparatory and follow-up materials. These materials were packaged with visual and print materials and interactive elements that could be organized via listening groups. The relationship between radio and instructional material became symbiotic: as materials to work with radio for instructional purposes became more effective, so too did radio broadcasts. Techniques were developed for using educational radio, including how to function as a one-way medium used for instruction. The methodology combined the radio with the teacher to facilitate the scripted radio broadcast with a room of students through a deferred response dialogue (Friend, 1989). A similar strategy is now applied by the popular children's television show *Dora the Explorer*, when Dora pauses after asking a question, leaving time for the viewer to respond. By 2001, radio had become the most important medium for development and social change worldwide (Dagron, 2001), deployed throughout the last century for reaching geographically dispersed groups often in need of cost-effective educational support.

The many affordances of radio as a technology adopted by education did not come without difficulty. For most emergent technologies, barriers to accessibility delayed more widespread adoption in education. Like the radio, instructional uses of XR technologies will increase, but at what rate? Will it take 100 years for XR to reach its potential? With time, costs will go down and access will go up. But access is not enough to bring about necessary paradigm shifts.

The Need for a Framework to Approach New Technologies

Education is changing because the world is changing. With technologies more accessible to students and increased educator understanding, we will see instructional shifts that better benefit learners (Shippee, 2019a). The rate at which we will see these shifts directly correlates with access to research-based, best-practice-tested guidance.

Research demonstrates that XR learning experiences are making an impact on learning (Lion-Bailey et al., 2020). The University of Maryland conducted one of the first in-depth analyses on whether people learn better through immersive virtual environments. Researchers analyzed these immersive experiences and compared them to traditional platforms like a computer or tablet. The researchers split participants (largely unfamiliar with VR) into two groups: one viewed information first via a VR head-mounted display and then on a desktop; the other did the opposite. The results showed an 8.8% improvement overall in recall accuracy using the VR headsets (Krokos et al., 2019), a statistically significant number according to the research team (Rogers, 2019). We have no doubt that this type of research will continue to become accessible and support what many of us already know—that XR has a growing future in education.

In a comprehensive review of research, Johnson and Aragon (2002) compared traditional classroom-based instruction to technology-supported instruction and found no significant difference in critical educational variables. Finding no significant impact of instructional technology on various educational variables seems counter intuitive to our efforts, but a deeper dive into the research reveals important, productive insights.

Johnson and Aragon (2002) point to more findings stating that the technology used is not as important as other instructional factors, such as pedagogy and course design (Phipps & Merisotis, 1999), a point supported by past researchers who have identified that learning is affected more by what is delivered than by the delivery medium (Schramm, 1977). Our work here is to better understand and support the delivery of emergent technologies (the medium) to improve learning and learning outcomes.

As we have found in the past with paradigm shifts, the most significant influence on the evolution of emergent technologies is not always the technical development of more powerful devices, but rather educators developing a better understanding of and familiarity with how these technologies can be used to improve learning and learning outcomes (Dede, 1996). It is in the adoption, rather than integration, of emergent technologies that we will start to see a meaningful shift in practice. Think about the difference between the language used: adoption versus integration. Adoption infers empowerment through choice whereas integration infers force without choice. Integrating new technology will not change our practice but adopting a positive approach to innovation will lead to a paradigm shift. More creative instructional solutions may come from the lessons learned from radio.

XR ABC Framework

The XR ABC Framework is a guide intended to focus our conversation around effective and efficient uses of XR in education (Lion-Bailey et al., 2020). We believe giving a platform that provides a voice for XR-experienced educators is paramount. The XR ABC Framework provides a common language for instructional practice around XR while comprehensively illustrating objectives and standards that can be used to communicate the effectiveness of instruction. The XR ABC Framework has evolved from both research-based and best-practice-tested cases demonstrating how XR can improve learning and learning outcomes.

In XR and classroom software solutions, we talk about consuming and creating as two levels of interactivity afforded by the technology. Through research and practice, we have found that an area exists between these two levels that is a combination or blend of capabilities. The XR ABC Framework describes the areas of interactivity in XR as absorb, blend, and create.

Absorb

Absorb refers to the use of readily available apps and experiences to engage students in virtual field trips and observations of 3D models. Absorbing experiences supports increased understanding and recall.

AR Absorb experiences observe content that augments the learning and adds minimal interactivity. AR Absorb means adding to our experience in a somewhat simple and static manner. This differs from Blend and Create where we are manipulating or creating objects in AR. These experiences can be accessed through AR targets, geographic locations, and mobile apps, whereas the applications of AR Absorb are WYSIWYG (what you see is what you get). The learning curve is low for AR Absorb; almost every student and educator can immediately take advantage of the benefits.

VR Absorb experiences allow users to visit distant and theoretical places to see things with their own eyes from a first-person perspective. VR Absorb experiences are WYSIWYG with a low-interactivity level, but we should not dismiss these types of experiences. Simple VR Absorb field trips can be incredibly powerful when paired with meaningful conversations and thoughtful instructional delivery.

As in the scenario described early in this chapter, Micah's students explored the Anne Frank house in VR and interacted with various artifacts while a young girl read portions of the diary aloud. After training half of the students on how to use the Oculus Go headsets, the students then trained their peers to operate the device (Shippee, 2019b). Micah found there was a relatively low learning curve for successfully navigating the experience. This immersive experience brought new life to a story that had previously existed for students only as words on a page. As another student shared,

> The Anne Frank House VR experience helped me understand Ann Frank's story because it allowed me to visualize what was happening to her for the better. For example, it showed how cramped the rooms were that Anne Frank was living in. The VR experience helped with this because it made it seem like I was actually in the rooms that Anne was in which gives you a better idea of how things actually were. Moreover, the VR experience showed me why they have to be very cautious of being quiet because the floors were all made out of wood that is very creaky and the only thing that is keeping them hidden is a bookshelf on hinges. Another way the VR experience helped me to understand why Anne and the others had to be very quiet is because they weren't allowed to look out the windows, which based on the VR experience, were very big windows. In conclusion, the VR experience helped me to put things into better perspective and understand what Anne was going through better.

Experiencing Anne Frank's story in this way elicits emotions that would be difficult to evoke through a simple reading of the diary. Students experience and empathize in ways only possible using immersive technology.

Blend

Blend means to modify existing content by employing available apps and experiences for modifying or moving objects to apply, analyze, and evaluate content. Blend experiences do not truly create; rather, they manipulate characters, objects, etc. that are preloaded into the XR applications. Blend is the in-between state of consuming content while manipulating it, but not creating something entirely new.

AR Blend learners can change the outcome of an experience while working within pre-existing content. This is a step beyond AR Absorb because manipulation and change take place in the experience: engaging for the learner while intuitive to those who are not ready for the concept of creation. In VR, the concept of Blend affords learners the opportunity to change the immersive experience's outcome while working within pre-existing content. VR Blend allows users to engage in their VR experience and make choices in a more meaningful and personalized encounter.

When looking at VR Blend in the learning environment, we can consider using immersive technology to provide students with an outlet from their current reality. For example, in a classroom where students are challenged with navigating the social cues of their peers, there is often frustration with the lack of control they may have in the moment. The students often display behavioural challenges that disrupt the learning environment for both themselves and their peers. A behaviour intervention chart is a tool often implemented as a means of assisting with controlling those behaviours. In one case, the VR experience *Beat Saber* served as therapeutic for students needing to control the environment in the moment. While many would dismiss *Beat Saber* as more of a traditional gaming experience, through their participation students were able to use their actions to control the outcomes of each stage while expending energy and reaping the reward of success in the environment. This led to direct observed improvements in classroom behaviour as well as students' abilities to recognize how their role within the classroom could lead to both positive and negative outcomes.

Create

Create means to develop new content by leveraging available technologies to synthesize and add new experiences. Create opportunities are used to truly demonstrate an understanding of content through the construction of XR experiences, objects, stories, etc. that did not previously exist within the XR applications.

AR Create learning experiences move the learner from simply consuming content to creating it. For learners to create their own content, educators need to have a different mindset toward the learning process. When educators design activities for their students with thought and intention, they are often elevating the types of thinking that their students are required to do and, in turn, creating more impactful learning experiences. For students to create these experiences themselves means learning at a much higher level. VR Create is also a game-changer for students since it allows them to use their ideas and imagination to demonstrate real learning and understanding. Students become owners of learning, architects of content, and developers of brave new worlds. However, in considering the ABC framework, it is important not to exclusively rely on Create. Instead, we should implement the framework and include all three levels of mastery.

Immersive Pedagogical Considerations

Each of the areas (absorb, blend, create) has the potential to positively impact instruction when leveraged appropriately. For example, taking students on a virtual field trip (VR Absorb) can be the perfect experience when aligned with lesson objectives, whereas having the students create a fictional world may not be as meaningful.

Over time, more and more high-quality experiences will become accessible. They may not be used today in our instruction, but it is important that we monitor them so we will be prepared to use them in the future. Through the XR ABC Framework, we have a common language to describe what is happening with XR in our classrooms. The various areas of interactivity found in XR, both now and in the future, promise to magnify positive instructional experiences. By referring to these experiences in terms of Absorb, Blend, and Create, we can dive deep into harnessing the power of these exciting new technologies in our classrooms. Additionally, the framework can be used alongside other learning objectives. We have found strong connections to the framework in the following: Five Es (STEM), Four Cs, ISTE Student Standards, ISTE Educator Standards, and the SAMR Model.

It is important to consider best practices in instruction when determining pedagogical approaches in the classroom (Shippee, 2019c). The XR ABC Framework provides best practices for levels of adoption of immersive technologies while paying homage to other important pedagogical structures and objectives. When considering the Five Es (STEM) stages of learning, the XR ABC Framework empowers students with the ability and wherewithal to construct their own learning (Duran & Duran, 2004). Through immersive learning experiences, students tap into the Five Es (engagement, exploration, explanation, elaboration, and evaluation) as they navigate their learning (Duran & Duran, 2004). Similarly, the XR ABC Framework calls upon the Four Cs (critical thinking, communication, collaboration, and creativity), which originated in the *Framework for twenty-first Century Learning,* (National Education Association, 2012) to encourage students to tap into skills that lead to a future-ready learner.

When considering the connections between the XR ABC framework and the SAMR model (Puentedura, 2010), we begin by *Substituting* our existing strategies for ones that are supported by emergent technologies. We then *Augment* the strategy when we find that technology can improve (rather than replace) the strategy. Next, we use technology to *Modify* the strategy, and finally we *Redefine* the entire strategy when we discover technology may offer us a better way of doing things. Simply put, the SAMR model helps each of us to rethink individual lessons, units, and instructional practice (Shippee, 2019a).

The standards with which we align our content and objectives are also important considerations for the design of any learning experience. The ISTE Standards for Students are designed to empower student voices and ensure that learning is a student-driven process. Through the application of these standards, we can intentionally design learning experiences that empower our learnings, promote digital citizenship, and foster innovative designers through unique learning opportunities. Similarly, when considering connections to the ISTE Standards for Educators, the XR ABC framework supports educators in helping students become empowered learners. By applying the ISTE Educator Standards, the XR ABC framework promotes educators to serve as leaders, learners, citizens, collaborators, designers, facilitators, and analysts all within an idiosyncratic learning environment (ISTE, 2017).

Strategies for Implementation of Design

Many powerful instructional design theories and principles can prescribe effective learning practices for educators. Among them is the work of M. David Merrill (2002), who describes five principles of instruction. We can take these principles of instruction and apply them to creating and implementing immersive learning experiences in the following manner:

- **Solving real world problems**. "Learning is promoted when learners are engaged in solving real-world problems" (Merrill, 2002, p. 43). Through VR Create, students can develop sustainability practices for our global neighbors to improve the care of the earth as well as living conditions for many. Using programs like Google Earth and Google Blocks (https://vr.google.com/blocks), students can conduct a survey of regions where sustainability measures are needed and then design solutions to meet the needs of those communities. Through creating content, students are engaged in solving real-world problems in a meaningful and impactful way.
- **Drawing on existing knowledge**. "Learning is promoted when existing knowledge is activated as a foundation for new knowledge" (Merrill, 2002, p. 43). Through AR Blend, students can explore the solar system not only through the planets, but the celestial bodies and orbits that accompany them. This level of exploration and self-navigation through the solar system allows students to access their existing knowledge while exploring outer space through a new perspective. Access through the Merge Cube and Galactic Explorer apps provides students with unique self-navigated learning experiences.
- **Demonstrating new knowledge**. "Learning is promoted when new knowledge is demonstrated to the learner" (Merrill, 2002, p. 43). Utilizing a VR Absorb experience, students can engage with *The Blu* app to discover underwater ecosystems, fostering new knowledge through an immersive experience that promotes interactions with sea life. In this way, the VR experience provides students with an irreplaceable learning opportunity.
- **Application of new knowledge**. "Learning is promoted when new knowledge is applied by the learner" (Merrill, 2002, p. 43). In the VR Blend learning experience, *Becoming Homeless: A Human Experience* (Asher et al., 2018), students are presented with a journey through a day in the shoes of a homeless individual.

By interacting with the experience, taking in new knowledge along the way, and applying this knowledge as the user makes decisions that impact their journey, students are applying their learning throughout the experience. *Becoming Homeless: A Human Experience* is true experiential learning.

- **Integration of new knowledge**. "Learning is promoted when new knowledge is integrated into the learner's world" (Merrill, 2002, p. 43). Through AR Absorb, students can access museum artifacts brought into the learning environment. For example, the *BBC Civilizations* app provides students with access to historical artifacts of great relevance to world history. Because these artifacts are transported right into the learning environment, students can interact with them in meaningful ways.

Conclusion

Technology is a disruptor. Similar to how the radio changed the way we learned about the world, the Internet has changed how we can access knowledge. Emergent technologies will continue to change us by redefining how we work and play (Aviles et al., 2020; Konopelko & Lubinsky, 2021). At first, we integrate these technologies by adding them to what we do, but eventually, if we find real meaning-making and value, we will adopt them. In education, we do not talk about learning with a pencil since we have adopted the pencil as a learning tool. This is just what we do with emergent technologies (Hackl & Buzzel, 2021).

The XR ABC framework was developed for educators to provide context on how to adopt VR/AR technologies for teaching and learning. Developed by experienced educators from research-based examples, the framework illustrates how XR can improve teaching and learning outcomes while providing us with a common language to guide our growth and our meaningful adoption of XR technologies in education. Providing educators with this common language and a global understanding of how adopting XR shifts the instructional paradigm, we are not only preparing our learners for the future but also leveling the playing field for all global learners. Thus, the physical walls (or lack thereof) of schools and instructional institutes will no longer be barriers to education.

The beauty of having a framework available to educators for this type of technology adoption is that it provides us with an opportunity to be thoughtful, intentional, and reflective about designing instructional experiences for our students (Ardito et al., 2021). As we begin to evaluate the effectiveness of using VR/AR in our instruction, we can gain a better understanding of the desired outcomes during the design phase of our lessons based on this framework. With time, more accessibility to XR technologies, and an increased understanding of how XR learning practices can engage learners in meaningful and purposeful educational experiences, the XR ABC framework will enable educators to share and collaborate on the development of instruction using a common language.

References

Ardito, G., Shippee, M., & Lubinsky, J. (2021). Fusion+SNA: A new model for understanding and influencing technology innovation as a function of communication networks in K-12 schools. In M. J. Loureiro, A. Loureiro, & H. R. Gerber (Eds.), *Global education and the impact of institutional policies on educational technologies* (pp. 196–225). IGI-Global Publishing.

Asher, T., Ogle, E., Bailenson, J. N., & Herrera, F. (2018). Becoming homeless: a human experience. *ACM SIGGRAPH 2018* Virtual, Augmented, and Mixed Reality. https://doi. org/10.1145/3226552.3226576.

Aviles, C., Isaacs, S., Lion-Bailey, C., & Lubinsky, J. (2020). *The Esports education playbook: Empowering every learner through inclusive gaming.* Dave Burgess Consulting.

Berman, S. D. (2008). The return of educational radio? *International Review of Research in Open and Distance Learning, 9*(2), 1–8.

Blin, B. (1997). The first half century (1895–1945): Milestones in radio. *The UNESCO Courier, 2*, 16.

Cuban, L. (1986). *Teachers and machines: The classroom use of technology since 1920.* Teachers College Press.

Dagron, G. (2001). Making waves. *Rockefeller Foundation.* https://www.cfsc.org/content/ uploads/2018/04/making_waves_english.pdf

Dede, C. (1996). The evolution of distance education: Emerging technologies and distributed learning. *The American Journal of Distance Education, 10*(2), 4–36.

Duran, L. B., & Duran, E. (2004). The 5E instructional model: A learning cycle approach for inquiry-based science teaching. *The Science Education Review, 3*(2), 49–58. https://files.eric. ed.gov/fulltext/EJ1058007.pdf

Friend, J. (1989). Interactive radio instruction: Developing instructional methods. *British Journal of Educational Technology, 20*(2), 106–114. http://onlinelibrary.wiley.com/doi/10.1111/j.1467- 8535.1989.tb00270.x/full

Hackl, C., & Buzzell, J. (2021). *The augmented workforce: How artificial intelligence, augmented reality, and 5G will impact every dollar you make.* Renown Publishing.

ISTE. (2017). *ISTE Standards.* https://www.iste.org/standards

Johnson, S. D., & Aragon, S. R. (2002). An instructional strategy framework for online learning environments. In T. M. Egan & S. A. Lynham (Eds.), *Proceedings of the academy for human resource development* (pp. 1022–1029). AHRD. http://citeseerx.ist.psu.edu/viewdoc/download ?doi=10.1.1.114.7888&rep=rep1&type=pdf

Konopelko, D., & Lubinsky, J. (2021). Powerful partnerships for continued esports success and growth. *EdTech Magazine.* https://edtechmagazine.com/k12/article/2021/11/ powerful-partnerships-continued-esports-success-and-growth

Krokos, E., Plaisant, C., & Varshney, A. (2019). Virtual memory palaces: Immersion aids recall. *Virtual Reality, 23*, 1–15. https://doi.org/10.1007/s10055-018-0346-3

Lion-Bailey, C., Lubinsky, J., & Shippee, M. (2020). Reality bytes: Innovative learning using augmented and virtual reality.. Dave Burgess Consulting.

Merrill, M. D. (2002). First principles of instruction. *Educational Technology Research and Development, 50*, 43–59. https://doi.org/10.1007/BF02505024

National Education Association. (2012). *Preparing 21st century students for a global society: An educator's guide to the four Cs.* Washington, DC. http://www.nea.org/assets/docs/A-Guide-to- Four-Cs.pdf

Phipps, R. A., & Merisotis, J. P. (1999). What's the difference? *A review of contemporary research on the effectiveness of distance learning in higher education.* Institute for Higher Education Policy.

Puentedura, R. (2010). *The SAMR model.* http://hippasus.com/resources/sweden2010/SAMR_ TPCK_IntroToAdvancedPractice.pdf

Rogers, S. (2019, March 15). Virtual reality: The learning aid of the 21st century. *Forbes.* https://www. forbes.com/sites/solrogers/2019/03/15/virtual-reality-the-learning-aid-of-the- 21st-century/.

Romiszowski, A. J. (1974). The selection and use of instructional media.. Kogan Page Limited.

Schramm, W. L. (1977). *Big media, little media: Tools and technologies for instruction*. Sage Publications.

Shippee, M. (2019a). *WanderlustEDU: An educator's guide to innovation, change, and adventure*. Dave Burgess Consulting, Inc.

Shippee, M. (2019b) Streaming VR with a participant and their experience with green screen. *Tech & Learning*. https://www.techlearning.com/news/streaming-vr-with-a-participant-and-their-experience-with-green-screen

Shippee, M. (2019c) Augmented reality – The art of BYOD in the classroom. *Tech & Learning*. https://www.techlearning.com/news/augmented-reality-the-art-of-byod-in-the-classroom

Traub, D. (2004). The shift to seamless augmentation and "humane" applications via mobile/wireless devices: A view to a future for lifelong learning. In J. Attewell & C. Savill-Smith (Eds.), *Mobile learning anytime everywhere* (pp. 201–202). Yumpu. https://www.yumpu.com/en/document/view/31536338/mobile-learning-anytime-everywhere/210

Vardhan, H. (2002, January). Radio broadcast technology. *Resonance*, 53–63.

Christine Lion-Bailey is Chief Strategy Officer of Ready Learner One. She serves as a director of Tech & Innovation and an elementary principal as well as a college professor. She is co-author of *Reality Bytes: Innovative Learning Using Augmented & Virtual Reality* and *The Esports Education Playbook: Empowering Every Learner Through Inclusive Gaming*.

Jesse Lubinsky is Chief Learning Officer of Ready Learner One. He is co-author of *Reality Bytes: Innovative Learning Using Augmented and Virtual Reality* and *The Esports Education Playbook: Empowering Every Learner Through Inclusive Gaming*. Jesse is an international keynote speaker, a CoSN CETL, and co-host of the Partial Credit Podcast.

Micah Shippee, PhD is Chief Executive Officer of Ready Learner One. He is the author of *WanderlustEDU: An Educator's Guide to Innovation Change and Adventure* and the co-author of *Reality Bytes: Innovative Learning Using Augmented and Virtual Reality*. Micah serves as an educator, professor, and speaker.

From Abstract to Concrete: How Immersive Virtual Reality Technology Enhances Teaching of Complex Paradigms

Sarune Savickaite and David Simmons

Abstract We demonstrate how topics in developmental psychology may be taught via immersive virtual reality (VR). We give a brief overview of each topic, demonstrate our immersive VR rendition of the task, and describe the advantages of immersive technology for teaching abstract concepts. We also offer additional suggestions and best-practice advice.

Keywords Abstract concepts · Active learning · Developmental psychology · Immersive education

Introduction

Virtual reality (VR) is as difficult to define as the experience itself. It is often described as an artificial environment experienced through sensory stimuli, such as sights and sounds, provided by a computer, in which one's actions partially determine what happens in the environment. However, the general understanding of VR is narrower and often refers to an artificial environment experienced through a variety of senses, created by a computer, and accessed via a display, often a Head-Mounted Display (HMD). Due to the recent increased interest in VR, there are already several comprehensive literature reviews on VR applications for education (Jensen & Konradsen, 2018; Merchant et al., 2014; Radianti et al., 2020). The most popular domains covered in recent reviews are medicine, social science, and psychology. Spatial knowledge, social skills, and evacuation strategies training are just a few examples of how VR has been used in education (Radianti et al., 2020). Radianti et al. (2020) also highlight several gaps in knowledge in the education literature, which we aim to address in this chapter.

S. Savickaite (✉) · D. Simmons
University of Glasgow, School of Psychology and Neuroscience, Glasgow, Scotland
e-mail: sarune.savickaite@glasgow.ac.uk; david.simmons@glasgow.ac.uk

© The Author(s), under exclusive license to Springer Nature Switzerland AG 2022
P. MacDowell, J. Lock (eds.), *Immersive Education*,
https://doi.org/10.1007/978-3-031-18138-2_9

In this chapter, we demonstrate how complex and abstract topics in undergraduate psychology, specifically developmental psychology, can be taught in immersive VR. We use three well- known concepts in developmental psychology: the Perspective Taking task, the Conservation task, and the False Belief task, which are regularly taught in undergraduate psychology courses. We will briefly outline each task, present our version of the task in immersive VR (using the immersive VR platform) and discuss the benefits of immersive VR technology for complex and abstract concept teaching. We will also suggest further recommendations and best-practice tips.

Vignette

Teaching abstract or complex concepts in psychology is challenging at the best of times. After months of lockdown and restriction due to the COVID-19 pandemic, Jennifer found it even harder to communicate such complex psychological problems to students. Students often disengage in live sessions, so there is little hope for active engagement with all, or most, of the teaching being online. Jennifer started researching immersive education technologies, such as Eon and Labster, where students can engage with the three-dimensional content remotely with only minimal guidance from the teacher. However, most of the topics available for teaching were around applied or medically oriented subjects. Jennifer then turned to immersive education software, such as Edify. Jennifer used a free trial provided by her institution (other similar VR teaching apps are also free or provide free trials). She soon found that, after the initial learning curve of getting familiar with the VR teaching environment, she could easily import her own 3D models and lecture slides and deliver these lessons via broadcasting tools (VR-by-proxy). With pandemic restrictions easing, Jennifer hopes she can invite her students to the classroom to learn psychology in a VR-mediated learning environment, without the proxy broadcasting interface used in her distance-learning courses.

Background

Digital technology has shaped the evolution of education for decades (Savickaite et al., 2022). The early 1990s saw the introduction of networked computers for collaborative learning (Harasim, 2000). Soon came the movement to online digital learning, which has boomed in recent years via MOOC (Massive Open Online Course) platforms like Coursera and Udemy as well as LMS (Learning Management Systems) such as Moodle or Blackboard. VR, an interplay of technology and human perception, initially emerged in the 1980s and 1990s. For a while, VR systems faded from prominence largely due to limitations in core technology and prohibitive costs. But as these barriers have lifted and immersive user experience has improved, industrial, professional, and entertainment uptake of VR has increased. Early research in military and aviation simulations proved that practice-based training in VR is highly effective (Mesa-Gresa et al., 2018). The education sector is now in the process of adapting this pathfinder knowledge and application of visual immersion to modern teaching environments, creating new learner-centered approaches, and seeking paradigm-shifting changes in teaching success.

Moreover, the next generation of learners, Gen Z (Mohr & Mohr, 2017), and Gen Alpha (Jha, 2020; Tootell et al., 2014), are arguably digital citizens with intrinsically strong associations between play and technology, especially in early-years education. They can hold a universe of content in their hands with an endless textbook of knowledge at their fingertips, delivered through user-friendly devices and seamlessly integrated with their everyday lives (Savickaite, 2020). Many are also skills-focused, self-sufficient, creative individuals with an interest in fast-paced advancement and sustainability. Generation theory is contested in places (Jauregui et al., 2020); however, the need for adaptation to match the tenacity of this next generation of learners remains a crucial part of research in education.

Recommendations on the most effective methods for teaching complex concepts have evolved since the 1990s, but the main principle—that some form of active learning is effective—remains. Active learning is an umbrella term for teaching methods that put students in charge of their own learning. To different people, active learning entails different things, and/or different people highlight different aspects of the concept. There is consensus that children learn best by performing their own learning in an active, mental and/or physical way; students develop their own knowledge structures by discovering for themselves; and learning actively leads to the ability to think critically and solve problems (see Page, 1990, for an historical overview). In this chapter, we focus on the broader terms, which align with Jesionkowska et al.'s (2020) recent definition of active learning for augmented reality (AR).

Over two decades ago, Stearns (1994) identified the importance of active learning strategies for complex and abstract concepts. Teaching complex concepts is often challenging as students tend to find lower-level learning of the material, such as memorization and definitions, easier while struggling with critical evaluation and problem solving. Stearns (1994) further proposed that teaching complex concepts should start with standard lectures and individual learning, where the lower-level learning is accomplished. Then small- and large-group active learning can enhance the basic concepts, encourage peer learning, avoid unnecessary repetition, and encourage critical thinking. In a critical review, Tsai and Huang (2001) discussed the effects of students' internal control of learning. They propose that one role of technology in learning is to help students develop appropriate epistemological commitments, metacognitive skills, and critical thinking (Tsai & Huang, 2001).

Active learning and self-reflection are successful strategies in a carefully considered and appropriate curriculum (Butler et al., 2009; Heriot et al., 2008; Salisbury & Irby, 2020), but like any learning strategy it has also been criticized and questioned (Michael, 2006; Sanders et al., 2017). Active learning seems to be particularly effective in teaching strategies involving gamification (Kiryakova et al., 2014;

Silva et al., 2019; Wood & Reiners, 2012) and immersive technology (Hobson et al., 2019; Jesionkowska et al., 2020; Roberts & Roberts, 2014). Current teaching curricula are extremely wide. As a result, critics contend that students have only a rudimentary comprehension of numerous subjects. Switching from lecture-based frontal teaching to an active learning approach that facilitates deeper understanding of theory and principles, we believe, is the pedagogical solution to this challenge. Such practical, hands-on, project-based learning allows students to create, challenge, actualize, and evaluate ideas in a more holistic manner, while also rewarding their efforts with tangible results through cooperatively produced learning outcomes (Jesionkowska et al., 2020).

With the development of VR technologies over the last 10–20 years, interest has increased in applying this emerging technology to support instructional design methods in both K–12 and higher education (Pellas et al., 2021). Rapid adoption of VR technology as a pedagogical method has challenged our definition of what constitutes a digital learning environment and what aspects of this immersive technology are appropriate and effective in education (Hamilton et al., 2009). High-quality graphics, customizable environments, and immersive content allow students to explore complex subjects in a way that traditional teaching methods simply cannot. Despite this, research on learning outcomes and effectiveness of the interventions has been sparse (Hamilton et al., 2009). Immersive technology, including VR and AR, has been successfully adopted in the teaching of healthcare and medical concepts (Qiao et al., 2021) where learners can explore three-dimensional structures in VR, step into locations which would be difficult (if not impossible) to visit in real life, and experience controlled social situations in psychological interventions. However, the teaching of complex or abstract topics in VR has been under-researched. We propose that with careful consideration, standard teaching strategies in developmental psychology, for example, can be enhanced with the use of immersive VR.

Immersive VR learning environments have already been shown to offer a powerful alignment of learner engagement and knowledge retention (de Freitas et al., 2010; Freina & Ott, 2015; Ummihusna & Zairul, 2021). The move towards active learner engagement pedagogies in VR is driven by the knowledge that active engagement offers significant benefits over passive observation, forming new experience-based learning methodologies for students. The application of technology in education has mostly focused on making information more accessible and interactive (Mesa-Gresa et al., 2018; Radianti et al., 2020). VR introduces new methods for the delivery of active learning: potentially enhancing learning experiences by innovative, realistic presentation of information, manipulating the learner's cognitive load, and providing repeated opportunities to practice (Andersen et al., 2018; Lin et al., 2021). Teaching, therefore, must adapt to this innovative medium and move from an abstract 2D to a practical 3D pedagogy. This applies to both VR-by-proxy (for online and distance education) and face-to-face teaching.

Immersive Teaching Platforms

Immersive Teaching platforms such as *Edify* (www.edify.ac) use VR and video conferencing to enable accessible, immersive, and engaging educational experiences. Educators can demonstrate concepts in virtual laboratories and spaces which are normally challenging to access. New medical students, for example, may struggle in the standard post-COVID-19 teaching environment. *Edify* provides 3D immersive anatomical and physiological environments where students can utilize active learning strategies in safe and controllable virtual worlds.

In the vignette, we briefly outlined the challenges teachers face. Teaching abstract or complex psychological constructs can be difficult at the best of times. Learners need to have good spatial awareness and imagination as well as a concept of scale and dimension, and to apply these abilities in the learning contexts. Because of its flexibility, *Edify* was chosen as a test bed for the three key developmental psychology paradigms that could be successfully delivered directly in VR or as VR-by-proxy. We also believe that these classical paradigms can be enhanced and empowered when presented in a virtual environment (VE), where users can manipulate dimension and perspective without the physical restrictions of the real world.

Illustrative Examples

We present three illustrative examples of how VR can be used in teaching developmental psychology at middle years and high school education and at the undergraduate level. We outline the steps of creating these lessons once careful consideration of the pedagogical design has been evaluated. The aim of these illustrative examples is to demonstrate how abstract concepts such as Perspective Taking, Conservation, or Theory of Mind can be taught in VR and enhance students' understanding of developmental psychology. We also wish to explore what VR adds to these lessons: for example, the ability to manipulate the three-dimensional environment, such as scaling the models, which is not possible in the real world. The illustrative examples we present are well-developed design frameworks, and we aim to test the validity and feasibility of these lessons with teachers and students in future undergraduate courses on developmental psychology. In the following sections, we present the key design elements to be considered when devising a VR lesson on an abstract concept.

Perspective Taking Task

Social interaction often requires a good understanding of another individual's interpretation of the surroundings, and that often includes visual perspective. Failure to recognize these individual viewpoints can often lead to miscommunication or conflict (Ferguson et al., 2017). Children generally behave egocentrically when assessing another individual's perspective. We can infer that accurate perspective taking is a skill children develop. This does not mean, however, that adults lose the egocentric perspective later in life. We often find ourselves still taking a very self-centred view; for example, we generally believe that others have more access to our internal states than they actually do (Gilovich et al., 1998). Theory of Mind (ToM) or Mentalizing refers to our ability to make inferences about mental states of others. It is suggested that ToM develops around the first 4–5 years of life (Frith & Frith, 2003). The ability to adopt the viewpoint of someone else is a constitutive part of both spatial and social cognition (Vogeley & Fink, 2003). Thus, spatial perspective taking refers to the ability to translocate one's own egocentric viewpoint to somebody else's viewpoint in space. The Perspective Taking Task (or VPT for Visual Perspective Taking) is a psychological paradigm based on egocentrism in early childhood (Kesselring & Müller, 2011) and it is now often used to assess Theory of Mind (Harwood & Farrar, 2006) (Fig. 1). To our knowledge, there have been no attempts to create a VR version of this task. Yet due to its three-dimensional nature, it seems appropriate to explore this task using immersive technology.

For our VR Perspective Taking Task (VR-PTT), we have used the *Edify* platform's blank environment and imported three-dimensional models we obtained from online 3D content websites (a full list of the models used is available in Appendix). For VR-PTT, we have selected an island with mountains and trees (like the standard three-mountain VPT task; see Foorman et al., 1984; Light & Nix, 1983). We selected an animated character of a cat and created several copies in different colours. In the experimental set-up we used two versions: orange and brown. We placed cats in two locations on the island, with their view obstructed (Fig. 2). The *Edify* platform allows placement of cameras, which can then be broadcast to a

Fig. 1 Example of the visual perspective taking task

Fig. 2 Visual perspective taking task set up in VR: two screenshots show different viewpoints

viewer via video conferencing. This allows an alternative teaching method of VR-by-proxy, where the teacher can allow students to view the scene from various angles and assume the viewpoint of the characters placed in the three-dimensional scene. In our example, we placed cameras behind each of the cats, with an additional camera showing the overall scene where both characters were visible.

Lesson set-up is simple and requires an immersive teaching platform, such as *Edify*, and several three-dimensional models freely available online. These concepts can be taught remotely and actively allow students to assume variable viewpoints, which is suitable for blended or remote teaching. Also, with appropriate VR equipment available, students can enter the three-dimensional lesson themselves and actively explore by teleporting, or just moving around, in the scene.

Conservation Task

The Conservation Task is another classical test in Piagetian developmental psychology. In one version, a Piagetian number conservation task, children are asked if two aligned rows of objects have the same number of objects or if one of the rows has more (Piaget, 1952). After the child agrees that the lines are the same, the experimenter transforms one of the lines so that it is longer, and the child is asked again if the two rows have the same number of objects or if one of the rows has more. When asked the second time, pre-operational-aged children (intuitive period; approximately ages four to seven years old) typically answer that the longer row has more (Fig. 3).

In our VR Conservation Task (VR-CT), we set up two scenarios (Fig. 4). The first was a coliseum environment in *Edify*, where we placed three-dimensional coins following the classical number conservation task from Fig. 3. With careful placement of coins in three dimensions, the widely dispersed display and the initial display appear the same (see Fig. 3 for reference). Alongside the conventional way of describing this task, VR-CT also has the potential to spark critical thinking, with more possibilities to explore and a greater variety of presentation options. Moreover, it could be expanded to experimental applications.

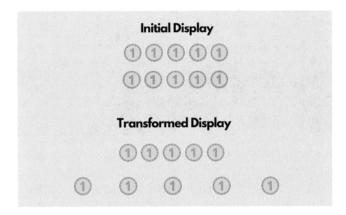

Fig. 3 Example of the Piagetian number conservation task

Fig. 4 VR conservation task set up

The second example we created was set in the gallery environment of the *Edify* platform. Using three-dimensional golf balls (Fig. 4), we once again followed the classical conservation tasks set-up. Additionally, we set up golf balls in variable arrangements to demonstrate how perception of the size and dispersion of objects changes with the different perspective. If students are able to experience this VR lesson themselves, they can also actively manipulate the objects (golf balls in this example) and investigate how their perception changes from different viewpoints. Three-dimensional models can be resized, moved around, rotated, scaled, and viewed from multiple perspectives. For example, with careful placement of the camera, the view broadcast to the learner would show an array of coins or balls of the same size. However, by moving the objects around and changing the perspective, the learner would be able to see how the size of the golf balls changes. This active exploration of the environment and knowledge of how placement of objects can alter our perception of size and dimension can help students develop advanced critical skills and novel ideation: an embodiment of the principles of active learning.

Note The top screenshot shows the gallery environment and golf balls arrangement (the camera is also visible to demonstrate how it is viewed from the teacher's perspective in VR-by-proxy mode). The lower image shows coin placement in the coliseum environment in *Edify*.

False Belief Task

The False Belief task is a classical method used to assess Theory of Mind (ToM). Bloom and German (2000) suggest that there is more to passing the False Belief task than ToM and there is more to ToM than passing the False Belief task. However, it has been successfully used in developmental (Setoh et al., 2016; Zaitchik, 1990) and evolutionary psychology (Call & Tomasello, 1999; Krachun et al., 2009) and for research into autism (Surian & Leslie, 1999; Tager-Flusberg & Joseph, 2012), schizophrenia (Fernandez-Gonzalo et al., 2015), and Alzheimer's (Fernandez-Duque et al., 2009). One of the most well-known versions of the False Belief task is the Sally-Anne task (Baron-Cohen et al., 1985) (Fig. 5). In this scenario, Sally and Anne are presented as puppets by the experimenter and the child (or adult, depending on the experimental set up) acts as an observer. Sally places a marble in a basket and leaves. Anne takes the marble from the basket and places it in a box. When Sally returns, the experimenter asks the participant where Sally will look for her marble. A participant with fully developed ToM will deduce what Sally is thinking and that she did not see the marble being placed in the box, and will say that Sally will look for the marble in the basket where she placed it before leaving. However, a child under a certain age (the exact age is variable) or some neurodivergent individuals (e.g., autistic) might not assume the point of view of Sally, and therefore will say that Sally will look for the marble in the box, because that is where the marble actually is.

Fig. 5 Example of the false belief task

Fig. 6 VR false belief task set up

In our VR False Belief task (VR-FBT), we used another *Edify* environment (Da Vinci Lab) which has a realistic room set-up with tables, a bed, chairs, and windows (Fig. 6). In this room we placed 2 three-dimensional children's characters (we used the same model of a child with a onesie and changed colours as in the VR-PTT), 2 baskets, a ball, and a dog. In this set-up, a teacher can decide what would be the best way to present the False Belief task. Learners can enter the three-dimensional VE and place the objects at variable locations and attempt to explain the concept themselves. Alternatively, the teacher can use the VR-by-proxy method and move the figures while describing the False Belief (or Sally-Anne) task. The addition of a dog and an environment with other objects present (although learners cannot move the furniture) encourage the thinking behind the ecological validity of the task, including how additional cues and setting the task in a realistic environment could influence performance in the task.

Strategies for Implementation of Design

Each of the three examples we presented demonstrates a unique aspect of immersive teaching. VR-PTT allows assuming multiple viewpoints; VR-CT allows investigation of scale and dimensionality, which is unavailable in the standard version; VR-FBT allows the learner to think about how being part of the social scenario is important, rather than being a passive observer.

- **Enable active learning.** We discussed active learning and reflective pedagogical strategies in the introduction. The three illustrative examples we provide demonstrate how, with careful planning, immersive technology can help teachers communicate complex and abstract psychological paradigms more effectively. VR allows the use of teaching tools simply not available in a real-world teaching scenario. The VR-PTT task allows the assumption of multiple viewpoints, sometimes at once (if you view the broadcasting tool bar). In the active VR-PTT task, learners can walk or teleport around the objects. The active version of the task also allows further manipulation and resizing of the objects placed in the scene. Freedom of exploration coupled with teachers' active engagement has the potential for a promising immersive lesson. VR-CT follows the basic principles of the classical Conservation task and extends them further. Users can manipulate, resize, and move the subjects. In the VR-by-proxy version this task is demonstrated by the teacher, whereas in the active version of VR-CT students can explore the environment themselves. Moreover, students can attempt to set up an arrangement of objects and present it to other students using the VR-by-proxy method, which would make learners assume the role of a teacher. Explaining complex ideas that we have learned to another learner (e.g., peer assisted learning) has been demonstrated as a way to prove our own understanding (Pi et al., 2021). Such collaborative strategies enhance critical thinking and reflection (Gokhale, 1995; Scheffler, 2012).
- **Use an instructional VR-by-proxy method.** Critics of classic False Belief tasks argue that it is difficult to demonstrate the link between understanding the false belief in the task and real-world scenarios (Gopnik & Astington, 1988; Zaitchik, 1990). Our VR-FBT allows users to manipulate three-dimensional objects in a realistic environment. Teachers can choose to use an instructional VR-by-proxy method, moving objects around and explaining the classical Sally-Anne task. However, if learners can access the VR environment themselves, they can use the previously mentioned learner-becomes-teacher method and explain the concept to their peers, move objects around, and reflect on how the classical False Belief task can be translated into three dimensions.

- **Be aware of the overheads involved.** Although immersive technology, particularly VR, seems to present huge potential for teaching complex and abstract paradigms, it is not without problems. VR capabilities rely heavily on the sophistication of the hardware used. Just comparing the capabilities of the first Oculus Rift or HTC Vive Pro (tethered and bulky HMDs) to the recent stand-alone Meta Quest 2, it is clear the technology is improving rapidly. Therefore, teachers need to make sure they are aware of these technological advancements and the benefits they bring to the classroom. With research in immersive education still in its infancy, teachers are expected to be active researchers. This can often create problems with time and resources. Future research should explore the importance of competency and cognitive load from the teachers' perspective (Savickaite & Millington, 2021) and how these issues could be addressed.
- **Consider the importance of immersion.** Literature in immersive education is further complicated by the lack of clear definitions and a better understanding of the link between hardware sophistication and the level of immersion (Savickaite et al., 2022). Active engagement and an ability to navigate and manipulate the immersive environment is likely to be important in successfully adopting immersive technology for teaching. Immersive VR is arguably better than the standard teaching methods in teaching crime scene investigation (Mayne & Green, 2020), language learning (Parmaxi, 2020), history (Ben Ghida, 2020) and even mathematics (Cabero-Almenara et al., 2021). For example, Mayne and Green (2020) showed that VR applications helped students develop practical crime scene processing skills through qualitative and quantitative evaluations. VR-based practical sessions demonstrated the potential to enhance forensic science courses by providing a cost-effective practical experience. Students expressed high levels of engagement with the app, with few reports of negative effects (such as motion sickness). All these examples note that the methodology should be carefully considered before it is fully integrated in the teaching curriculum. Increasing evidence suggests that fully immersive environments are beneficial and should be a focus for future pedagogical design frameworks. The VR-by-proxy methods discussed in our chapter, although initially designed as a temporary solution to the COVID-19 pandemic, will still be applicable in distance learning or other situations where there is a physical separation between teacher and student.
- **Pay attention to accessibility.** Accessibility is an emerging topic in the field of immersive technology. Hardware, software, and acquisition of appropriate teaching materials (3D models and animations) can be costly. Cybersickness and other factors related to student diversity should be considered (Mott et al., 2020; Teófilo et al., 2018; Trewin et al., 2008). Moreover, new research initiatives such as XRAccess (https://xraccess.org/research/) are seeking to broaden the question of accessibility. Research is emerging on how individuals with visual impairments can access VR. For example, Rector (2018) has explored adaptations of interactive technologies (especially around exercise and outdoor activities) for blind or low-vision individuals. Work on accessibility is also making headway in the field of neurodiversity (Boyd et al., 2018). Addressing issues of accessibility is likely to be an integral part of future design frameworks for immersive education.

Conclusion

We have presented three frameworks demonstrating how complex and abstract concepts in developmental psychology can be translated into VR lessons. In future, we aim to test the concepts we have outlined in the three illustrative examples and gather feedback from learners and teachers. VR has considerable potential for teaching a variety of subjects, but it also needs to be evaluated responsibly. Technology is taking over our everyday lives: we have smart phones, smart TVs, and AI technology to help us navigate the world more efficiently. Researchers and educators are often seduced by the flashy promise of these technologies and their benefits for teaching. We should always be critical of what new methodologies bring to our existing pedagogical frameworks and understand whether they help or hinder the learning process. Our three illustrative examples from developmental psychology demonstrate how carefully selected technologies can shift our perspective and help us to re-evaluate active learning methodologies.

As technology advances further and more users adopt VR-mediated approaches to education, expertise in best practices for learning will increase. Our vision of the future is that there will be multi-user VR teaching labs in every institution and libraries of pedagogical content generated (Savickaite et al., 2022). VR-by-proxy approaches will expand availability to those who cannot access campuses directly. There are even more possibilities as users adopt VR technologies at home and enter the Metaverse (Park & Kim, 2022). This chapter is an early step in building the pedagogical literature for this exciting new venture.

Acknowledgements and Conflict of Interest Declaration Special thanks to Elliot Millington and Gabriella Rodolico for kind feedback on early versions of the manuscripts. We also thank content creators at *Edify*, who helped us modify some of the models.

We wish to declare a potential conflict of interest. Sarune Savickaite is funded by an ESRC/SGSSS collaborative studentship with ***Edify***. She spends 10% of her time working with ***Edify*** as part of her PhD studies.

Appendix: Models Used in the Lessons

Video explaining and demonstrating each experiment is available at https://www.youtube.com/watch?v=ODRDA6nKg-A

Perspective taking	Conservation task	False belief task
Toon cat by Omabuarts studio at Sketchfab https://sketchfab.com/3d-models/toon-cat-free-b2bd1ee7858444bda366110a2d960386	*Roman coin* by Serafim123 from Sketchfab https://sketchfab.com/3d-models/roman-coin-b153a9c736b0463abcb423e8515587cc	*Bunny Child* by sofiemhoffmann from Sketchfab https://sketchfab.com/3d-models/bunny-child-c5dfe6059e034e75af3f527286eb38d6
		Shiba by zixisun02 from Sketchfab https://sketchfab.com/3d-models/shibafaef9fe5ace445e7b29889d1c1ece361c
Lowpoly Island by alfance at Sketchfab https://sketchfab.com/3d-models/lowpoly-island-26c3f2f271ab41a5a0c9178ac5304df8	*Golf ball* by germydan at Sketchfab https://sketchfab.com/3d-models/golf-ball-5f158949c1084575abf02437f6b43028	*Warn baseball* by Alex Bes from Sketchfab https://sketchfab.com/3d-models/worn-baseball-ball-fdf3de6ae225421ea78961b897b9608a
		Basket by Mikko Haapoja from Sketchfab https://sketchfab.com/3d-models/basket-83f888e2736e4d49b7f66a945492f6c4
		Wicker basket from cgtrader https://www.cgtrader.com/free-3d-models/architectural/decoration/wicker-basket%2D%2D3 

References

Andersen, S. A. W., Konge, L., & Sørensen, M. S. (2018). The effect of distributed virtual reality simulation training on cognitive load during subsequent dissection training. *Medical Teacher, 40*(7), 684–689. https://doi.org/10.1080/0142159x.2018.1465182

Baron-Cohen, S., Leslie, A. M., & Frith, U. (1985). Does the autistic child have a "theory of mind"? *Cognition, 21*(1), 37–46. https://doi.org/10.1016/0010-0277(85)90022-8

Ben Ghida, D. (2020). Augmented reality and virtual reality: A 360 immersion into Western history of architecture. *International Journal of Emerging Trends in Engineering Research, 8*(9), 6051–6055. https://doi.org/10.30534/ijeter/2020/187892020

Bloom, P., & German, T. P. (2000). Two reasons to abandon the false belief task as a test of theory of mind. *Cognition, 77*(1), B25–B31. https://doi.org/10.1016/s0010-0277(00)00096-2

Boyd, L. E., Day, K., Stewart, N., Abdo, K., Lamkin, K., & Linstead, E. (2018). Leveling the playing field: Supporting neurodiversity via virtual realities. *Technology & Innovation, 20*(1–2), 105–116. https://doi.org/10.21300/20.1-2.2018.105

Butler, K. W., Veltre, D. E., & Brady, D. (2009). Implementation of active learning pedagogy comparing low-fidelity simulation versus high-fidelity simulation in pediatric nursing education. *Clinical Simulation in Nursing, 5*(4), e129–e136. https://doi.org/10.1016/j.ecns.2009.03.118

Cabero-Almenara, J., Barroso-Osuna, J., & Martinez-Roig, R. (2021). Mixed, augmented and virtual, reality applied to the teaching of mathematics for architects. *Applied Sciences, 11*(15), 7125. https://doi.org/10.3390/app11157125

Call, J., & Tomasello, M. (1999). A nonverbal false belief task: The performance of children and great apes. *Child Development, 70*(2), 381–395. https://doi.org/10.1111/1467-8624.00028

De Freitas, S., Rebolledo-Mendez, G., Liarokapis, F., Magoulas, G., & Poulovassilis, A. (2010). Learning as immersive experiences: Using the four-dimensional framework for designing and evaluating immersive learning experiences in a virtual world. *British Journal of Educational Technology, 41*(1), 69–85. https://doi.org/10.1111/j.1467-8535.2009.01024.x

Ferguson, H. J., Apperly, I., & Cane, J. E. (2017). Eye tracking reveals the cost of switching between self and other perspectives in a visual perspective-taking task. *The Quarterly Journal of Experimental Psychology, 70*(8), 1646–1660. https://doi.org/10.1080/17470218.2016.1199716

Fernandez-Duque, D., Baird, J. A., & Black, S. E. (2009). False-belief understanding in frontotemporal dementia and Alzheimer's disease. *Journal of Clinical and Experimental Neuropsychology, 31*(4), 489–497. https://doi.org/10.1080/13803390802282688

Fernandez-Gonzalo, S., Turon, M., Jodar, M., Pousa, E., Rambla, C. H., García, R., & Palao, D. (2015). A new computerized cognitive and social cognition training specifically designed for patients with schizophrenia/schizoaffective disorder in early stages of illness: A pilot study. *Psychiatry Research, 228*(3), 501–509. https://doi.org/10.1016/j.psychres.2015.06.007

Foorman, B., Leiber, J., & Fernie, D. (1984). Mountains and molehills: Egocentricism in recent research. *Oxford Review of Education, 10*(3), 261–270. https://doi.org/10.1080/0305498840100303

Freina, L., & Ott, M. (2015, April). *A literature review on immersive virtual reality in education: State of the art and perspectives* [Conference session]. Elearning and Software for Education, Bucharest, Romania. https://www.researchgate.net/publication/280566372_A_Literature_Review_on_Immersive_Virtual_Reality_in_Education_State_Of_The_Art_and_Perspectives

Frith, U., & Frith, C. D. (2003). Development and neurophysiology of mentalizing. *Philosophical Transactions of the Royal Society of London. Series B: Biological Sciences, 358*(1431), 459–473. https://doi.org/10.1098/rstb.2002.1218

Gilovich, T., Savitsky, K., & Medvec, V. H. (1998). The illusion of transparency: Biased assessments of others' ability to read one's emotional states. *Journal of Personality and Social Psychology, 75*(2), 332–346.

Gokhale, A. A. (1995). Collaborative learning enhances critical thinking. *Journal of Technology Education, 7*(1). https://doi.org/10.21061/jte.v7i1.a.2

Gopnik, A., & Astington, J. W. (1988). Children's understanding of representational change and its relation to the understanding of false belief and the appearance-reality distinction. *Child Development*. https://doi.org/10.1111/j.1467-8624.1988.tb03192.x

Hamilton, A. F. D. C., Brindley, R., & Frith, U. (2009). Visual perspective taking impairment in children with autistic spectrum disorder. *Cognition, 113*(1), 37–44. https://doi.org/10.1016/j.cognition.2009.07.007

Harasim, L. (2000). Shift happens: Online education as a new paradigm in learning. *The Internet and Higher Education, 3*(1), 41–61. https://doi.org/10.1016/S1096-7516(00)00032-4

Harwood, M. D., & Farrar, M. J. (2006). Conflicting emotions: The connection between affective perspective taking and theory of mind. *British Journal of Developmental Psychology, 24*(2), 401–418. https://doi.org/10.1348/026151005X50302

Heriot, K. C., Cook, R., Jones, R. C., & Simpson, L. (2008). The use of student consulting projects as an active learning pedagogy: A case study in a production/operations management course. *Decision Sciences Journal of Innovative Education, 6*(2), 463–481. https://doi.org/10.1111/j.1540-4609.2008.00186.x

Hobson, W. L., Hoffmann-Longtin, K., Loue, S., Love, L. M., Liu, H. Y., Power, C. M., & Pollart, S. M. (2019). Active learning on center stage: Theater as a tool for medical education. *MedEdPORTAL, 15*. https://doi.org/10.15766/mep_2374-8265.10801

Jauregui, J., Watsjold, B., Welsh, L., Ilgen, J. S., & Robins, L. (2020). Generational 'othering': the myth of the Millennial learner. *Medical Education, 54(1), 60–65.*

Jensen, L., & Konradsen, F. (2018). A review of the use of virtual reality head-mounted displays in education and training. *Education and Information Technologies, 23*(4), 1515–1529. https://doi.org/10.1007/s10639-017-9676-0

Jesionkowska, J., Wild, F., & Deval, Y. (2020). Active learning augmented reality for STEAM education—A case study. *Education Sciences, 10*(8), 198. https://doi.org/10.3390/educsci10080198

Jha, A. K. (2020, June 20). Understanding Generation Alpha. https://doi.org/10.31219/osf.io/d2e8g

Kesselring, T., & Müller, U. (2011). The concept of egocentrism in the context of Piaget's theory. *New Ideas in Psychology, 29*(3), 327–345. https://doi.org/10.1016/j.newideapsych.2010.03.008

Kiryakova, G., Angelova, N., & Yordanova, L. (2014. October). *Gamification in education* [Paper presentation]. 9th International Balkan Education and Science Conference, Edirne, Turkey.

Krachun, C., Carpenter, M., Call, J., & Tomasello, M. (2009). A competitive nonverbal false belief task for children and apes. *Developmental Science, 12*(4), 521–535. https://doi.org/10.1111/j.1467-7687.2008.00793.x

Light, P., & Nix, C. (1983). "own view" versus "good view" in a perspective-taking task. *Child Development, 54*(2), 480–483.

Lin, H. C. S., Yu, S. J., Sun, J. C. Y., & Jong, M. S. Y. (2021). Engaging university students in a library guide through wearable spherical video-based virtual reality: Effects on situational interest and cognitive load. *Interactive Learning Environments, 29*(8), 1272–1287. https://doi.org/10.1080/10494820.2019.1624579

Mayne, R., & Green, H. (2020). Virtual reality for teaching and learning in crime scene investigation. *Science & Justice, 60*(5), 466–472. https://doi.org/10.1016/j.scijus.2020.07.006

Merchant, Z., Goetz, E. T., Cifuentes, L., Keeney-Kennicutt, W., & Davis, T. J. (2014). Effectiveness of virtual reality-based instruction on students' learning outcomes in K-12 and higher education: A meta-analysis. *Computers & Education, 70*, 29–40. https://doi.org/10.1016/j.compedu.2013.07.033

Mesa-Gresa, P., Gil-Gómez, H., Lozano-Quilis, J. A., & Gil-Gómez, J. A. (2018). Effectiveness of virtual reality for children and adolescents with autism spectrum disorder: An evidence-based systematic review. *Sensors, 18*(8), 2486. https://doi.org/10.3390/s18082486

Michael, J. (2006). Where's the evidence that active learning works? *Advances in Physiology Education, 30*(4), 159–167. https://doi.org/10.1152/advan.00053.2006

Mohr, K. A., & Mohr, E. S. (2017). Understanding Generation Z students to promote a contemporary learning environment. *Journal on Empowering Teaching Excellence, 1*(1), 9. https://doi.org/10.15142/T3M05T

Mott, M., Tang, J., Kane, S., Cutrell, E., & Ringel Morris, M. (2020, October). "I just went into it assuming that I wouldn't be able to have the full experience": Understanding the accessibility of virtual reality for people with limited mobility. In T. Guerriero, H. Nicolau, & K. Moffat (Eds.), *Proceeding: ASSETS '20, 22nd International ACM SIGACCESS conference on computers and accessibility* (pp. 1–13). Association for Computing Machinery. https://doi.org/10.1145/3373625.3416998

Page, M. (1990). *Active learning: Historical and contemporary perspectives* [Unpublished doctoral dissertation]. University of Massachusetts. https://www.academia.edu/63141263/Active_Learning_Historical_and_Contemporary_Perspectives

Park, S. M., & Kim, Y. G. (2022). A metaverse: Taxonomy, components, applications, and open challenges. *IEEE Access, 10*, 4209–4251. https://doi.org/10.1109/ACCESS.2021.3140175

Parmaxi, A. (2020, May 22). Virtual reality in language learning: A systematic review and implications for research and practice. *Interactive Learning Environments*, 1–13. https://doi.org/10.1080/10494820.2020.1765392

Pellas, N., Mystakidis, S., & Kazanidis, I. (2021). Immersive virtual reality in K-12 and higher education: A systematic review of the last decade scientific literature. *Virtual Reality, 25*, 835–861. https://doi.org/10.1007/s10055-020-00489-9

Pi, Z., Zhang, Y., Zhou, W., Xu, K., Chen, Y., Yang, J., & Zhao, Q. (2021). Learning by explaining to oneself and a peer enhances learners' theta and alpha oscillations while watching video lectures. *British Journal of Educational Technology, 52*(2), 659–679.

Piaget, J. (1952). Jean Piaget. In E. G. Boring, H. Werner, H. S. Langfeld, & R. M. Yerkes (Eds.), *A history of psychology in autobiography* (Vol. 4, pp. 237–256). Clark University Press. https://doi.org/10.1037/11154-011

Qiao, J., Xu, J., Li, L., & Ouyang, Y. Q. (2021). The integration of immersive virtual reality simulation in interprofessional education: A scoping review. *Nurse Education Today, 98*, 104773. https://doi.org/10.1016/j.nedt.2021.104773

Radianti, J., Majchrzak, T. A., Fromm, J., & Wohlgenannt, I. (2020). A systematic review of immersive virtual reality applications for higher education: Design elements, lessons learned, and research agenda. *Computers & Education, 147*, 103778. https://doi.org/10.1016/j.compedu.2019.103778

Rector, K. (2018). Enhancing accessibility and engagement for those with disabilities. *IEEE Pervasive Computing, 17*(1), 9–12. https://doi.org/10.1109/MPRV.2018.011591056

Roberts, D., & Roberts, N. J. (2014). Maximising sensory learning through immersive education. *Journal of Nursing Education and Practice, 4*(10), 74–79. https://doi.org/10.5430/jnep.v4n10p74

Salisbury, J. D., & Irby, D. J. (2020). Leveraging active learning pedagogy in a scaffolded approach: Reconceptualizing instructional leadership learning. *Journal of Research on Leadership Education, 15*(3), 210–226.

Sanders, K., Boustedt, J., Eckerdal, A., McCartney, R., & Zander, C. (2017, August). Folk pedagogy: Nobody doesn't like active learning. In *ICER '17: Proceedings of the 2017 ACM conference on international computing education research* (pp. 145–154). Association for Computing Machinery. https://doi.org/10.1145/3105726.3106192

Savickaite, S. (2020). An immersive education. Immerse UK Org. https://www.immerseuk.org/news/an-immersive-education/.

Savickaite, S. & Millington, E. (2021, June 8) *teaching in VR and cognitive load: A teacher's perspective* [Paper presentation.] 17th Annual Conference of the Immersive Learning Research Network (iLRN), iLRN Virtual Campus. https://ilrn2021.sched.com/list/descriptions/

Savickaite, S., McDonnell, N., & Simmons, D. (2022, January 31). Defining virtual reality (VR). Scoping literature review on VR applications in autism research [Pre-print]. https://doi.org/10.31234/osf.io/p3nh6

Scheffler, P. (2012). Theories pass. Learners and teachers remain. *Applied Linguistics, 33*(5), 603–607.

Setoh, P., Scott, R. M., & Baillargeon, R. (2016). Two-and-a-half-year-olds succeed at a traditional false-belief task with reduced processing demands. *Proceedings of the National Academy of Sciences (PNAS), 113*(47), 13360–13365. https://doi.org/10.1073/pnas.1609203113

Silva, J. B. D., Sales, G. L., & Castro, J. B. D. (2019). Gamification as an active learning strategy in the physics education. *Revista Brasileira de Ensino de Física, 41*(2), e20180309.

Stearns, S. A. (1994). Steps for active learning of complex concepts. *College Teaching, 42*(3), 107–108. https://doi.org/10.1080/87567555.1994.9926835

Surian, L., & Leslie, A. M. (1999). Competence and performance in false belief understanding: A comparison of autistic and normal 3-year-old children. *British Journal of Developmental Psychology, 17*(1), 141–155. https://doi.org/10.1348/026151099165203

Tager-Flusberg, H., & Joseph, R. M. (2012, March). How language facilitates the acquisition of false-belief understanding in children with autism. In J. W. Astington & J. A. Baird (Eds.), *Why language matters for theory of mind*. Oxford Scholarship Online. (Original work published 2005). https://doi.org/10.1093/acprof:oso/9780195159912.003.0014

Teófilo, M., Lucena, V. F., Nascimento, J., Miyagawa, T., & Maciel, F. (2018, January) Evaluating accessibility features designed for virtual reality context. In *2018 IEEE international conference on consumer electronics (ICCE)* (pp. 1–6). IEEE. https://doi.org/10.1109/ICCE.2018.8326167

Tootell, H., Freeman, M., & Freeman, A. (2014, January). Generation alpha at the intersection of technology, play and motivation. In *2014 47th Hawaii international conference on system sciences* (pp. 82–90). IEEE. https://ieeexplore.ieee.org/document/6758614

Trewin, S. M., Laff, M. R., Cavender, A., & Hanson, V. L. (2008). Accessibility in virtual worlds. In *CHI'08 extended abstracts on human factors in computing systems* (pp. 2727–2732). https://doi.org/10.1109/HICSS.2014.19.

Tsai, C. C., & Huang, C. M. (2001). Development of cognitive structures and information processing strategies of elementary school students learning about biological reproduction. *Journal of Biological Education, 36*(1), 21–26. https://doi.org/10.1080/00219266.2001.9655791

Ummihusna, A., & Zairul, M. (2021). Investigating immersive learning technology intervention in architecture education: A systematic literature review. *Journal of Applied Research in Higher Education, 14*(1), 264–281. https://doi.org/10.1108/JARHE-08-2020-0279

Vogeley, K., & Fink, G. R. (2003). Neural correlates of the first person-perspective. *Trends in Cognitive Sciences, 7*(1), 38–42. https://doi.org/10.1016/S1364-6613(02)00003-7

Wood, L. C., & Reiners, T. (2012). Gamification in logistics and supply chain education: Extending active learning. In P. Kommers, T. Issa, & P. Isaías (Eds.), *IADIS international conference on internet technologies & society 2012* (pp. 101–108). IADIS Press.

Zaitchik, D. (1990). When representations conflict with reality: The preschooler's problem with false beliefs and "false" photographs. *Cognition, 35*(1), 41–68. https://doi.org/10.1016/0010-0277(90)90036-J

Sarune Savickaite is a PhD candidate at the School of Psychology and Neuroscience, University of Glasgow. Sarune is also a consultant at Edify.ac through the industrial partnership studentship (ESRC/SGSSS). Sarune holds a BA Hons Illustration & Graphic Design, HEDip Life Sciences, BSc Hons Psychology, and MSc Hons in Psychological Research Methods.

David Simmons is a Lecturer in the School of Psychology and Neuroscience at the University of Glasgow. Despite having a first degree in Physics (Imperial College, London), and a D.Phil, in Physiological Sciences (University of Oxford), the earlier phase of David's research career focused on visual perception, especially stereo vision and colour vision. This included post-doctoral research at Keele University and McGill University. However, in the past 20 years David has refocused his research on perception in autism, most recently how to use virtual environments to explore, and accommodate, the perceptual differences common in neurodivergent individuals.

Teaching the Teachers with Immersive Technology: Preparing the Next Generation of Educators at Ithaca College

Becky Lane and Christine Havens-Hafer

Abstract This chapter analyzes the implementation of a training program utilizing virtual reality (VR) and augmented reality (AR) as educational technologies for teacher education students to enhance their lessons. The students benefitted professionally from effective training to use the technology and practice planning lessons that integrate VR/AR in specific activities.

Keywords Constructivism · Differentiated instruction · Immersive technology · Instructional technology · Pedagogy · Secondary education · Simulated learning environments · Teacher education · Virtual reality

Introduction

Secondary education continues to evolve alongside technology, challenging our teachers with discovering new ways to be more intentional with their planning. The question we often ask ourselves and are asked by other stakeholders is, *what is the advantage of teaching with emerging technology?* One argument is that using immersive technology can dilute the content being learned and result in cognitive overload, with the added concern about the logistical and cost issues that arise from employing the technology (Graeske & Sjöberg-Aspling, 2021). Others may argue that a traditional method of teaching, such as direct instruction, results in a passive model of learning that requires little interaction, with few opportunities to make authentic connections to the content (Ormrod, 2020). While face-to-face learning is key for creating and building community between instructors and students and

B. Lane (✉)
Ithaca College, Ithaca, NY, USA
e-mail: blane@ithaca.edu

C. Havens-Hafer
Piedmont University, Athens, GA, USA
e-mail: chafer@piedmont.edu

© The Author(s), under exclusive license to Springer Nature Switzerland AG 2022   153
P. MacDowell, J. Lock (eds.), *Immersive Education*,
https://doi.org/10.1007/978-3-031-18138-2_10

should continue to be implemented in classroom models, blended, online, and immersive learning have developed as additional resources that can give supplemental as well as alternative instructional support. Implementing classroom simulation activities is beneficial for students because these provide the closest approximation to an authentic experience in a controlled environment. Such experiences either prepare learners for real-life situations or expose them to interactive learning that allows them to make choices and manipulate information (McHaney et al., 2018). As instructors of higher education, we are realizing the need to address incorporating immersive technologies into pedagogy as we guide education students through teacher preparation programs.

While education innovators understand the imminent need for media fluency in this arena, implementing a successful change process presents challenges for adoption. Active learning sessions allow attendees to identify resources required, create a strategy for adoption, and review examples of successful collaborations for consideration at their campuses. This chapter details the collaboration of Becky Lane (Ithaca College Learning and Innovative Technology Department) and Christine Havens-Hafer (Ithaca College Department of Education) to implement a teacher training program—VR in Education—that utilizes virtual reality (VR) as a teaching tool and an asset for professional development. We discuss our rationale for and process of incorporating VR-assisted teaching and learning into the teacher training program at Ithaca College: highlighting how immersive technology supports activities used in a lesson to improve learning outcomes for students. We give examples of what worked well and what did not, and we include comments and feedback from students who participated in the project.

Vignette

The COVID-19 pandemic caused face-to-face courses at Ithaca College to come to a screeching halt. Students were sent home from campus, and the campus was closed. Online teaching suddenly became the norm, and students and professors were thrown into a whirlwind of navigating various platforms with mixed results. Our education students were studying to be middle grade teachers and needed real-life experience teaching in front of a group of learners. But the lack of a physical classroom made that impossible. Like many professors, we were immediately in a quandary. How do you instruct teacher education students to walk through teaching a lesson when there are no people in front of them to teach? The challenge convinced us that it was the time to find ways to integrate VR technology with pedagogy that would satisfy curriculum requirements while also engaging our students. We took lessons learned from our previous workshop experience and created the foundation for our first pilot program using VR as a student teaching tool.

VR in Teacher Education: Our First Steps

In 2019, we embarked on a series of workshops aimed at middle school teachers on how to incorporate VR into grades 7–12. The school districts were primarily in rural and suburban settings, chosen because of their participation with the teacher education program at Ithaca College. Providing mentoring for future student teachers and preparing them for working with immersive technology in their classrooms, the schools had a range of technological accessibility, with one leading the charge to develop their technology program to include augmented reality (AR) and VR. Statistics for this district showed that 40% of families reported having a tablet device, 72% used a mobile device, 42% of low-income families had access to high-speed internet, and 51% of low-income families had access to smartphones (Ithaca, n.d.).

Based on this knowledge, we tailored our VR training to reflect the limited experience of both the students and the teachers who would be using it. We offered a series of professional development workshops to the teachers working in this district, and approximately 15 teachers in a variety of content areas attended the sessions. In the workshops, we introduced VR technology and how educators are using it for teaching. The teachers were then allowed to put on the VR headsets and explore and experiment with different VR applications. We followed up by providing instruction specific to lesson planning via a template that directed teachers to create a specific learning objective using VR. Teachers were then instructed in how to create a mock lesson and write an outline for a lesson plan for implementing VR in their content areas.

Attendees completed a survey at the end of the workshop. The teachers indicated they were able to identify the resources—staff, space, hardware, and software—necessary for them to incorporate extended reality (XR) technologies such as VR/AR in their content areas by tapping into current technologies provided within their district. For most users, this included basic AR-capable cell phones and headsets designed to pair with these phones for VR use. In addition, they were able to develop an outline of strategies, utilizing the examples we provided, to ensure a successful campus adoption process. By providing this workshop, we were able to introduce teachers to the use of immersive technology in the curriculum before our student teachers were placed in these classrooms.

VR in Teacher Education: Pilot #1

We identified one course, *Pedagogy and Practices*, in the secondary education teaching program (grades 7–12) to create a pilot group. Students were sent an Oculus Go headset with the goal of having them use the headset to attend meetings and participate in discussions in a social VR environment. We decided to use the Oculus Go headset because it was relatively inexpensive and available at local retail stores. Students were also required to conduct microteaching sessions (via VR headsets) performed in front of their peers in a virtual classroom setting created by Dr. Lane's team. This team also facilitated onboarding students to the headsets and virtual environment and attended student teaching sessions.

After assessing the need for teachers to be properly trained in immersive technology, it became clear that incoming cohorts of students would benefit professionally if given the opportunity to train with the equipment and to practice planning lessons integrating elements of VR/AR in specific activities. Students learned different teaching models and strategies that they put into practice through collaborative partnering, lesson planning, and co-teaching to the rest of the class, which meant leading the class as if they were the actual instructors and developing activities for the class to complete. The use of immersive technology in this pilot included three interdependent components: teachers' knowledge and skill, students' engagement in their own learning, and academically challenging content. The outcome was directly observable. Students created the VR content and taught the activity to their peers, faculty, and the immersive technology team, after which the creators received feedback. The students in turn used this information to improve their lessons as well as troubleshoot different ways to use technology to appropriately deliver the concepts they were teaching.

VR in Teacher Education: Pilot #2

In Fall 2021, it was evident that the Oculus Go would no longer meet the needs of the pilot. We briefly used the Oculus Quest for a summer course, but we did not like the requirement to have a Facebook account associated with the headset. We began looking for a new VR system better suited to the education space and discovered that Lenovo, a Chinese-American technology company, had recently launched a new iteration of their Mirage VR S3 Classroom system. In our review of the Mirage system, we found that we liked Lenovo's included learning and headset management system and associated software packages, and so we began to integrate the new Mirage VR S3 equipment into our pilot program.

Our goal was to establish a *teach to the teacher* program, allowing students to practice teaching with VR content across the disciplines to learners in grades 7–12. We also aimed to empower these student teachers with the knowledge and skill to take VR into their own student teaching assignments in the public-school districts. Upon completing the class, students were allowed to take the Mirage VR S3 units into the field, incorporating VR into their own student teaching experiences. We utilized the software components included with the headset: *Mozilla Hubs* as a social VR space, *UpTale.io* as a VR construction tool, and *Veative* as a lesson content provider. In each class, we explored the how and why of using immersive learning in the classroom and discussed the real-world lessons learned from the previous pilot. Students learned how to create instructional lesson plans using the software provided. As part of the final assignment, students presented a VR lesson in their

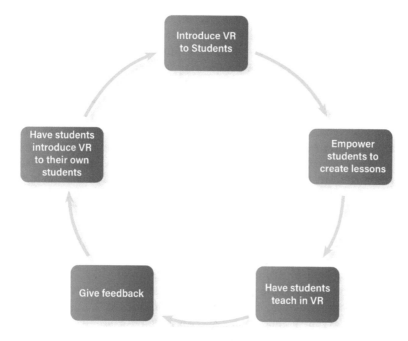

Fig. 1 Immersive design process for educators

area of study, designed for grades 7–12. When they began their own teaching experiences in the field, they were well-prepared to bring VR technology into their own classrooms (Fig. 1).

Design Framework: Immersive Design Process for Educators

In the teacher education program at Ithaca College, students who have not taught in the field need basic skills and strategies to support their lesson planning and teaching, and this instruction is key to their development as educators. Constructivism as a conceptual framework provides a foundation for this. Based on the theories and research of Jean Piaget and Lev Vygotsky, constructivism is a model of learning that supports students in the way they acquire and process information (Ormrod, 2020). When students construct meaning from the world around them, they are better able to achieve fluency and even mastery in the skill or concept they are learning (Chen, 2009). Whereas passive learning occurs with direct instruction and lecture formats with the teacher at the centre of the lesson, active learning requires a flexible classroom environment to engage students, with the teacher serving as a support system to guide and monitor students' progress.

The shift to active learning requires self-regulation on the part of students, who must employ an evolved set of strategies for problem-solving for addressing a variety of tasks assigned to them within a lesson. Developing metacognitive skills alongside motivation is key to ensuring student success. But much like a muscle that loses its tone when it lacks consistent exercise (Zepeda et al., 2015), such skills may not develop when the student does not receive information in an engaging fashion that allows them to have control over the outcome. Cognitive perspectives of learning employ activation of long-term memory storage and retrieval processes (Schunk & DiBenedetto, 2020). Understanding the factors affecting long-term memory storage, including forgetting key information that impacts student learning, is key to crafting innovative strategies such as implementing VR. This understanding connects with the constructivist pedagogy of teaching wherein students interact with the material in a way that feels more personalized to their individual learning needs.

Constructivism is a strategy or activity that allows students to learn in situations requiring them to take the initiative in solving problems and build on their prior knowledge; the teacher provides stimulation that leads the students to create their own hypotheses and conclusions. According to Aiello et al. (2012), "a constructivist point of view makes us recognize the potential of an 'inverted reality', strongly influenced by the individual's capacity for perception and action" (p. 319). This is what led our charge into finding unique methods that would take our students' classrooms to the next level in creating a vibrant and interactive learning environment. VR provides the type of stimulation that leads to active learning: encouraging students to transfer learning by applying it to new situations and to create hypotheses that may change their initial perspectives on a topic. The learning that occurs in VR centres on key concepts that students engage with and respond to through critical thinking activities shared with the class, for which the instructor can provide feedback. The teacher can use feedback from VR experience to change instructional practices to fit the cognitive development of the class. Computer-based simulations have been used in education for some time to support students, particularly those whose cognitive styles of learning are not supported by traditional direct instruction. These simulations provide opportunities for students to have an empowered role in their education, which makes the move to the hands-on experience provided by VR logical as well as inevitable (De Freitas & Neumann, 2009).

Analysis of the VR in the Teacher Education Pilot Study

As part of the debriefing on integrating immersive technology in education, we asked students to share their thoughts about the experience via an anonymous survey. The following questions were posed: (1) Inclusion of immersive technology in lesson planning: if you were the student, how valuable would you find the activity you planned? (2) Learning curve: what suggestions do you have that would make learning and mastering this technology easier for you? (3) Product offered: what content or modules were missing, or you wished had been offered that would have been useful to your lesson planning? and (4) As a learner: how would using immersive technology help you or classrooms in general?

Overall, students' responses were favourable and positive, while also including useful feedback. The feedback offered a range of comments, giving insight into how the immersive pilot impacted the teacher education students and their ability to successfully use different types of technology in their teaching practice. One response revealed that it could be seen as "beneficial, because it gives students the opportunity to see what these environments are like in real life. Many students may have never seen inside an agriculture, industrialized company and this experience will help them with our overall unit." This relates to what we know about constructivism, which is that learners would benefit from an immersive activity that provides an exploratory learning environment they would not easily be able to experience within the four walls of a classroom.

This ability to explore was confirmed by another student, who commented they would find their VR activity useful as it was a demonstration of Stonehenge. This student stated,

> A lot of what makes Stonehenge so interesting is being able to see the giant rocks and wonder how they got there. While pictures can suffice, it truly gives a better understanding of the significance of a place when you can immerse yourself virtually next to the henge. It also allows for a museum-like activity to be conducted, this means that students can learn at their own pace and actually see what is being taught.

Speaking to the idea of converting an activity traditionally completed within a face-to-face classroom to VR, one student noted,

> I think utilizing the VR technology creates an engaging space for the students to get excited about the information they are learning. I think I would find this activity valuable because it would be a new way of learning and working with the information being presented, rather than just working through another group activity like everything else in the unit.

The comments about the realistic and interactive aspects of this platform were consistent with the findings in other studies in classroom use of VR (Han, 2019), with students reporting an increased feel of "presence" or connection to the material. Regarding the learning curve necessary to follow when using immersive technology, one student stated it would make learning and mastering this technology easier had they been able to become adjusted to the technology through "actual tasks/activity examples that would be used in lessons we could practice going through. This is more specific to using platforms such as Hubs and getting used to using all the controls and moving around in the space." Additionally, they recommended practicing in person and not online as it was "difficult during some of our VR classes to fully get the technology working correctly when we couldn't physically use and see each other's headsets." Another student concurred, stating that depending on one's age and familiarity with the technology, it may be wise to "start out maybe with an easier component of VR ... if it was for younger classroom grades, I would start out [using] simpler [tools]." Inconsistent WiFi continues to be an issue, with more than one student stating, "If it were a guarantee that all headsets could easily connect, or already be connected to the WiFi, that would be extremely helpful." Another asked about the ability to add text or voiceovers, particularly to 360 YouTube videos.

We asked our students about missing content or modules and discovered there was some inconsistency with content support, particularly with English and Social Studies, which suffered from a dearth of already created immersive models they could use within their planned lessons. A student reflected,

> Many of the modules were very interesting and I thought they would fit great in lesson plans, but my group had a difficult time finding one that specifically fit into our lesson because of our subject. I think content focused on English, reading, and writing could be really useful for both students and teachers because this is an area that many individuals struggle with, so the VR component may help since it is such an engaging way to get students excited about the lesson material.

We also heard about how the navigation could be improved, such as when allowing students to take a tour of virtual space. The student who used this module in their lesson said, "As teachers, when learning about how to teach, knowing when to be present during an activity like this would be helpful. I was concerned with what I was going to be doing while the students were in the module." Having control over the pace of the lesson came up in another student's response, which suggested the addition of a "speed through button" for instructors to use so they can control the amount of time students spend in specific areas. Finally, another student noted that a more hands-on experience would "allow students to view a lesson from a different point of view or perspective," if they had the ability to actually "touch something and have that actual experience even if it was through technology."

Our final question focused specifically on immersive technology by asking for students' perspectives as learners. These responses were particularly insightful, with comments about being intentional about when and how VR is used. One student said, "Specifically, I think it can give them a more personal and emotional aspect to what they are learning. Teachers should use it to enhance their lesson, and not have it be the central focus of their lessons." Others saw the benefit of creating a more interactive learning environment by pointing out,

> The lessons and activities we saw in class would work well for visual and hands-on learners. It also allows the students to participate in activities that would be otherwise impossible. If they are going to surround our real world, nevertheless, why should we not include them in education?

There was support for the alternative method of learning that immersive technology offers, with comments such as,

> I often got very frustrated in high school because each day would blur to become one and it felt like every class, I went through had the exact same teaching routine for the entire year. I think utilizing immersive technology adds some excitement to the classroom and gets kids thinking more about the material. I know I would have liked to use immersive technology in classes such as history, where I typically struggled with getting engaged in and often felt behind.

Making connections to the material was key to feelings of success, as this student noted: "I think connecting examples helps because even if you cannot remember the definition or concept, but you can remember the example, you can figure out the first part. Using VR would just make these connections stronger."

Evaluation of VR Hardware and Software

We learned much about the capability of the VR hardware and software during each iteration of the VR in Education implementation. Each semester had highs and lows that helped inform the choices we made for the following cohort. Next, we outline some of the points and issues we encountered and the solutions we tried as the program evolved.

We began our project with the Oculus Go, an entry-level headset providing three degrees of freedom (3 DoF) operation and a single hand controller. For software, we used *Rumii 2.0* by Doghead Simulations (Fig. 2) a social VR platform that offers simple, prebuilt rooms with spatial audio, whiteboard functionalities, media imports, and 3D model viewing. The VR site could also be customized with our college logo.

The Oculus Go was a readily available and reasonably priced VR headset in March 2020, when we were looking for an accessible solution to providing education students a means to share an embodied space with their peers to practice their teaching skills. We were able to buy them locally during the height of COVID-19 pandemic-related restrictions, and we had ample time to prepare each headset for mailing to the students' homes.

The *Rumii* cloud-based software solution was a simple yet powerful social VR application that ran well on the Oculus Go headset. Students were able to enter a shared space and successfully practice teaching skills using a white board and such limited 3D objects as a self-designed avatar, as well as interact using spatial audio. This pairing was not without significant disadvantages, as the Oculus Go did not have sufficient battery life and sometimes overheated and shut down. The Oculus Go was discontinued shortly after the end of our 2020 pilot. Despite the issues we

Fig. 2 Rumii session with students presenting lectures and lesson plans to peers

Table 1 Analysis of learning experiences using the Oculus Go and Rumii

Strengths	Challenges	Neutrals
Oculus Go was affordable and available. Oculus Go was a consumer product designed to be used and understood by the general public; the students were able to get up and running in a short time. *Rumii* was a free social VR solution that was easy to use and had few lag or bandwidth issues.	Oculus Go was prone to overheating, and the battery life often did not last for the entire 50- minute class. The Oculus Go units needed to be managed individually. The Oculus Go was discontinued June 2000. *Rumii* was limited in customization options, and customer support was unreliable.	The 3DoF headset was not an issue for the students, as most of them used it in a seated position. *Rumii* was functional, but harder to use when importing items such as 3D objects. Students were unable to create more elaborate environments related to their fields of study.

encountered during the pilot, we considered the endeavour to be a success based on students' performance and feedback. We decided to repeat the pilot using a more powerful hardware/software combination. In Table 1, we outline the strengths, challenges, and items considered neutral in our experience with the combination of the Oculus Go and *Rumii*.

Based on the success of and the lessons learned from our experience with the Oculus Go and *Rumii*, we decided to run the program again, this time using higher-end headsets and a more sophisticated social VR platform. We chose the Oculus Quest, a wireless six degrees-of-freedom headset with superior graphics, speed, and battery life compared to the Oculus Go. Like the Oculus Go, the Oculus Quest is a consumer-based product that required individual setup to be usable for the class. We chose *AltspaceVR* by Microsoft (Figs. 3 and 4) as the social VR platform because it had a more fully realized metaverse, was free to use, and offered students the opportunity to design and build sophisticated and complex environments.

The VR in Education Program using the Oculus Quest and *AltspaceVR* was very successful in that we received overwhelmingly positive feedback from the class, the students made significant virtual worlds in which to teach, and the students were able to successfully teach a self-created lesson in VR related to their program of study. The upgrade to the Oculus Quest added a significant cost increase as each headset was $400 USD. We were fortunate to have a small grant to complete this program, but acknowledge that many, if not most, educational institutions would not have the funding available to outfit 15+ students in headsets. It is also disappointing that Oculus does not provide, at least as of this writing, a way for educational institutions to use enterprise-level features. Table 2 summarizes the strengths, challenges, and neutral aspects of the Oculus Quest/AltspaceVR combination.

In Fall 2021, we entered a partnership with Lenovo to pilot their newest headset, the VRS3, a three-degrees-of-freedom headset designed specifically for the education market. Lenovo provided a suite of immersive applications for use with the headset: *Mozilla Hubs*, a web-based social VR program; *Veative* (Fig. 5), a suite of premade lessons relating to K-12 education; and *UpTale*, a VR creation tool that

Fig. 3 AltspaceVR session with student-created Walden pond environment to teach on Thoreau

Fig. 4 Students presenting on Aztec civilization in a student-created environment in AltspaceVR

Table 2 Analysis of learning experiences using the Oculus Quest and AltspaceVR

Strengths	Weaknesses	Neutrals
The Oculus Quest provided adequate battery life, powerful processing power, and was easy to set up. *AltspaceVR* is an established social VR platform with many features to empower users, including world design and presentation tools. The students were especially excited to be receiving the newest Oculus headset.	Similar to the Oculus Go, the quest required individual setup with an individual Facebook account. The Oculus Quest Enterprise solution was not offered to educational institutions. *AltspaceVR* at times involved using some public spaces, and sometimes had random, unaffiliated users disrupting the flow of the class.	Students were required to set up their headsets as if they were the owners, including creating an Oculus account on their personal phones. Oculus was in the process of requiring a Facebook account to be linked to both the headset and Oculus online platform.

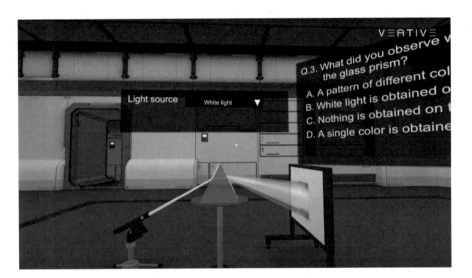

Fig. 5 Screen shot from the Veative science module

requires no programming skills. Students were taught how to use each program and were required to choose one in which to prepare and teach a lesson to their peers.

This pilot was a departure from the initial model in that we gave the students choices of which application to use in their teaching and provided pre-built lessons with which to work. The level of student engagement varied within the class, as some chose to create elaborate and original lessons using *UpTale* (Fig. 6), including taking their own 360 photos and videos.

Others created worlds within *Mozilla Hubs* (Fig. 7), including a walk-through environment where embodied avatars visited individual spaces to learn about language and grammar. Some students used a pre-built module, such as a chemistry lab, and built a lesson around it.

Fig. 6 UpTale VR experience created by students on using sheep in solar farms to control grasses

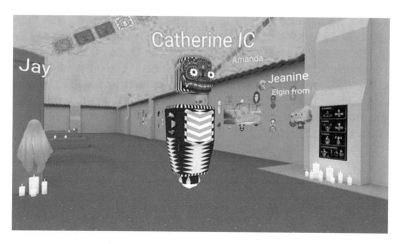

Fig. 7 Students gathering in Mozilla Hubs

At the end of the course, students gave a presentation outlining how they used the hardware and software and demonstrated how their proposed lesson would be used by learners in their prospective classrooms.

This iteration using the Lenovo system differed from the first two using the Oculus system in that the Lenovo hardware and software was specifically designed for classroom use. The Lenovo headset shipped with a hardware and software management system which saved a significant amount of time when administering content. The headsets are constructed of non-porous materials, making them easy to disinfect and keep clean. We, as the IT/VR specialists, found the degrees of freedom somewhat lacking, but the students did not seem to mind or notice the difference. The education software—*Veative*, *UpTale*, and *Hubs*—offers enough coverage to enable educators to create effective VR integrations in the classroom. The Lenovo content ecosystem system is not as polished as the Oculus environment but is not designed as a consumer product. Table 3 outlines the strengths and challenges when using the Lenovo headset:

Both Lenovo and Oculus have advantages, disadvantages, and best use cases. The Oculus is a sleek consumer product, has six degrees of freedom, and offers an active online store with many independent developers creating entertaining content. At this time, it is priced at under $300 USD and is easily available. But there is no central management system, and users are required to have a Facebook account to use the hardware, creating privacy and data collection concerns. Content is plentiful, but it is up to the educator to find appropriate content and apply it to their curricula. Lenovo is designed for classroom use, ships with a built-in central management system and targeted educational software that is easy to deploy in a classroom setting. The available content is a fraction of what can be found in the Oculus environment, however, and the headset uses only three degrees of freedom. The Lenovo headset is not as accessible in retail outlets as Oculus.

For K–12, Lenovo offers advantages over other platforms, even though the current headset is not as robust as the Oculus. The Lenovo unit is superior in terms of privacy, ease of use at scale, and washability. The Oculus Quest unit is best for higher education and comes with a higher cost in terms of money and user data collection. We mitigated reliance on a Facebook account by ascribing a work-only Facebook account to one lab employee and sharing that account across multiple headsets. Based on our experience, we recommend Lenovo for K–12 and Oculus Quest for college and university use.

Table 3 Analysis of learning experiences using the Lenovo headset

Strengths	Weaknesses	Neutrals
The Lenovo headset was very easy to use and clean. The Lenovo headset comes paired with a very effective device management system. The Lenovo headsets are shipped in school- ready, mobile suitcases with 10 units and a tablet to control them.	There is a definite learning curve in using some of the included software programs and back-end management system. This class was offered in the summer, and the compressed schedule didn't allow adequate time to create the experiences learners would have liked. *Mozilla Hubs,* a free web-based social VR program, was sometimes glitchy with more than 10 people in a single space.	The cost of the headset is higher than the quest at over $500. The price includes *ThinkReality* and *Lanschool air*, which are very effective hardware and software management tools. Overall content for the Lenovo headset is not as plentiful as that of the Oculus products. Development is possible using the Pico SDK.

Immersive Technology in Teacher Education: Lessons Learned

We have learned several lessons that apply to effective hardware solutions when implementing a VR program in a classroom. Teachers might find these suggestions helpful to begin their own VR programs:

- Allow adequate time for users, especially those new to VR, to acclimate to the technology. We found that students needed extra time to explore the headset and its operation and that erring on the side of too many introductory and demonstration activities saved time later when students used headsets on their own.
- Pay attention to accessibility and be sensitive to user comfort around immersive technology. A small percentage of students mentioned motion sickness and were encouraged to remove the headset and, if they wanted to continue, were advised to use it for shorter periods.
- Acquire IT help if available at your institution. These professionals can often assist with projecting headset activities onto large monitors or tablets, manage multiple headsets, and assist with hardware maintenance.
- Keep current with VR in education user groups. Facebook has several active groups easily found via search, and AltspaceVR has a lively user group that offers free workshops and meetups.
- Browse current offerings in each platform's marketplace; each company releases new games and experiences that may apply to teaching and learning. Don't overlook free content such as YouTube 360 videos, which can be incorporated as part of a lesson or implemented within a 3D environment for viewing in social VR.
- Keep VR fun! At some point, the technology will let you down at the wrong moment, and that can feel overwhelming. Take a breath, restart, and move on.

Strategies for Implementation of Design

The following is a list of strategies we found helpful when integrating immersive technology into our teacher education course. The points represent our reflection on the process, along with feedback we received from the students in the course and from our technology partners.

- **Identify educational gaps in immersive instruction.** Research the school districts in which the teacher education students will be completing their teaching practicum. Understanding the needs of the student body is key to developing a program based on the district's resources and budget. With this knowledge, we were able to identify which districts had the equipment available to implement immersive technology in their classrooms and which would need assistance from our program to deliver the necessary equipment and training for the students to be successful.

- **Instruct teacher education students in cognition and active learning.** Give students the opportunity to learn different teaching models and best-practices strategies with an emphasis on collaborative partnering, lesson planning, and co-teaching. The goal in effective lesson planning is to assist students in retaining information that they will be able to use in future learning scenarios. This requires activating cognitive strategies for applying this information, which can be effectively harnessed by implementing immersive platforms.
- **Integrate conceptual learning.** Social VR platforms allow for a live, embodied experience that mimics in-person events to give students a more realistic, robust, and synchronous teaching practice opportunity. Students should be instructed in conceptual learning by covering cognitive perspectives about the nature of knowledge, which include procedural, declarative, explicit, and implicit styles. This material can be delivered via readings and pedagogical videos featuring researched strategies—such as schemes, scripts, personal theories, and world views—that students can utilize when crafting their own lesson plans. Students should show their ability to identify foundational concepts and applications of these types of knowledge. They should also understand the implications for classroom practices and experiences when knowledge is translated into immersive activities, with a specific emphasis on using VR experiences while wearing headsets.
- **Apply immersive technology to address students' diverse learning needs.** One of the core areas of pedagogy and practice in teacher education is relating findings and implications from research in learning and cognition to one's own content area and classroom practices to better understand students' diverse needs. Showing teacher education students how immersive learning is employed to support differentiated instruction that uses artificial and/or simulated environments will allow them to see how their students can control the outcomes of their learning. This is accomplished through connections with real experiences—for example, a virtual trip to Stonehenge as part of a history lesson—that would not otherwise be possible because of financial and logistical constraints within the school system.
- **Employ actionable improvements to the model.** Feedback from observers and participants allows content creators to make real-time improvements to their VR activities. Feedback also helps the faculty and immersive technology team improve the rollout of the pilot, with increased instructional time to use the VR technology and application within lesson plans.

Conclusion

The pilot studies conducted at Ithaca College are a valuable blueprint for educators seeking funding to build their own labs and create learning spaces that offer differentiated instruction to support the learning of all students. The studies also demonstrate how to implement a pilot within school districts, including the amount of time and information needed to train staff in immersive learning technologies, along with financial considerations and funding possibilities for purchasing equipment and supporting professional development.

This chapter connects to a broader strategy of improvement that can be implemented before teacher education students lead VR activities in school classrooms during their teaching practicums. Testing VR activities with peers allowed students to have a safe space for identifying technological challenges, such as insecure WiFi or a glitch in the simulation, and weak areas in their lesson planning where the activity failed to connect with the content they were teaching. A key component of the training program at Ithaca College is improving students' ability to provide cognitive and conceptual learning to best support the diverse needs of contemporary classrooms. We believe immersive technology is a valuable tool for teacher education students to explore innovative and engaging avenues of instruction.

References

Aiello, P., D'Elia, F., Di Tore, S., & Sibilio, M. (2012). A constructivist approach to virtual reality for experiential learning. *E-Learning and Digital Media, 9*(3), 317–324. https://doi.org/10.2304/elea.2012.9.3.317

Chen, C. J. (2009). Theoretical bases for using virtual reality in education. *Themes in Science and Technology Education, 2*(1–2), 71–90. http://earthlab.uoi.gr/theste/index.php/theste/article/view/23

De Freitas, S., & Neumann, T. (2009). The use of "exploratory learning" for supporting immersive learning in virtual environments. *Computers & Educations, 52*(2), 343–352. https://doi.org/10.1016/j.compedu.2008.09.010

Graeske, C., & Sjöberg-Aspling, S. (2021). VR-technology in teaching: Opportunities and challenges. *International Education Studies, 14*(8), 76–83. https://doi.org/10.5539/ies.v14n8p76

Han, I. (2019). Immersive virtual field trips in education: A mixed-methods study on elementary students' presence and perceived learning. *British Journal of Educational Technology, 51*(2), 420–435. https://doi.org/10.1111/bjet.12842

Ithaca City School District New York State Report Card. *NYSED Data Site.* (n.d.). https://data.nysed.gov/essa.php?year=2019&instid=800000036448

McHaney, R., Reiter, L., & Reychav, I. (2018). Immersive simulation in constructivist-based classroom e-learning. *International Journal on E-Learning, 17*(1), 39–64. https://www.learntechlib.org/primary/p/149930/

Ormrod, J. (2020). *Human learning* (8th ed.). Pearson.

Schunk, D. H., & DiBenedetto, M. K. (2020). Motivation and social cognitive theory. *Contemporary Educational Psychology, 60*, 101832. https://doi.org/10.1016/j.cedpsych.2019.101832

Zepeda, C. D., Richey, J. E., Ronevich, P., & Nokes-Malach, T. J. (2015). Direct instruction of metacognition benefits adolescent science learning, transfer, and motivation: An in vivo study. *Journal of Educational Psychology, 107*(4), 954–970. https://doi.org/10.1037/edu0000022

Becky Lane, PhD, is an Immersive Media scholar, filmmaker, and creative content developer focused on applying emerging technologies to traditional methods of teaching, learning, and storytelling. She currently leads the Center for Creative Technology at Ithaca College and is part of their Learning and Innovative Technologies group.

Christine Havens-Hafer has a BA in English from Pennsylvania State University, an MAT in secondary education from Binghamton University, and a PhD in English from Binghamton University. After several years of teaching grades 7–12 for various public schools, she began her career as an assistant professor of education at Ithaca College. Her work centres around the preparation of teaching candidates, with an emphasis on implementing immersive technology in the classroom. Her goal is to study its impact on the development of curricula to differentiate learning in support of students. She recently relocated to Georgia, where she is an assistant professor of education at Piedmont University and is continuing her work with teacher candidates.

Teachers Designing Immersive Learning Experiences for Environmental and Sustainability Education

Paula MacDowell

Abstract Addressing the ongoing challenges of environmental and sustainability education (ESE), a virtual reality course was developed for teachers to explore new pedagogical approaches with technologies for ESE. The chapter contributes practical insights for empowering and supporting teachers in designing immersive learning experiences with connections to natural environments and sustainability targets.

Keywords Immersive learning · Immersive teaching · Instructional design · Environmental and sustainability education · Virtual reality · World building

Introduction

Recent research shows that engaging students with immersive learning experiences can be a meaningful and affordable solution for visualizing complex environmental issues like climate breakdown and increasing awareness and empathy for conservation efforts (e.g., Chirico et al., 2020; Fauville et al., 2020b; Harrington, 2011; Harrington et al., 2021; Huang et al., 2020; Makransky & Mayer, 2022; Markowitz et al., 2018; Markowitz & Bailenson, 2021; Petersen et al., 2020; Schott, 2017). Immersive learning experiences have unique capabilities to enhance curriculum and instruction in ways that have not been previously possible or accessible. They can provide awe-inspiring, first-hand encounters that prime students for deeper engagements by igniting an emotional response (Chirico & Gaggioli, 2019). In so doing, they can make abstract and complex sustainability issues more concrete and psychologically closer for students, increasing their sense of presence or *being there* (Cheng & Tsai, 2019). Immersive environments allow students to step into the

P. MacDowell (✉)
College of Education, University of Saskatchewan, Saskatoon, SK, Canada
e-mail: paula.macdowell@usask.ca

© The Author(s), under exclusive license to Springer Nature Switzerland AG 2022
P. MacDowell, J. Lock (eds.), *Immersive Education*,
https://doi.org/10.1007/978-3-031-18138-2_11

teaching space and move around with peers, offering an interactive and contextualized knowledge exchange. Students can see from other points of view, which raises awareness of bias and provides opportunities to apply their new perspectives and empathy skills in safe and controlled settings (Fauville, Queiroz, et al., 2020a; Herrera et al., 2018). Participation in immersive environments is not limited to special occasions or affected by inclement weather conditions, and administrative logistics are minimized compared to traditional field trips.

In this chapter, I explore how immersive learning experiences can mitigate the ongoing challenges of environmental and sustainability education (ESE) in teacher education and school systems. First, I begin by discussing the gap in policy and curriculum around ESE, highlighting the significance of empowering teachers to lead change and the need for students to form personal connections and respectful relations with the topic of study. Second, I outline a new university course elective, *Designing Immersive Experiences for K-12 Learning Environments,* that prepares and inspires teachers to apply instructional design principles in creating immersive learning experiences and environments. Third, I explore a collaborative design-based approach for building educational virtual worlds, guided by IDEO's (2020) *Co-Designing Schools Toolkit and Change Framework.* The chapter contributes practical insights and pedagogical strategies that teachers and designers can use to create or implement an immersive experience in classroom settings, with an ethical foundation that integrates the Sustainable Development Goals (SDGs).

Vignette

After experiencing months of lockdown restrictions due to the COVID-19 pandemic, Elaine, an instructor in ESE, noticed her graduate students had discussion forum and online-meeting fatigue. Few were turning on their webcams, and it was challenging for Elaine to stay personally connected with her class. She wanted to develop more authentic and engaging ways for students to participate. An opportunity opened to create a new course elective, so she took a risk and scheduled it to take place entirely in virtual reality. Elaine was sure of two things: (1) The course would focus on designing virtual worlds for pro-social and environmental change, and (2) Students needed creative freedom and inspiration for designing immersive learning experiences that address sustainability targets in meaningful ways. Utilizing a collaborative design-based approach, Elaine developed a genuine rapport with her team and supported their journeys in becoming immersive storytellers.

Empowering Teachers to Lead Change

As unsustainable consumption patterns, biodiversity loss, air pollution, clean water scarcity, deforestation, and land degradation continue to threaten human and planetary well-being, the need intensifies to prepare teachers with the knowledge, skills, and best practices for leading sustainability education in K–12 classrooms. As Elshof (2009) warns, "the sustainability challenge is emerging as the global challenge facing young people because, without significant advances on this front, other important human development agendas like security, health and well-being will be impossible to meet" (p. 134). More than ever before, faculties of education in Canada are recognizing their responsibilities for preparing teachers to integrate ESE across the curriculum, including climate action, environmental protection, biodiversity conservation, preservation of Indigenous cultural heritage, and learning to live within the limits of the Earth's carrying capacity (Berger et al., 2015; Elshof, 2009; Falkenberg & Babiuk, 2014; Læssøe & Mochizuki, 2015). The goal for educators is to "empower learners with knowledge, skills, values and attitudes to take informed decisions and make responsible actions for environmental integrity, economic viability and a just society" (UNESCO, n.d.).

While ESE is arguably the most significant and urgent issue of our time nationally and globally, there have been ongoing and persistent challenges in integrating this study area into formal educational settings. At present, Canada has no clear strategy or education policy for preparing students or teachers, intellectually and emotionally, to be sustainability leaders and changemakers in the uncertain future that lies ahead (Aikens & McKenzie, 2021; Falkenberg & Babiuk, 2014; Howard, 2012). For example, extensive research led by Bieler et al. (2018) finds that K–12 education policy across Canada minimally attends to climate change initiatives. There is little attention to supporting priority areas; cognitive knowledge is prioritized over affective and action-oriented initiatives. Worldwide, a lack of suitable data is available (in terms of quantity and quality) to analyze and monitor the effectiveness of climate education activities (McKenzie, 2021). As a result of minimal progress tracking, many students and teachers from early childhood through higher education are uninvolved in taking action to catalyze the societal transition needed for a sustainable future.

In 2015, the United Nations General Assembly articulated a set of 17 interconnected SDGs with specific targets for resolving the challenges humans face to achieve a just, peaceful, and sustainable planet for all people (United Nations, n.d.). These global goals have the power to create a better world by 2030; however, they are highly complex, interdisciplinary, and challenging to teach in traditional classroom settings with an already overcrowded curriculum (Læssøe & Mochizuki, 2015). Also problematic for educators is knowing how to teach the SDGs such that students will understand how their actions impact the health and well-being of other people and the planet (Elshof, 2009; MacDowell, 2021). Many students take our natural resources for granted, including clean water, air, energy, and food abundance. Today's children and youth can be far removed from the natural world in their daily lives—hence the need for enriching or re-establishing relationality and connectivity between students and what they are learning in the classroom (Harrington, 2011; Markowitz et al., 2018; Petersen et al., 2020).

Hollweg et al. (2011) define an environmentally literate person as "someone who, both individually and together with others, makes informed decisions concerning the environment; is willing to act on these decisions to improve the well-being of other individuals, societies, and the global environment; and participates in civic life" (p. 3). This definition brings forth many questions for practitioners. How do teachers move from an endorsement of the SDGs to students having a sense of personal responsibility for taking care of the Earth (MacDowell, 2021)? What are effective strategies to engage uninterested or overwhelmed youth in environmental stewardship (Petersen et al., 2020)? How might digital games and social media be used to mobilize student interest and action on sustainability issues (Wu & Lee, 2015)? How might new digital assessment tools measure learning outcomes, perception shifts, responsible citizenship, and community impact (McKenzie, 2021)? Who will teach the teachers (Howard, 2012)?

Since teaching in schools traditionally occurs indoors with occasional outdoor activities, virtual spaces offer a third place for instruction. The recent pivot to emergency remote education due to the COVID-19 pandemic provided a timely opportunity to experiment with the pedagogical potential of immersive learning environments. Addressing this opportunity and the current gap in curriculum, resources, and knowledge of teaching ESE, I designed a virtual reality (VR) education course that explores new possibilities for guiding and empowering teachers to be sustainability leaders in their classrooms and school communities. This course elective was designed to use immersive learning experiences that enhance real-life learning opportunities for cultivating healthy relationships between students and the Earth's living systems.

Designing a VR Education Course Elective for Teachers

Designing Immersive Experiences for K-12 Learning Environments is a special-topic three-credit course for pre-service and in-service teachers in the College of Education at the University of Saskatchewan. The content introduces user experience (UX) and user interface (UI) design principles applied to the development of extended reality (XR) applications that support teaching and learning in K–12 contexts. Students have the opportunity to explore a topic of interest and relevance to their profession or program of studies. The main goal is for students to develop design skills and confidence in creating immersive learning environments for pro-social and environmental change. A secondary goal is to explore pedagogical strategies for guiding immersive learning experiences in their classroom settings.

The VR education course was delivered using three virtual communication platforms: *AltspaceVR* (https://altvr.com), *EngageVR* (https://engagevr.io), and *Virbela* campus (https://virbela.com). Each student needed to have or borrow a stand-alone head-mounted display (HMD) such as the Meta Quest 2, Pico Neo 3, or HTC Vive Focus 3. Five graduate and four upper-level undergraduate students completed the course during the 2020 summer term. Class discussions were oriented around the pedagogical benefits of immersive technologies, such as differentiating instruction, situating learning, managing cognitive load, increasing knowledge retention and transfer, and facilitating relational connections to the course activities and resources (e.g., Lion-Bailey et al., 2020; Southgate, 2020; Thompson et al., 2019). Students engaged in reflective dialogue on a range of internal and external barriers to educational VR, including technical support, teacher preparation, teacher confidence, administrative resistance to change, funding, Internet access, and availability of suitable learning materials.

The course challenged students to create immersive experiences designed for pro-social and environmental change related to the SDG targets. The syllabus included 21 recommended readings and 15 immersive applications for students to explore and inform their work. The course was well-grounded in a growing body of research that examines teacher perceptions of VR as a learning tool (Bower et al., 2020; Domingo & Bradley, 2018) and the transformation of teachers in immersive learning environments (Bailenson et al., 2008; Billingsley et al., 2019). Two specific learning objectives focused on: students developing skills in designing an immersive learning environment to inspire change in thinking or behaviour; and students analyzing the implementation and facilitation of immersive experiences in formal educational settings.

A memorable feature of the course was virtual world-hopping. Synchronous weekly class meetings were scheduled in highly creative and insightful immersive learning environments. During our first class, we met as avatars in an *AltspaceVR* world called *Food Waste*, designed by Gibson-Hylands (n.d.-a) to advance understanding of the unsustainable cycle of production and consumption in the overdeveloped and under-developed countries on our planet (Fig. 1). Student comments emphasized that the hour we spent learning in *Food Waste* was equivalent to a week's worth of field trips on reducing waste generation from human activity. We were fortunate to have Gibson-Hylands as a guest speaker at our inaugural class

Fig. 1 "Food Waste" AltspaceVR world designed by Gibson-Hylands (n.d.-a)

Fig. 2 "Plastic Mountain" AltspaceVR world designed by Gibson-Hylands (n.d.-b)

Fig. 3 "The Ocean" AltspaceVR world designed by Gibson-Hylands (n.d.-c)

meeting. She inspired everyone with powerful visual storytelling and impactful design strategies to ignite thinking on pressing environmental issues.

Other worlds designed by Gibson-Hylands include *Plastic Mountain* (Gibson-Hylands, n.d.-b), which communicates risks about the hazardous effects of toxic plastic waste on the planet, wildlife, fish, and human health. In *The Ocean* (Gibson-Hylands, n.d.-c), our avatars dove into a heavily polluted ocean to swim alongside abandoned trash and accumulated marine litter (Figs. 2 and 3). We discussed how these virtual worlds are pedagogically structured to support scenario-based learning and catalyze conversations about global problems and sustainable solutions. Further, we analyzed the meaningful integration of SDG targets, including responsible consumption and production (SDG 12) and life below water (SDG 14).

Pre-service and in-service teachers often receive inadequate professional development around the pedagogical uses of educational technology (MacDowell, 2021). Hence, practice sessions were scheduled to enhance students' design fluency and pedagogical knowledge of immersive technologies. For example, we teleported to the Moon and then to Mars to experiment with learning possibilities using the *EngageVR* library assets, including 3D models, template environments, special effects, and audio effects. Scheduling time for the team to engage in imaginative play enabled creative confidence and innovative ideas to flourish. Playful experimentation with spatial interactions facilitated lived experiences of what to do (and what not to do) for designing immersive spaces that inspire and influence learning. This practical knowledge informed the application of UI/UX design principles in the course assignments. During class meetings in *Virbela*, we explored the virtual campus and used our time to discuss progress, challenges, and insights for the term projects. During breaks, we enjoyed watching our avatars dancing together, doing synchronous backflips, and playing soccer by the beach.

Assessment methods were essential for motivating and challenging the students to take creative risks and demonstrate their knowledge in new and innovative ways (e.g., through world building and immersive storytelling). I put great effort into planning the assignments and ongoing evaluation stages. For example, students had flexibility and choice in how they would meet the assignment expectations. They were encouraged to explore personal interests and integrate real-world problems to help increase relevance and intrinsic motivation throughout their course work. For the term design project, it was essential to break the components into smaller, easier-to-understand parts, beginning with an outline, followed by a prototype for peer and instructor feedback, and planning sufficient time for evaluating and revising. This timeline supported students to experience ongoing success and feel empowered rather than overwhelmed by the complexity of the large learning task. Weekly team check-ins were energizing and enjoyable, inspiring students to learn from and with peers. We had lively and insightful group discussions around tasks in process and roadblocks that needed clearing. My typical questions were: "What have you completed? What is getting in your way?" Not only did the ongoing peer feedback help resolve creative and technical issues quickly, but it also fostered meaningful relationships, teamwork, and trust.

Introducing a Design-Based Toolkit for Teachers to Make Change

IDEO's *Design Thinking for Educators* is a renowned approach that guides teachers to think like a designer and think outside the box to question assumptions and find new ways to solve problems. Using a design mindset, teachers can develop the confidence to create impactful and feasible solutions for small or significant challenges in their classrooms and school communities: "Wherever they fall on the spectrum of scale – the challenges educators are confronted with are real, complex, and varied. And as such, they require new perspectives, new tools, and new approaches. Design thinking is one of them" (IDEO, 2013).

Building on a decade of meaningful feedback and robust research around the classic *Design Thinking for Educators*, IDEO (2020) partnered with esteemed collaborators and foundations to develop a new resource called the *Co-Designing Schools Toolkit*. This toolkit supports teachers in making equitable change and transformation in their classrooms and schools through a co-design and community-led process. The toolkit's compilation of instructional resources, facilitator guides, change frameworks, and student activities are available for free download in PDF and Google Doc formats. The content can be remixed and distributed under a Creative Commons licence, which aligns with the aim of SDG 4 to "ensure inclusive and equitable quality education and promote lifelong learning opportunities for all" (United Nations, n.d.). Educators and school leaders can connect with and learn from others through the professional learning network organized by the Teacher's Guild x School Retool (TG x SR), an affiliated IDEO initiative.

The *Co-Designing Schools Toolkit* is structured as a collaborative design process with six interconnected phases: build your team, define your aspiration, know your students, start hacking, observe and understand impact, and showcase your work. This approach challenges teachers to think critically about the complexities and uncertainties involved with making meaningful and equitable change in educational settings. Five building blocks are identified for developing teachers' belief in their ability to create change: trusting relationships, belonging and feeling seen, resilience, evidence, and collaboration (IDEO, 2020). While there are other effective models for leading educational change, such as John Kotter's 8-Step Change Management Model and Kurt Lewin's 3-Stage Model of Change, these approaches do not fully address the human emotions at the core of any effort to catalyze change within school systems. The *Co-Designing Schools Toolkit* philosophy states that change starts with people (not policies) and by building teams who believe in each other and pursue collective action together. The goal is to empower teachers as changemakers and engage students as valuable problem finders and problem solvers.

Integrating the Co-designing Schools Toolkit and Change Framework

Recognizing the benefits of a collaborative and empathy-centered design approach, I put the *Co-Designing Schools Toolkit* to the test for developing and instructing a new course. *Designing Immersive Experiences for K-12 Learning Environments* was a design experiment to explore virtual possibilities for meaningful ESE. This course was ground-breaking in teacher education, amongst the first in Canada to be offered in VR with world building assignments for students. Due to the innovative nature of the course, I did not have other syllabi to build upon or follow. Hence, it was essential for me to pay close attention to the design process as we navigated our way forward. In this section, I report on how the toolkit strategies and co-design phases empowered my instructional skills and confidence in supporting the students' needs and aspirations.

Phase 1 highlighted the importance of building a community of committed teammates. To build team energy and a sense of belonging, we went world-hopping and explored virtual worlds together. Not only was this fun and inspiring, but it helped to form a unique group identity and team bond as we taught each other how to fly and throw portals for teleporting to other worlds. The term design projects required a range of knowledge, skills, and perspectives beyond my instructional capacity.

Hence, I invited students to take on leadership roles and relied on their contributions and expertise throughout the course. We greatly benefitted from the generous technical and design support offered by the Educators in VR team and *AltspaceVR* communities, with communication typically through Discord channels. In this phase, consideration must be given for what expertise is missing and who is needed to join your team. How will you show appreciation for the contributions of all team members?

Phase 2 outlined how to align the team by co-defining aspirations. I crafted a syllabus with a design vision to guide students through their new journey as world builders and immersive storytellers. To get students to believe in the design vision, I invited them to contribute their ideas and resources, and then I improved the course outline with their valuable suggestions. We also negotiated the design milestones, progress indicators, and deadlines. Including student insights helped to put them in charge of their learning and establish an equitable team environment. My role in the course was not as a knowledge disseminator but as an innovation leader dedicated to challenging students' thinking and championing their use of immersive technologies for learning. While we were fortunate not to have unresolvable conflicts, I will be more proactive in mitigating potential concerns in the future. For example, I may lead the team in generating a list of obstacles, assumptions, and biases that could interfere with the students' design progress.

Another vital aspect of the co-design process was developing empathy. Thus, Phase 3 involved spending time with students to understand their needs. By listening to and building trusting relationships with my team, I knew who needed support or a creative push. Activities like design sprints and sharing circles helped build empathy for multiple perspectives and develop concern for others. The term projects were refined based on ongoing empathy insights. Simple but effective strategies for students to practice and cultivate empathy include imaginatively putting themselves in the shoes of others and perspective-taking: "What is this person feeling? How might I feel in this situation?" Ongoing team reflection can lead to empathic responses and mindfulness for discussing deeply human issues involving privilege, oppression, inequity, inclusion, and belonging.

Test big ideas by starting small was the focus of Phase 4. We began the course with more questions than answers about technologies and pedagogies for designing immersive learning experiences. Scrappy experiments with different features in various platforms were helpful for students to discover what and how they wanted to build their term projects. I broadened the team's horizons with various immersive environments, knowing these lived experiences would generate creative ideas and enhance their design intuition. First-time or less experienced immersive creators can be their own worst critics. They need sufficient time to master new design skills, permission to learn from failure, and continuous reminders to trust the design process and keep experimenting. Good design ideas result from collaboration, experimentation, taking risks, and small achievements over time.

Phase 5 emphasized observing and understanding impacts. To move students closer to achieving their goals, they needed critical and creative feedback on how to evolve their ideas. I scheduled team meetings where the students reflected on what was working well, how they delivered on learning objectives, and where they needed to pivot. Using an organic, open-ended approach to feedback was efficient, meaningful, and enjoyable for the team. However, I recommend using more formal methods of collecting feedback for group discussions on controversial or sensitive topics. Ongoing reflective practice was also necessary for fostering self-confidence and self-directed learning. Finally, students needed to reflect on their design projects as teachers or future teachers. They were required to document their design process by collecting evidence of professional growth, such as pedagogical insights and design decisions, strategies for resolving technical challenges, changes in thinking, and sources of inspiration.

To build enthusiasm and support for student work, in Phase 6, we held a team Celebration of Learning in *AltspaceVR*. Students were proud to dress up their avatars and present their term projects. We recognized the individual and collective contributions that made our journey as world builders and immersive storytellers possible. To invite the broader community to participate in the students' design work, we presented at the 2021 Immersive Learning Research Network (iLRN) international conference using the *Virbela* platform. This professional opportunity allowed the students to showcase their pedagogical expertise with immersive technologies. The one-hour team panel, *Instructional Design Principles for Guiding Immersive Learning Experiences,* focused on instructional design principles for enhancing student learning experiences in XR-enabled classes. Panellists highlighted pedagogical strategies for integrating XR in distance education to support learner interaction, creativity, and collaboration.

During iLRN 2021, we also led a Guided Virtual Adventure (GVA): *Designing Relational Land-Based Connections through Immersive Learning for Middle-Years and Secondary Education*. Guests had the opportunity to experience a well-designed VR classroom. They participated in a scavenger hunt and learning experience with Myrtle O'Brien, a Cree Traditional Knowledge Keeper, herbalist, crafter, and educator. As she demonstrated knowledge of Indigenous plants, language, and traditions, we discussed cross-curricular connections related to respecting the environment and the human impact on the land. The GVA included two public worlds on *AltspaceVR*: (1) *SDGs 2030 Global Agenda* (Fig. 4), designed by Lavoie

Fig. 4 "SDGs 2030 Global Agenda" AltspaceVR world designed by Lavoie (n.d.)

Fig. 5 "Boreal Forest Biome" AltspaceVR world co-designed by Lavoie et al. (n.d.)

(n.d.) and (2) *Boreal Forest Taiga Biome* (Fig. 5), co-designed by Lavoie et al. (n.d.). These worlds had enchanting landscapes and interactive activities for learning about environmental and human well-being. Hidden Easter egg objects were embedded in the pathways to evoke curiosity and wonder. The talking circle in Lavoie's (n.d.) virtual world included a series of questions for guided reflection:

- What do we mean by needs and wants? How are they different?
- What do we need to do well in life?
- Do you think everyone in the world has the things they need to do well in life? Why or why not?

Presenting and demonstrating at the iLRN 2021 conference was a leadership opportunity that enabled the students to connect with and learn from world builders and designers who were not part of our course. This experience exemplifies how Phase 6 (showcasing) is associated with Phase 1 (building community), as the students benefitted from observing a global audience interact with their worlds. Conference guests offered valuable suggestions for integrating new technical features and mindfulness activities to enhance learner agency. Our design journey is ongoing; we completed a design cycle, generating momentum for moving forward beyond the course. Further plans involve integrating the virtual worlds in classrooms and starting a ripple effect for SDG awareness and action in students' lives, homes, and school communities. The goal is to continue creating sustainable change through real-life and virtual dialogues that advance understanding, spark imagination, build connections, and catalyze helpful solutions.

Strategies for Implementation of Design

Educators and designers can consider the following five pedagogical strategies when creating or implementing an immersive learning experience.

- **Focus on the learning.** Be intentional and clarify why you want to use immersive learning rather than another pedagogical approach. What is the problem or focus of the learning? For example, VR is a good solution for learning in rare, impossible, dangerous, or expensive (RIDE) scenarios. What are the learning objectives? Without clearly defined learning objectives, an immersive experience can quickly devolve into a random series of events and activities without educational value or purpose. Pedagogy needs interact with technology; enhancing student learning should be the primary reason for selecting an immersive experience. While immersive technologies are powerful and engaging, they are not the best choice for every classroom or learning situation.
- **Redefine engagement to support creativity.** What does student engagement look like in an immersive environment? Check assumptions and do not be tempted to replicate a traditional classroom or lecture experience. Be deliberate in using immersive technologies to enhance human-computer interaction and spatial capabilities. Explore new dimensions of student connection, collaboration, and creation. Expand your team's capacity for innovation by scheduling practice sessions for students to experiment with new ideas and pedagogical techniques without undue criticism. Immersive environments can enhance a sense of co-presence and make personal connections stronger. Utilize this spatial design advantage to foster a learning community where students build trusting relationships and develop the creative confidence to take on new learning challenges.
- **Empower students as world builders and immersive storytellers.** Invite students to demonstrate their competencies and proficiencies in new ways, such as world building and immersive storytelling assignments. Ensure that design challenges have a manageable scope and well-defined criteria. Avoid hinting at a solution. The goal is for students to come up with unexpected or novel possibilities. Empower students by demonstrating a curious mindset, unsettling assumptions, supporting risk-taking and experimentation, and asking questions that push them to think critically about the quality and impact of their work. Guide students to evaluate and refine their immersive creations for UX/UI design considerations and pedagogical implications.
- **Value critical perspectives.** Whether students are content creators or consumers, thinking critically about immersive learning experiences is an essential skill that must be taught. Although immersive environments can feel real and legitimate, students need to understand they are not typically primary source material; designers create them with goals and intentions. Consider who the creator of the experience is. Whose points of view are represented or omitted? What are the messages conveyed? Is the content accurate? It is insufficient for students to participate in or create an immersive experience without critical discussions to evaluate real-life implications. Reflect on what worked well and what could be improved from a technical and design standpoint. Value the critical perspectives of educational researchers studying the influence of immersive technologies on teaching and learning; their recommendations and concerns should be included in class discussions.

- **Create for a cause.** Schedule guided learning explorations in virtual worlds that address one or more SDG targets to deepen connections between students and the issues that affect their lives. Invite students to consider how they can be environmental and sustainability changemakers, and part of the solution for cultivating a more resilient and sustainable future. Provide opportunities for students to use their creativity and problem-solving skills to design immersive experiences that teach about ecological limits and planet conservation. Challenge students to consider how they might tell immersive stories that help others practice empathy for the world's social and environmental concerns (this is not easy to do). Remember that good design takes time. It is unnecessary to develop or revise an entire course. Instead, start by making a small change, such as enhancing a lesson or module with an immersive experience, followed by a reflective activity to synthesize the learning.

Conclusion

Climate leader Bill Scott (2012) observed, "In the end, we will conserve only what we love, we will love only what we value, and we will value only that we have come to appreciate through experience." His thoughts about the conservation of nature reflect the hard truths about sustainability that we face today and in the future. Meeting the needs of all people and the planet will require sacrifices and changes that are daunting to consider. It is not surprising that action for the SDGs has been slow in Canada and around the world and that "Despite the growing global problems of unsustainable consumption and environmental degradation, which threaten the health of the planet and our survival, many students and teachers are not taking action for sustainable living" (MacDowell, 2021). What role should teacher education play in addressing our social-environmental issues? How might faculties of education offer learning opportunities to foster sustainability knowledge and values in pre-service and in-service teachers?

This chapter addresses the ongoing challenges of ESE in teacher education programs and school systems by supporting teachers in designing immersive learning experiences with connections to natural environments and SDG targets. The VR course *Designing Immersive Experiences for K-12 Learning Environments* integrated the teachers' technological pedagogical content knowledge to design intentional and meaningful learning immersive learning experiences. Although the relationship between technology and ESE is arguably contentious, we need to explore new approaches for engaging and connecting students with sustainability education for greater planetary resilience. Immersive technologies are evolving rapidly as the world's leading technology companies invest in what they predict will become a primary mode of human communication and interaction. It is imperative to build an ethical foundation for the positive change that new technology can bring and advance knowledge for designing immersive environments toward goals that benefit the lives of people and the planet. Further, we need multi-disciplinary partnerships to unite our efforts and study how immersive learning technologies can help shift the world onto a sustainable and resilient path for present and future generations.

References

Aikens, K., & McKenzie, M. (2021). A comparative analysis of environment and sustainability in policy across subnational education systems. *The Journal of Environmental Education, 52*(2), 69–82. https://doi.org/10.1080/00958964.2021.1887685

Bailenson, J., Yee, N., Blascovich, J., Beall, A. C., Lundblad, N., & Jin, M. (2008). The use of immersive virtual reality in the learning sciences: Digital transformations of teachers, students, and social context. *The Journal of the Learning Sciences, 17*(1), 102–141. https://doi.org/10.1080/10508400701793141

Berger, P., Gerum, N., & Moon, M. (2015). "Roll up your sleeves and get at it!" Climate change education in teacher education. *Canadian Journal of Environmental Education, 20*, 154–172. https://cjee.lakeheadu.ca/article/view/1370

Bieler, A., Haluza-Delay, R., Dale, A., & McKenzie, M. (2018). A national overview of climate change education policy: Policy coherence between subnational climate and education policies in Canada (K-12). *Journal of Education for Sustainable Development, 11*(2), 63–85. https://doi.org/10.1177/2F0973408218754625

Billingsley, G., Smith, S., Smith, S., & Meritt, J. (2019). A systematic literature review of using immersive virtual reality technology in teacher education. *Journal of Interactive Learning Research, 30*(1), 65–90. https://www.learntechlib.org/primary/p/176261

Bower, M., DeWitt, D., & Lai, J. W. M. (2020). Reasons associated with pre-service teachers' intention to use immersive virtual reality in education. *British Journal of Educational Technology, 51*(6), 2215–2233. https://doi.org/10.1111/bjet.13009

Cheng, K., & Tsai, C. (2019). A case study of immersive virtual field trips in an elementary classroom: Students' learning experience and teacher-student interaction behaviors. *Computers & Education, 140*(2), 103600. https://doi.org/10.1016/j.compedu.2019.103600

Chirico, A., & Gaggioli, A. (2019). When virtual feels real: Comparing emotional responses and presence in virtual and natural environments. *Cyberpsychology, Behavior and Social Networking, 22*(3), 220–226. https://doi.org/10.1089/cyber.2018.0393

Chirico, A., Scurati, G. W., Maffi, C., Huang, S., Graziosi, S., Ferrise, F., & Gaggioli, A. (2020). Designing virtual environments for attitudes and behavioral change in plastic consumption: A comparison between concrete and numerical information. *Virtual Reality, 25*, 107–121. https://doi.org/10.1007/s10055-020-00442-w

Domingo, J., & Bradley, E. (2018). Education student perceptions of virtual reality as a learning tool. *Information Technology Systems, 46*(3), 329–342. https://doi.org/10.1177/2F0047239517736873

Elshof, L. (2009). Toward sustainable practices in technology education. *International Journal of Technology and Design Education, 19*(2), 133–147. https://doi.org/10.1007/s10798-008-9074-4

Falkenberg, T., & Babiuk, G. (2014). The status of education for sustainability in initial teacher education programs: A Canadian case study. *International Journal of Sustainability in Higher Education, 15*(4), 418–430. https://doi.org/10.1108/IJSHE-10-2012-0088

Fauville, G., Queiroz, A. C. M., Hambrick, L., Brown, B. A., & Bailenson, J. N. (2020a). Participatory research on using virtual reality to teach ocean acidification: A study in the marine education community. *Environmental Education Research, 27*(2), 254–278. https://doi.org/10.1080/13504622.2020.1803797

Fauville, G., Muller, A., & Bailenson, J. (2020b). Virtual reality as a promising tool to promote climate change awareness. In J. Kim & H. Song (Eds.), *Technology and health: Promoting attitude and behaviour change* (pp. 91–108). Academic Press. https://doi.org/10.1016/B978-0-12-816958-2.00005-8

Gibson-Hylands, K. (n.d.-a). *Food waste*. AltspaceVR join code: FAK094. https://account.altvr.com/worlds/1110409405431546666/spaces/1437234598701432973

Gibson-Hylands, K. (n.d.-b). *Plastic mountain*. AltspaceVR join code: CHR370. https://account.altvr.com/worlds/1110409405431546666/spaces/1255057002795630764

Gibson-Hylands, K. (n.d.-c). *The ocean*. AltspaceVR join code: JAE160. https://account.altvr.com/worlds/1110409405431546666/spaces/1199136371516638093

Harrington, M. (2011). Empirical evidence of priming, transfer, reinforcement, and learning in the real and virtual trillium trails. *IEEE Transactions on Learning Technologies, 4*(2), 175–186. https://doi.org/10.1109/TLT.2010.20

Harrington, M., Bledsoe, Z., Jones, C., Miller, J., & Pring, T. (2021). Designing a virtual arboretum as an immersive, multimodal, interactive, data visualization virtual field trip. *Multimodal Technologies and Interaction, 5*(4), 18. https://doi.org/10.3390/mti5040018

Herrera, F., Bailenson, J., Weisz, E., Ogle, E., & Zaki, J. (2018). Building long-term empathy: A large-scale comparison of traditional and virtual reality perspective-taking. *PLoS One, 13*(10), 1–37. https://doi.org/10.1371/journal.pone.0204494

Hollweg, K. S., Taylor, J. R., Bybee, R. W., Marcinkowski, T. J., McBeth, W. C., & Zoido, P. (2011). Developing a framework for assessing environmental literacy. *North American Association for Environmental Education.*. https://cdn.naaee.org/sites/default/files/devframewkassessenvliton-lineed.pdf

Howard, P. (2012). Who will teach the teachers? Reorienting teacher education for the values of sustainability. In K. Bartels & K. Parker (Eds.), *Teaching sustainability and teaching sustainably* (pp. 149–157). Stylus Publishing.

Huang, J., Lucash, M. S., Scheller, R. M., & Klippel, A. (2020). Walking through the forests of the future: Using data-driven virtual reality to visualize forests under climate change. *International Journal of Geographical Information Science, 35*(6), 1155–1178. https://doi.org/10.108 0/13658816.2020.1830997

IDEO. (2013, January). *Design thinking for educators*. https://www.ideo.com/post/design-thinking-for-educators

IDEO. (2020). Tools for creating equitable change in your school. *Co-designing Schools Toolkit.* https://www.codesigningschools.com

Læssøe, J., & Mochizuki, Y. (2015). Recent trends in national policy on education for sustainable development and climate change education. *Journal of Education for Sustainable Development, 9*(1), 27–43. https://doi.org/10.1177/2F0973408215569112

Lavoie, J. (n.d.). *SDGs: 2030 global agenda*. AltspaceVR join code: RZH206. https://account.altvr.com/worlds/1508417509638800367/spaces/1672683625046343783

Lavoie, J., Banow, J., & Stange, J. (n.d.). *Boreal forest (taiga) biome*. AltspaceVR join code: KHT243. https://account.altvr.com/worlds/1508417509638800367/spaces/1510450070388998593

Lion-Bailey, C., Lubinsky, J., & Shippee, M. (2020). *Reality bytes: Innovative learning using augmented and virtual reality*. Dave Burgess Consulting.

MacDowell, P. (2021). Design principles for teaching sustainability within makerspaces. In D. Scott & J. Lock (Eds.), *Teacher as designer: Design thinking for educational change* (pp. 133–147). Springer. https://doi.org/10.1007/978-981-15-9789-3_10

Makransky, G., & Mayer, R. E. (2022). Benefits of taking a virtual field trip in immersive virtual reality: Evidence for the immersion principle in multimedia learning. *Educational Psychology Review, 34*, 1771–1798. https://doi.org/10.1007/s10648-022-09675-4

Markowitz, D. M., & Bailenson, J. N. (2021). Virtual reality and the psychology of climate change. *Current Opinion in Psychology, 42*, 60–65. https://doi.org/10.1016/j.copsyc.2021.03.009

Markowitz, D. M., Laha, R., Perone, B. R., Pea, R. D., & Bailenson, J. N. (2018). Immersive virtual reality field trips facilitate learning about climate change. *Frontiers in Psychology, 9*, 23–64. https://doi.org/10.3389/fpsyg.2018.02364

McKenzie, M. (2021). Climate change education and communication in global review: Tracking progress through national submissions to the UNFCCC secretariat. *Environmental Education Research, 27*(5), 631–651. https://doi.org/10.1080/13504622.2021.1903838

Petersen, G., Klingenberg, S., Mayer, R., & Makransky, G. (2020). The virtual field trip: Investigating how to optimize immersive virtual learning in climate change education. *British Journal of Educational Technology, 51*(6), 2099–2115. https://doi.org/10.1111/bjet.12991

Schott, C. (2017). Virtual field trips and climate change education for tourism students. *Journal of Hospitality and Leisure Sport and Tourism, 21*, 13–22. https://doi.org/10.1016/j.jhlste.2017.05.002

Scott, B. (2012, February 3). *Will we really understand only what we are taught?* Bill Scott's Blog. https://blogs.bath.ac.uk/edswahs/2012/02/03/will-we-really-understand-only-what-we-are-taught

Southgate, E. (2020). *Virtual reality in curriculum and pedagogy: Evidence from secondary classrooms.* Routledge.. https://doi.org/10.4324/9780429291982

Thompson, M., Kaser, D., & Grijvala, K. (2019). *Envisioning virtual reality: A toolkit for implementing VR in education.* Carnegie Mellon University Press. https://doi.org/10.1184/R1/9700397.v1

UNESCO. (n.d.). *Education for sustainable development: A roadmap.* https://www.unesco.org/en/education/sustainable-development

United Nations. (n.d.). *About the sustainable development goals.* https://www.un.org/sustainabledevelopment/sustainable-development-goals

Wu, J. S., & Lee, J. J. (2015). Climate change games as tools for education and engagement. *Nature Climate Change, 5*(1), 413–418. https://doi.org/10.1038/nclimate2566

Paula MacDowell, PhD, is an Assistant Professor in the College of Education, University of Saskatchewan. Her area of specialization is Educational Technology and Design (ETAD) with research interests in immersive education, emerging technologies, instructional design, and education for social and environmental change. Paula serves as the Practitioner Chair for the Immersive Learning Research Network (iLRN).

Part III
Teachers and Students as Designers of Immersive Learning

Teachers Facilitating Student Virtual Reality Content Creation: Conceptual, Curriculum, and Pedagogical Insights

Erica Southgate

Abstract This chapter contributes insights into how teachers can make curriculum design and pedagogical choices that enhance students' agency to meet learning outcomes through virtual reality (VR) content creation. The focus is on achieving deeper learning by unleashing student creativity through easy-to-use VR authoring tools that enable students to design their own virtual environments.

Keywords Children · Digital learning · Metaverse · School · STEM education · Virtual reality

Introduction

Educators and researchers have become increasingly interested in empowering students as active learners through new media content creation (Grizioti & Kynigos, 2021), including learner design of immersive virtual reality (VR) (Southgate, 2020b). VR can be defined as a 3D computer-generated environment—highly imaginative or a realistic simulation—that can be experienced via a computer or mobile device screen, a surround-screen projection room, or via a head-mounted display (a VR headset or goggles). This chapter focuses on VR mediated by a headset, known in scholarly circles as immersive VR (Slater & Sanchez-Vives, 2016).

The aim of this chapter is to present insights into how teachers can make curriculum design and pedagogical choices that enhance students' student agency and ability to meet learning outcomes through VR content creation, especially using 'no code create' sandbox applications. These insights derive from the VR School Study (www.vrschoolresearch.com), a multi-site research project that commenced in 2016

E. Southgate (✉)
University of Newcastle, Newcastle, Australia
e-mail: Erica.southgate@newcastle.edu.au

© The Author(s), under exclusive license to Springer Nature Switzerland AG 2022
P. MacDowell, J. Lock (eds.), *Immersive Education*,
https://doi.org/10.1007/978-3-031-18138-2_12

and continues to this day. This chapter begins with a vignette from the case studies, followed by a succinct review of the literature. The research methodology is then outlined. A set of conceptual frameworks are subsequently discussed and woven together into a new curriculum development process for student VR content creation. Each phase of this process is then elaborated on with examples from two VR School case studies: one in junior secondary science and the other in senior drama. The chapter concludes with a set of suggestions for teachers on embedding student VR content creation into their classrooms.

Vignette

Three girls in junior high school science have formed a group to create a model of the human heart in Minecraft VR. They set about researching the form and function of the heart. Working on screen and in VR, they create a human heart that they can fly around and into when in VR. The heart is huge, and its chambers can be toured in the correct direction of blood flow which pulsates through the organ like a river. Fun facts are posted inside each of the chambers, and after the tour, they leave the heart by flying out its aorta.

   Meanwhile, at another school, students in senior drama work in groups to prototype a set design using the 3D painting application Tilt Brush. They seek to understand how the symbolism of a Gothic play might be represented in a set to realize a directorial vision. They create designs on paper and then take turns in Tilt Brush to develop their design. With one student in VR, the others look at the creation process in action on the computer screen, making suggestions. In these interactions, learning in the virtual design studio of Tilt Brush merges seamlessly with learning in the real drama studio.

Immersive VR for School Education

While there is significant research on learning in screen-based virtual worlds (Peachey et al., 2010), this review concentrates on immersive VR and school education. A recent systematic review on the topic in K–12 and higher education (Pellas et al., 2021) located 46 journal articles published between 2009 to mid-2020, of which 21 reported on research conducted in schools. The review found that students in many K–12 studies achieved learning of complex material and developed creativity, problem-solving, and metacognitive skills. Only two of the 21 studies in the review mentioned a collaborative or participatory methodology, which assumed teacher-as-researcher involvement.

   There is evidence that VR experiences can produce positive learning outcomes for elementary and secondary school students (Calvert & Abadia, 2020; Wu et al., 2020), generate increased interest in science careers for secondary students, including girls (Makransky et al., 2020a), and develop empathy in middle school students via an anti-bullying intervention (Ingram et al., 2019). Some research comparing the effects of learning the same material with VR versus other media shows more equivocal results (Makransky et al., 2020b; Parong & Mayer, 2018). Most research concentrates on evaluating the effect of VR experiences on learning outcomes where university researchers give students VR applications (either in their labs or in school) and then measure impact on specified areas of learning such as content knowledge, procedural mastery, or affective domains. Exceptions are work by Chang et al. (2020), who document the positive influence of peer feedback on improving VR design, and Yiannoutsou et al. (2021), who explore embodied pedagogy through designing a non-visual VR math application for children with visual impairment.

As the systematic review by Pellas et al. (2021) indicates, there are very few examples of studies where teachers are genuine co-researchers. Such research is participatory in nature and focuses both on exploring student learning through VR and understanding pedagogical and curriculum choices that can facilitate learning. The VR School Study is the first and longest continuous investigation of how different types of VR can be embedded in elementary (primary) and secondary school classrooms as a regular part of learning across a variety of subject areas. The study differs from experimental, short-term intervention research. It is conducted over extended periods of time (6 months to 2 years) in classrooms with teachers as co-researchers. The study has yielded findings on the ethical and safe use of VR schools (Southgate et al., 2017) as well as on organizational facilitators and constraints to embedding the technology (Southgate et al., 2019). It has investigated peer-to-peer collaboration, metacognition, problem-solving, and creativity in-situ in virtual worlds (Southgate, 2020b). A key focus across school sites and subject areas has been theorizing curriculum development and pedagogical practice that can leverage VR for deeper student learning (Southgate, 2019).

Methodological Snapshot of the Two Case Studies

As participatory inquiry, the VR School Study seeks to enable people to investigate aspects of their lives, including work and education, so they can be empowered to make change for the better (Kemmis & McTaggart, 2005). It is research *with* teachers and students, not *on* them, and reflects a commitment to teachers being part of building the evidence base for their profession. The study is guided by a number of research questions investigated across sites, including: (1) What pedagogical approaches work best with VR? and (2) How can the curriculum be tailored to use VR for deeper learning? The case studies discussed in this chapter implemented a mixed methodology design in two secondary schools (see Table 1 for a description of the setting, participants, method, and scope of data).

The research was approved by the University of Newcastle Human Ethics Committee (Approval No. H-2017-0229) and the New South Wales Department of

Table 1 Overview of setting, participants, and data type and scope from two case study sites

Study setting	Callaghan College junior secondary science	Dungog high school senior drama
	Two junior high school campuses in an urban setting serving a low-income school community	One high school in a rural setting serving a low-income school community
Sample	48 students (21F, 27 M) from 2 mixed ability classes of year 9 students (ages 13–15). Control group knowledge test ($n = 134$)	9 students (6F, 3 M) from 1 class of mixed ability year 11 students (ages 16–17)
Type and scope of data	In-class observation (38 h) Audio recording in VR room (15 h, 50 mins) Hand-held video (3 h, 26 min) Screen capture of students in VR (21 h) In-class student interviews ($n = 35$) 6377 word written real-time reflection (university researcher) Teacher ($n = 4$) interviews VR work samples for all students Pre- and post-test knowledge test for VR and control group Empirical data collection duration 5 months (does not include the planning, analysis, write-up phases)	In-class observational hours (4 h, 30 min) Hand-held video recording (1 h, 59 min) Screen capture of students in VR (1 h, 50 min) Photos of design work in VR ($n = 56$) Photos of design work outside of VR ($n = 53$) Student group interviews (all students, 19 min 50 sec) Teacher ($n = 3$) interviews (1 h 12 min) 3506 word written real-time reflection (university researcher) 1876 word written real-time reflection (teacher-researcher) VR work samples for all students Empirical data collection duration 2 months (does not include the planning, analysis, write-up phases)
Technological aspects	6 × Oculus Rift and touch controllers (3 rifts per class at each school) paired with Alienware laptops and Minecraft VR software	2 × Oculus Rift and touch controllers paired with Alienware laptops and Tilt Brush software

Education (Approval No. 2017396). Parents/caregivers were provided with a printed and video information statement and parental consent and child assent form that allowed for the collection of grades, work samples, interviews, and deidentified still and video photography.

This chapter draws on insights from the case studies and uses conceptual tools (discussed in the next section) and data, such as student and teacher-interview extracts and VR work samples, to illustrate phases in curriculum development for student VR content creation.

Conceptualizing Curriculum Design for Student VR Content Creation

Three conceptual frameworks are relevant to this chapter. The first is that of learning affordances. Affordance refers to the actual or perceived properties of something and how these can suggest how it might be used or interacted with (Kaptelinin & Nardi, 2012). By extension, learning affordance implies the potential (utility) of a technology for learning (Bower, 2008). The learning affordances of VR are

- First-person perspective experiences. Viewing the virtual world directly through one's own eyes or the viewpoint of another (e.g., seeing the world through the eyes of a child).
- Natural semantics. Understanding the basis of something abstract before explicit learning (e.g., manipulating angles before learning about angles in mathematics).
- Size and scale manipulation. Learners changing the size of themselves, objects, or environments to interact with micro/macro worlds (e.g., travelling through the body as a blood cell).
- Reification. Transforming abstract ideas into perceptible representations (e.g., understanding the concept of instinct by embodying a fish avatar that swims with the school to survive).
- Transduction. Extending capability to feel data that is beyond the range of senses or experiences (e.g., flying above a simulated migration path of whales) (Dalgarno & Lee, 2010; Mikropoulos & Natsis, 2011).

The second conceptual framework from Southgate (2020b) proposes that while educators and researchers often focus on the technical differences between VR hardware and the interactive potential of the software, it is more important to recognize that pedagogically, VR should not be conceived of as a singular phenomenon. There are different pedagogical uses for VR. For example, VR might be (1) a one-off learning experience that acts as a stimulus in a lesson, (2) a form of immersive digital media for student content creation, (3) an instructional tool for learning a bounded set of declarative or procedural knowledge, or (4) a total learning environment such as a fully developed virtual science lab. Pedagogically, VR can be conceived as any or all these things depending on its design, affordances for learning, and how it is used in the classroom through curriculum design.

Extending on the idea that pedagogically VR is not one thing, Southgate (2020b) presents a non-hierarchical typology (Table 2). This typology classifies VR by (1) the degree of embodiment (or what you can do with your real and avatar's body in the virtual environment); (2) potential to affect the virtual environment or objects or agents (avatars and non-player characters) in a meaningful way through interaction, navigation, and/or creation; and (3) the extent of learner autonomy over learning in and with VR.

The VR School Study focuses on using 'no code create' sandbox applications across a variety of subject areas and age levels. Sandbox applications, accessible to

Table 2 Typology of immersive VR environments by learner interaction and autonomy

Swivel	A ready-to-use environment relying on a relatively stationary learner rotating their head/body to experience the surrounding virtual world
Explore	A type of ready-to-use environment allowing for unguided or guided exploration, either through a handheld controller or gaze, to explore a fully simulated or 360° photograph or video environment
Discover	An environment with embedded, fully interactive activities and tools that enable learners to independently undertake learning and assessment tasks that are usually curriculum- or competency-based
No code create	An authoring or content creation toolbox (sometimes called a sandbox) allowing learners to produce their own 3D objects, models, designs, prototypes, and artwork without needing to code
Code to create	Game engines (e.g., Unity, unreal) and other programs that require coding to create virtual objects/worlds
Social VR	Commercial (mostly free to enter) permanent 3D virtual worlds that allow people in 3D (and sometimes 2D mode) to socialize, play games, and meet for leisure and learning

all regardless of programming knowledge, allow students to create fully realized 3D virtual objects, avatars, and virtual environments to tell a learning story. While Table 2 provides a scaffold for educators to better understand and select VR applications for their classrooms, it is also an idealized representation; there can be a crossover between categories. For example, social VR applications often have sandbox spaces that provide users with content creation tools.

The third theoretical framework applied in Southgate's (2020b) research is Shulman's (2005) idea of signature pedagogies. Signature pedagogy refers to favoured ways of teaching in a specific discipline (or school subject area derived from a discipline) and how it relates to the professional practice of the discipline. For example, a signature pedagogy of geography is the field trip; in second language teaching, acquiring foundational vocabulary is linked to practising everyday interactions with people and historical or cultural places. The idea of signature pedagogies can assist teachers to reflect on the foundational instructional approaches of their subject area and why these approaches figure so prominently in professions related to the disciplines. Identifying the strengths and limitations of signature pedagogies can offer a starting point for curriculum design for the use of VR in classrooms. Rather than trying to invent new instructional approaches, Southgate (2020b) argues that teachers should begin by leveraging their signature pedagogies to develop VR tasks integrated into units of work, a practice illustrated in the next section of this chapter.

It is useful to understand how these frameworks (pedagogies) look like in practice. Figure 1 illustrates the synergies between the frameworks by combining them to form the curriculum development process for student content creation. This process is particularly relevant for using 'no code create' VR applications.

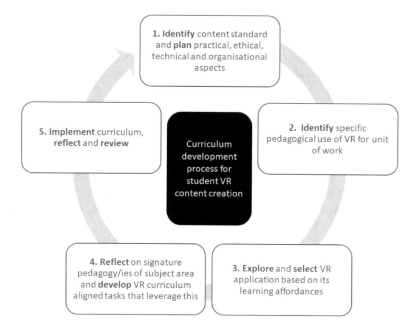

Fig. 1 Curriculum development process for student VR content creation

Unpacking the Five Phases of the Curriculum Development Process

Phase 1: Identifying Content Standards and Practical Planning

If the school is just beginning its VR journey, some initial research into technology options is required. What can certain hardware do in terms of the user and creator experience? What are the manufacturer's age recommendations for hardware? Does the software allow students to create virtual environments or participate in virtual environments easily? Teachers need as much time as students do to play with hardware and software. For an experiential technology, this is key to making informed hardware and software choices.

Investigating the school's network capability and reliability and whether applications require whitelisting is vital to ensure smooth learning experiences and easy firmware and software updates. With emerging technology such as VR, teachers and students should expect some degree of technical failure: screen-capture video of students working in Minecraft VR at Callaghan College indicated the technology stopped working around 13% of the time due to network drop-out, tracking issues, and unspecified causes. As one science teacher from the Callaghan study remarked:

> The biggest issues weren't so much around the pedagogy. All the teachers that were involved had really good ideas on how to implement to VR into it (the curriculum). It more the technology side (such as) learning to work within the Department's ... network and then

there's the hurdle of kid's access to technology because a lot of kids don't have the technology (mobile computing devices) to bring and the ones that perhaps do, it might not be the right type of equipment for the project … And interesting things like copying a (Minecraft) world from a (mobile) device to a laptop when connectivity is not all it should be, stopping and restarting servers, and keeping kids on track when their devices aren't working.

In both VR School case studies, Oculus Rift hardware was chosen because at the time it offered state-of-the-art six degrees of freedom (6DoF) VR with natural gestural control and fully tracked bodily interaction. Put simply, 6DoF refers to how hardware can facilitate a wide range of movement in VR, and this translates to full interactional opportunity and feelings of immersion. The need for reasonably sized play areas did cause issues in locating classroom or connected-classroom spaces large enough at Callaghan College to safely accommodate the areas needed for the tracking system to work. The idea was to embed VR into regular classrooms rather than have students travel to a specially set up VR lab. In one case, the VR equipment was set up in a (barely large enough) storeroom attached to the classroom (Fig. 2), while in the other, an old science preparation area attached to the classroom was used.

At Dungog High School, the drama studio was a large, open-plan room that easily accommodated the two VR play areas (Fig. 3). Even today's all-in-one headsets require reasonably large play areas. The spatial onfiguration of schools designed for the industrial age is not really suited to embedding VR into classrooms, so advanced timetabling of suitable spaces may be required.

Fig. 2 The VR set up in the smaller storeroom space off the classroom at Callaghan College

Fig. 3 The VR set up in the Dungog High School drama classroom

In this phase, small teams of teachers at both Callaghan College (science and ICT teachers) and Dungog High School (the drama teacher and librarians) explored with the university-researcher the syllabus-mandated content standards available within the current year's curriculum program sequence to identify possible units of work that might suit VR content creation. At Dungog High School, the drama teacher identified how an upcoming unit of work on directorial vision using a modern Gothic play as its centrepiece would be a great springboard for her students to develop set and costume designs in VR. The Callaghan College team identified a biology unit of work on the human body as one in which students might make models of body organs in VR.

Phase 2: Identify the Pedagogical Use of VR

After doing a preliminary identification of a possible unit of work within the program sequence, teachers turned their attention to which pedagogical use of VR they would adopt. Both case studies were based on the pedagogical conception of VR as a form of immersive media that could give students an opportunity to demonstrate their content mastery and collaborative and problem-solving skills through designing interactive objects or environments for an authentic audience. Opportunities for creative fun would be married to more serious learning endeavours such as collaborative research and prototyping.

Phase 3: Explore and Select VR Applications Based on Learning Affordances

Teachers explored appropriate 'no code create' sandbox applications, with Callaghan settling on Minecraft VR because students were already familiar with Minecraft and Minecraft Education Edition. As a networked application, Minecraft VR allowed groups of students to collaborate in screen mode and in VR. The experience of seeing friends as avatars in the same space and interacting together to create was exciting for students. The first-person perspective learning affordance allowed students to work together in VR as they would in real life, by collaboratively selecting a site, building their body-organ models by communicating about materials and engineering aspects for interactive design, and flying together to evaluate the creation from afar and close-up. The most promising learning affordance was that of size and scale manipulation. Students could build models that allowed for feelings of fully embodied interior exploration of the model as well as an exterior experience. There was also potential for reification, with abstract concepts about the human body being bought to life in more embodied ways.

Tilt Brush was selected for the senior drama class because it offered an infinite virtual design studio with the ability to easily 3D paint (and repaint), position, and resize objects for costume and set design. Its animation and theatrical lighting effects, including manipulation of the colour and tone of the lightbox, allowed students to explore mood and the ability to teleport around the created objects to get different perspectives (from the audience, an actor, or the director).

Phase 4: Reflect on Signature Pedagogies and Develop Curriculum

One of the signature pedagogies of science involves using models to deepen learning. Therefore, it was logical that science teachers would leverage this in their design of the VR task. The biology unit of work included direct instruction lessons and labs as well as self-directed learning through an online module. The VR task required students to work in small groups to research a body organ, build a model of it in VR to demonstrate understanding of form and function, and take peers, the teacher, or the researcher on a guided tour of it in VR. The unit of work ran over 6 to 7 weeks (21 h total with 12 one-hour lessons for VR). As each class had only three Oculus Rifts, groups cycled in and out of VR every 15–20 min. Students would design on screen and work incredibly quickly in VR to evaluate their progress and make changes. The limited access to VR time meant that most groups were on-task most of the time, as demonstrated in the analysis of screen-capture video of learners in VR (Southgate, 2020a).

The drama teacher also chose to weave the VR component through the unit of work on a directorial vision that spanned over 4 weeks with 5 one-hour VR lessons, although many students used the equipment at lunchtime. The unit of work involved direct instruction, self-directed research, visual art, and performative elements. Since students were required to produce a traditional cardboard set box design as well as the VR set and costume design component using Tilt Brush, the prototyping work in VR informed the production of the cardboard mock-up. The teacher leveraged VR to create a nexus between the traditional set box mock-up exercise, a signature pedagogy in theatre studies, with the opportunity to prototype at a real scale in VR. The drama teacher also drew on another signature pedagogy, improvisation, in her flexible pivoting during the unit of work. However, it became evident that costume design was less successful in Tilt Brush because some students did not have high-level drawing skills, so mid-unit of curriculum work, she shifted the focus to set design. The teacher was comfortable trusting a more open-ended creative process with students, concentrating on what they learned together in terms of collaboration and a deepening understanding of abstract ideas such as symbolism, rather than solely on the technical perfection of the end VR product.

Phase 5: Implement Unit of Work, Reflect, and Review

While not without its challenges, most of the students produced imaginative and novel designs in VR that demonstrated mastery of content knowledge, the power of collaboration, and the development of problem-solving skills. For example, one group of girls in the science class developed a model of the human heart that could be toured internally (Figs. 4 and 5) as described in the vignette that opened this chapter. In Fig. 5, the placard reads "This is not a model of the outside but the inside."

A group of boys built a skyscraper of a brain (Figs. 6 and 7) which was labelled correctly and used Minecraft engineering to represent its electrical impulses in an interactive way. Another group created an enormous eyeball that was toured via a

Fig. 4 External view of heart model with student avatars flying around it

Fig. 5 A student avatar enters the heart with fun fact placards ahead in the right atrium

Fig. 6 The model of the brain with spinal column with transparent side (right) demonstrating electrical functions of the brain

rollercoaster that went around and inside the eye to exit via the optic nerve (the internal part of the eye was labelled with fun facts).

The drama students revelled in Tilt Brush, commenting on how the first-person learning affordances of the application deepened their understanding of the abstract idea of directorial vision:

Fig. 7 A student avatar in the transparent side of the brain where Minecraft red stone material was used to represent electrical impulses

> I think it (Tilt Brush) helped all of us because we are basically coming from an audience perspective. We're looking at it. We're not just the creators of something on a piece of paper. We're basically sitting down like we're on a stage looking at this dark area and we have this piece of light and the costume or (elements of) the set design and we're able to see, 'Oh that doesn't look good (or) I don't understand what that means, and we're able to change it.'

The drama teacher reflected on what VR bought to learning in her classroom:

> The process of taking their directorial vision into the VR space allowed them to think more about the audience's experience and really immerse themselves in the director's role. ... In the design process there is a lot of experimentation and collaboration required. Tilt Brush has endless features that allow this to occur. Sketches could be saved, videoed, gifs made and photographed, and this process of documenting their ideas helped the students reflect on their ideas more. The quality of their ideas developed further. ... The Tilt Brush program was an endless space, which incorporated many amazing creative features. Designs could be instantly erased and then re-created quickly. ... As the teacher, I had to take a risk with new technology and not be frightened of not knowing absolutely everything about the software. After a while, the students were teaching each other and me. Just do it (use new technology)! It isn't scary and you don't have to know everything.

In both case studies, teachers reflected on the need to factor in enough time for students to familiarize themselves with the application before beginning the learning task. They felt they could have spent longer on the VR task if not constrained by the need to get through the mandated curriculum. They highlighted the unique learning that VR facilitated: from bringing scientific knowledge together with creativity to providing a virtual studio where rapidly prototyping set design was as easy as clicking a button on the controller.

Strategies for Implementation of Design

The following strategies have been developed by synthesizing key findings from the two case studies. Teachers considering the use of 'no code create' VR applications in their classrooms should

- **Experiment with VR technology**. VR is an experiential technology, and teachers need to seek out, experiment, and play with different types of VR to grasp its potential for learning in their subject area.
- **Start planning early**. Embedding an emerging technology like VR in school classrooms will involve technical, organizational, and curriculum decisions and problem-solving, and so early planning is vital. Teachers should factor in long lead times for practical implementation.
- **Integrate VR into the curriculum.** Design curriculum units of work that weave VR tasks *into* the curriculum rather have VR *be* the curriculum. VR can add variety to a teacher's instructional repertoire and offer unique student learning experiences in a well-developed unit of work that carefully considers how the learning affordances of the technology can best be leveraged in the subject area.
- **Empower students to be creators of VR content.** Student content creation, usually through small group work, is key to deeper learning. VR allows students to demonstrate content mastery by manifesting it through imaginative creations and sharing them with others. This is more important than teachers producing VR content for students.
- **Understand that the process of VR content creation is as important as the product.** Teachers should focus on what is being learned through the process of VR design, not just the final product, and formative and summative assessments should reflect this.
- **Play and have fun**. Use the curriculum design process for student VR content creation as a scaffold to guide your own progress and have fun learning with your students along the way. Recognize that when using new technology, students can sometimes scaffold teacher learning.

Conclusion

This chapter presented insights from the VR School Study on how curriculum design and pedagogical choices can enhance students' agency and enable them to meet learning outcomes through VR content creation. The chapter focused on 'no code create' VR sandbox applications that provided students with easy-to-use authoring tools to create their own virtual environments. Case studies from junior secondary science and senior drama classes illustrated how different types of sandbox applications can be integrated into a curriculum for deeper learning. The chapter also presented a new and practical framework to assist teachers with curriculum development decisions and pedagogical choices. It is important to conduct more research in the natural setting of the school with teachers as co-researchers so that curriculum and pedagogical frameworks focusing on VR can develop from practice as well as theory. Research in real classrooms highlights the tensions of embedding an emerging technology in schools and, importantly, the students' perspectives on using the technology for learning. Student creativity lies at the core of this chapter, and it is incumbent on teachers to scaffold student understanding of the affordances of VR so their imaginations can be truly unleashed in the learning process.

References

Bower, M. (2008). Affordance analysis - matching learning tasks with learning technologies. *Educational Media International, 45*(1), 3–15. https://doi.org/10.1080/09523980701847115

Calvert, J., & Abadia, R. (2020). Impact of immersing university and high school students in educational linear narratives using virtual reality technology. *Computers & Education, 159*, 104005. https://doi.org/10.1016/j.compedu.2020.104005

Chang, S. C., Hsu, T. C., & Jong, M. S. Y. (2020). Integration of the peer assessment approach with a virtual reality design system for learning earth science. *Computers & Education, 146*, 103758. https://doi.org/10.1016/j.compedu.2019.103758

Dalgarno, B., & Lee, M. J. (2010). What are the learning affordances of 3-D virtual environments? *British Journal of Educational Technology, 41*(1), 10–32. https://doi.org/10.1111/j.1467-8535.2009.01038.x

Grizioti, M., & Kynigos, C. (2021). Children as players, modders, and creators of simulation games: A design for making sense of complex real-world problems: Children as players, modders and creators of simulation games. In *Proceedings of Interaction Design and children* (pp. 363–374). Association for Computing Machinery. https://doi.org/10.1145/3459990.3460706

Ingram, K. M., Espelage, D. L., Merrin, G. J., Valido, A., Heinhorst, J., & Joyce, M. (2019). Evaluation of a virtual reality enhanced bullying prevention curriculum pilot trial. *Journal of Adolescence, 71*, 72–83. https://doi.org/10.1016/j.adolescence.2018.12.006

Kaptelinin, V., & Nardi, B. (2012). Affordances in HCI: Toward a mediated action perspective. In *Proceedings of the SIGCHI conference on human factors in computing systems* (pp. 967–976). Association for Computing Machinery. https://doi.org/10.1145/2207676.2208541

Kemmis, S., & McTaggart, R. (2005). Participatory action research: Communicative action and the public sphere. In N. K. Denzin & Y. S. Lincoln (Eds.), *The SAGE handbook of qualitative research* (pp. 559–603). SAGE.

Makransky, G., Petersen, G. B., & Klingenberg, S. (2020a). Can an immersive virtual reality simulation increase students' interest and career aspirations in science? *British Journal of Educational Technology, 51*(6), 2079–2097. https://doi.org/10.1111/bjet.12954

Makransky, G., Andreasen, N. K., Baceviciute, S., & Mayer, R. E. (2020b). Immersive virtual reality increases liking but not learning with a science simulation and generative learning strategies promote learning in immersive virtual reality. *Journal of Educational Psychology, 113*(4), 719–735. https://doi.org/10.1037/edu0000473

Mikropoulos, T. A., & Natsis, A. (2011). Educational virtual environments: A ten-year review of empirical research (1999–2009). *Computers & Education, 56*(3), 769–780. https://doi.org/10.1016/j.compedu.2010.10.020

Parong, J., & Mayer, R. E. (2018). Learning science in immersive virtual reality. *Journal of Educational Psychology, 110*(6), 785–797. https://doi.org/10.1037/edu0000241

Peachey, A., Gillen, J., Livingstone, D., & Smith-Robbins, S. (Eds.). (2010). *Researching learning in virtual worlds*. Springer.

Pellas, N., Mystakidis, S., & Kazanidis, I. (2021). Immersive virtual reality in K-12 and higher education: A systematic review of the last decade scientific literature. *Virtual Reality, 25*, 835–861. https://doi.org/10.1007/s10055-020-00489-9

Shulman, L. (2005). Signature pedagogies in the professions. *Daedalus, 134*(3), 52–59. https://www.jstor.org/stable/20027998

Slater, M., & Sanchez-Vives, M. V. (2016). Enhancing our lives with immersive virtual reality. *Frontiers in Robotics and AI, 3*, 74. https://doi.org/10.3389/frobt.2016.00074

Southgate, E. (2019). Virtual reality for deeper learning: An exemplar from high school science. In *2019 IEEE conference on virtual reality and 3D user interfaces (VR)* (pp. 1633–1639). IEEE. https://doi.org/10.1109/VR.2019.8797841

Southgate, E. (2020a). Using screen capture video to understand learning in virtual reality. In *2020 IEEE conference on virtual reality and 3D user interfaces abstracts and workshops (VRW)* (pp. 418–421). IEEE. https://doi.org/10.1109/VRW50115.2020.00089

Southgate, E. (2020b). *Virtual reality in curriculum and pedagogy: Evidence from secondary classrooms*. Routledge.

Southgate, E., Smith, S. P., & Scevak, J. (2017). Asking ethical questions in research using immersive virtual and augmented reality technologies with children and youth. In *2017 IEEE virtual reality (VR)* (pp. 12–18). IEEE. https://doi.org/10.1109/VR.2017.7892226

Southgate, E., Smith, S. P., Cividino, C., Saxby, S., Kilham, J., Eather, G., Scevak, J., Summerville, D., Buchanan, R., & Bergin, C. (2019). Embedding immersive virtual reality in classrooms: Ethical, organisational and educational lessons in bridging research and practice. *International Journal of Child-Computer Interaction, 19*, 19–29. https://doi.org/10.1016/j.ijcci.2018.10.002

Wu, B., Yu, X., & Gu, X. (2020). Effectiveness of immersive virtual reality using head-mounted displays on learning performance: A meta-analysis. *British Journal of Educational Technology, 51*(6), 1991–2005. https://doi.org/10.1111/bjet.13023

Yiannoutsou, N., Johnson, R., & Price, S. (2021). Non-visual virtual reality: Considerations for the pedagogical design of embodied mathematical experiences for visually impaired children. *Educational Technology & Society, 24*(2), 151–163.

Erica Southgate is Associate Professor of Emerging Technologies for Education (University of Newcastle, Australia) and lead researcher on the *VR School Study*, the longest-running research project on embedding VR into school classrooms across subject areas. She is author of *Virtual Reality in Curriculum and Pedagogy: Evidence from Secondary Classrooms* (Routledge).

PEGS: Pretraining, Exploration, Goal Orientation, and Segmentation to Manage Cognitive Load in Immersive Environments

Camila Lee and Meredith Thompson

Abstract As virtual reality (VR) becomes more affordable and available, educators need to understand how to evaluate VR experiences and how best to incorporate them into their classes. This article suggests evaluating VR experiences through presence and agency and incorporating VR experiences using PEGS: Pretraining, Exploration, Goal orientation, and Segmentation.

Keywords Biology · Cellular biology · Cognitive theory of multimedia learning · Pretraining · Segmenting · STEM · Virtual reality

Introduction

Educational technology allows teachers and students to access a wealth of information, enriching the classroom experience. Educators with access to the right resources and support can bring new dimensions of learning to their classroom through virtual experiences. Well-designed immersive virtual reality (VR) experiences have the unique ability to make users feel as if they are physically present and can have significant interactions with a context-rich simulated environment (Makransky & Petersen, 2021). VR has the potential to bring engaging, situated, and embodied learning experiences into the classroom (Cook & Thompson, 2021). Students can learn about ancient Egypt by exploring the tombs within the pyramids, understand deep-sea vents by swimming alongside them, walk with elephants on the African savannah as they read the book *Walking with Elephants*, and explore Mars without even leaving the Earth (Bailenson, 2018; Thompson, 2018). The increasing availability and affordability of VR technology gives educators even

C. Lee (✉)
Massachusetts Institute of Technology, Glendale, CA, USA
e-mail: camlee@mit.edu

M. Thompson
Massachusetts Institute of Technology, Winchester, MA, USA

© The Author(s), under exclusive license to Springer Nature Switzerland AG 2022
P. MacDowell, J. Lock (eds.), *Immersive Education*,
https://doi.org/10.1007/978-3-031-18138-2_13

more ways to engage students in learning (Kaser et al., 2019). Yet even as VR head-mounted displays (HMDs) become more available, barriers to including immersive technology in schools persist. In addition to acquiring and managing technology-related logistics, educators must also find enriching experiences, integrate the experiences into existing curricula, and account for limitations in the amount of time users can comfortably be in an immersive virtual environment (Cook & Thompson, 2021).

In this chapter, we focus on how educators can find and take existing VR experiences and design activities around them to successfully integrate existing immersive learning experiences into their classrooms. To explore options for embedding immersive learning into classrooms, we must first understand how learning happens in immersive environments. To that end, we draw from two theories of how learning happens in multimedia environments: the cognitive theory of multimedia learning (CTML) and the cognitive affective theory of immersive learning (CAMIL). CTML discusses broadly how individuals process multimedia environments (Mayer, 2020), and CAMIL applies that model specifically to immersive environments (Makransky & Petersen, 2021). We have reviewed a subset of strategies—specifically pretraining and segmenting (Mayer & Moreno, 2003)—for managing cognitive load in multimedia environments, focusing on the ways educators can bookend existing VR experiences as they plan to embed them in their classrooms. We have chosen to present pretraining and segmenting first as they have been well established in multimedia research and are easily applicable to VR. Then we integrate these strategies into a small study that we designed to examine two ways of framing VR activities: goal-oriented and exploration-oriented. Finally, we bring these ideas together in a set of strategies educators can use to evaluate and select experiences and integrate them into their classrooms.

Vignette

Tania's high school biology students are in a vocational technical program at an urban school in the northeastern US. Her students study topics such as plumbing, woodworking, and culinary arts, and describe themselves as hands-on learners and visual learners. The topic of cell biology can seem abstract to Tania's students, so when she heard about the game called Cellverse, she was eager to see if the game could appeal to her students' preferred learning modalities. During her planning, she found she had many questions about how to integrate the game into her class. What should she do to prepare her students? Should they do the entire game at once? Will her students be overwhelmed by the activity? Will her students get nauseous if they are in the activity for too long? What is the best way for her to help her students get the most out of this VR experience?

Making Cellular Biology Hands-on Through VR

In this chapter, we answer some of Tania's questions by exploring how educators can make use of the game *Cellverse* in their classes and how educators can prepare their students for success in using VR technology. Cells are central to the understanding of biology, so all high school biology teachers must find ways to get their students to learn about cells. Despite the advances made in the field of biology, most biology educational materials remain deeply rooted in traditional, two dimensional, simplistic, and schematic depictions of cells (Vlaardingerbroek et al., 2014). These representations portray the cell as a static, sparsely populated collection of organelles and do not capture the dynamic and complex environment of this building block of life (Thompson et al., 2021a). Often, one activity associated with the unit on cells is a project requiring students to design and build cell models using common household materials such as paper, macaroni, string, glue, and any other material they have on hand. However, students' cell design projects serve only to replicate students' notions of cells as flat, mostly empty entities (Thompson et al., 2021a, b).

To address the need for updated teaching materials, we designed a game called *Cellverse*. In *Cellverse*, students have a chance to learn about biology *from the inside out* by actively exploring and interacting with a virtual environment (Thompson et al., 2021a, b). *Cellverse* is designed to capture the complexity of cells by accurately representing both the types and structure of organelles and the numbers of each organelle in the cell. Using a combination of theory and experience, we describe how we have designed *Cellverse* and how we have scaffolded the experience using cognitive theories and principles of instructional design to provide the best possible learning experience.

Design Frameworks: How Does Learning Happen in Immersive Environments?

Any educator who intends to include immersive learning in their classroom will be confronted with the questions "But, why VR?" or "How is VR better than just watching a movie?" CAMIL answers this question by clarifying the two unique affordances of VR compared to other media: presence and agency. Presence is the psychological feeling that one is *in* the immersive environment (Slater & Sanchez-Vives, 2016), and agency is the degree to which the user is able to interact with the environment (Tapal et al., 2017). All learning is filtered through different constructs, including motivation and self-regulation, which are factors educators can influence even outside of the VR environment. A number of studies have supported the idea that VR experiences are motivating for learners (e.g., Makransky et al., 2019, Parong & Mayer, 2018). More recent research has shown that immersion alone positively affects learning when comparing video games with the same level of interactivity (Thompson et al., 2021a, b).

To maximize learning when using VR in the classroom, we suggest selecting experiences with rich and representative environments that can promote the feeling of being in the environment (presence) and allow the learner to interact with the environment (agency). If finding, filtering through, and selecting VR experiences may seem like a daunting task, consider involving students in the search. With a systematic approach to the search, students can be excellent researchers and evaluators of potential VR experiences. For example, Kaser et al. (2019) describe a high school VR class where students search for and evaluate VR experiences, share them with teachers who may be interested in them, and work closely with the teachers to help them integrate those VR experiences in their classes. The high school students bring and manage the equipment, help troubleshoot and provide technical support for the teacher during the lesson, and return and keep track of the equipment at the end of the session (Kaser et al., 2019).

While CAMIL is helpful for designers in creating immersive environments, the principles of CTML provide guidelines that educators can also use as they embed VR within their courses. CTML states that the primary mechanisms of learning are memory and processing (Mayer, 2005). When learning through multimedia, the brain processes visual and audio inputs in two separate channels and then joins them together. All learning requires a certain amount of cognitive load, which CTML deems essential processing. However, when a learner's essential processing exceeds their cognitive capacity, the processing does not facilitate learning, and the learner can experience excessive cognitive load. Mayer and Moreno (2003) provide some strategies designers can use to help manage cognitive load. The two strategies that educators can use in their classes are pretraining and segmenting.

Managing Cognitive Load Through Pretraining

In pretraining, learners are provided a summary of what they will see in the immersive experience (Checa & Bustillo, 2019). When the group described in this chapter played the game *Cellverse,* we provided them with a traditional schematic of a cell before they played the game. Research suggests that background knowledge is an important factor in how much individuals can learn from multimedia experiences (Thompson et al., 2020). Pretraining has been proven successful for reducing cognitive load during a VR experience (Meyer et al., 2019). In other VR experiences, it may be helpful to provide a map (if exploring a territory), or an overview of the characters learners may see while in the virtual world. Since giving learners a sense of what to expect in the virtual environment reduces cognitive load, we encourage educators to consider incorporating pretraining before the simulation to help students prepare for the virtual experience and manage cognitive load.

Managing Cognitive Load Through Segmenting

Segmenting breaks down the experience into smaller, more manageable pieces (Parong & Meyer, 2018; Rey et al., 2019). Segmenting can be designed into the experience or overlaid on the experience by controlling the time spent in the virtual environment. *Cellverse* incorporates three forms of segmenting. Participants start out in the "projection," a part of the cell that does not have many organelles. This allows participants to learn the hand controller functions and become familiar with parts of the cell. We designed a non-player character (NPC) named FR3ND, who also serves to segment the experience. FR3ND guides users through the tutorial and introduces them to the functions available in the game, as shown in Fig. 1. FR3ND accompanies players during the game, providing clues to ensure they are not too overwhelmed by the environment. In Fig. 2, FR3ND accompanies a player in the cell.

Another way to segment is to have participants vary their time in and out of the VR headset. In the game *BioDive* by Killer Snails, students put on the VR headsets to go on scientific expeditions, such as scuba diving to monitor coral colour and quantity of underwater creatures or taking a boat to collect water-quality data. They then remove the headsets so they can analyze the data in digital science journals (personalized websites) to create hypotheses and build models. One can also segment the experience by putting a time limit on VR. In the case of *Cellverse,* each student was given between 20 and 25 min in the environment. Segmenting helps

Fig. 1 FR3ND introduces the functions of the game

Note. **FR3ND, a non-player character, helps segment** *Cellverse* **by introducing the controls for the game. The tutorial starts in a projection of the cell, segmenting the introduction to the controls and introducing players to the more complicated cell environment.**

Fig. 2 FR3ND in the centre of the cell
Note. **After the tutorial, the player follows FR3ND to the central part of the cell, which shows a densely packed environment with many different organelles. FR3ND offers advice along the way, directing users' attention to important features in the game.**

with information processing, and limiting time in VR can also prevent nausea, especially for individuals who aren't frequently in VR.

Implementation: Goal-Oriented or Open Exploration

VR is a sensory rich experience, which makes it both highly engaging and potentially overwhelming. We were curious about additional ways to implement learning experiences that could manage cognitive load among learners. As we did not find research directly addressing this topic, we conducted a small study to learn more about these two options for educators. We were guided by the following two research questions:

- How would cognitive load differ if the learner were given a clear goal (goal-oriented) in the virtual world versus being able to explore freely (explore-oriented)?
- What impact would goal orientation versus open exploration have on learning and cognitive load?

One common critique of current research in VR is that many experiences are accessed only once; thus, potential outcomes of multiple uses are unexamined (Pellas et al., 2020). For this study, we designed a learning experience where participants would have two chances to interact with *Cellverse*. These multiple opportunities allow us to examine retention of the material over time as well as try different approaches to introducing the activity, such as starting with either a specific goal or open exploration. Providing multiple opportunities for the students to interact with the virtual environment also works well with the strategy of segmenting the material for learners.

Method

We recruited six college-level participants from a summer program at a technical institute in the northeastern US to try *Cellverse* twice, approximately one week apart. Participants accessed *Cellverse* using the Quest 1, a head-mounted display (HMD) manufactured by Facebook/ Oculus. Participants were assigned to one of two groups as they indicated interest in the study: either a "goal/explore" group or a "explore/goal" group. During the first session, the three participants in the "goal/ explore" group were given the goal of looking for a specific organelle when they tried *Cellverse* while the three participants in the explore/goal group were allowed to explore the cell freely. During the second session, those instructions were switched as shown in Fig. 3. Each session was approximately 40 minutes long. The goal-oriented group was instructed to find two specific organelles: the rough endoplasmic reticulum (RER) and the nucleus. The explore-oriented group was told they had the freedom to explore the cell in any way they wanted.

We measured learning through cell drawings, and measured cognitive load, presence, and agency through standardized surveys (Klepsch et al. 2017; Tapal et al. 2017; Vorderer et al. 2004). At the beginning of the first session, each participant drew a cell. Then, participants were given a cell schematic as a form of pretraining before putting on the HMD. Once participants entered *Cellverse,* they were taken through a tutorial and continued with the assigned activity for approximately 15–20 min. After completing the activity, participants were asked to draw another cell. The session concluded with some survey questions and a short semi-structured interview. The survey questions focused on the participants' cognitive load, sense of presence, and sense of agency while inside the HMD and experiencing *Cellverse*.

Fig. 3 Diagram of the Cellverse study *Note.* **The study setup shows six participants, timeline of pre- and post-research sessions, and activity framing (goal or explore) during the two sessions.**

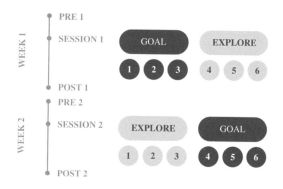

The short semi-structured interviews during the first session were designed to understand participants' attitudes toward the type of learning activity.

During the second session, participants were instructed to draw a cell to document how much information they retained from the previous session. Unlike the first session, participants were not given a form of pretraining. After the drawing, the participants put on the HMD and were in the virtual environment for 15–20 min. This time, the season ended with a short semi-structured interview to understand whether the participants perceived they learned more from the goal-oriented framing or the exploration framing for the activity.

Analysis

We analyzed cell drawings to address our research question as to whether learning was impacted by the framing of the learning activity (goal/explore or explore/goal). First, for each cell drawing we looked at the number of organelles labeled by the student. To ensure we were not misinterpreting what was drawn, we counted only organelles that were drawn and labeled by the participant. Then, we totalled the number of organelles in the drawing to give an overall score of the participants' mental model of cells at that point in the study. This score served as a proxy to measure an individual's knowledge gain compared with that of other participants to evaluate the treatment order. Figure 4 shows an example of one participant's drawings at those four time points.

This participant began with a very basic idea of a cell with a cell membrane, nucleus, mitochondria, and "organelle" and "riboids" (the participant may have meant ribosomes here). This image of a cell is similar to many other images we have collected during the *Cellverse* project (Thompson et al., 2020). Between the pre session 1 drawing and post session 1 drawing, this participant's ideas about cells became more accurate. This participant's drawings illustrate a typical example of the progress participants made during each learning session. On average, participants' first drawing showed they had extremely minimal recall of prior knowledge of cells before the study. Then after the first learning session, participants drew and labelled more organelles. The third set of drawings showed that participants retained information from the previous learning session and were able to clearly draw a diagram of the cell. The final cell drawings revealed that participants learned more from the second learning session.

Figure 5 shows the total number of organelles present and labelled for all six participants. As the figure shows, participants learned new organelles during their first session (pre 1 to post 1), retained that knowledge in the 7–10 days between the two sessions (post 1 to pre 2), and continued to learn more organelles in the second session (pre 2 to post 2). All six participants gained knowledge of cellular organelles between the first and final drawing. The learning progress shown through the drawings supports the importance of multiple learning sessions to allow participants to continue learning.

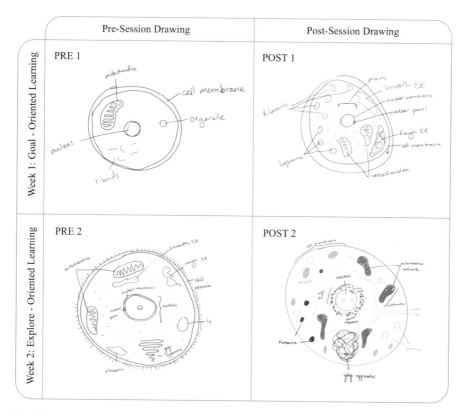

Fig. 4 Participant's drawings of cells at four time points during the study

Figure 6 shows a disaggregation of results for each individual with an upward trend for five of the six participants, suggesting that almost all individuals continued to learn new organelles after each session of playing *Cellverse*. Two participants did not have the same number of organelles between their post 1 drawing and their pre 2 drawing, which means they could have forgotten some information about cells during the time between session 1 and session 2. Only one participant, participant 6, had fewer organelles in their post 2 drawing than in their other drawings. We did not find any particular reason why participant 6 had fewer organelles in their final drawing.

We were curious about whether participants learned more during the goal sessions versus the explore sessions. To isolate the effect of the actual session type from the sequence of sessions, we used the change in the number of organelles as a measure of learning, rather than the absolute number of organelles present. We wanted to focus on new knowledge the participant gained in the form of knowledge about cell organelles. The change for each participant in the number of organelles between pre 1 and post 1 and pre 2 and post 2, according to the treatment (goal or explore), is shown in Fig. 7.

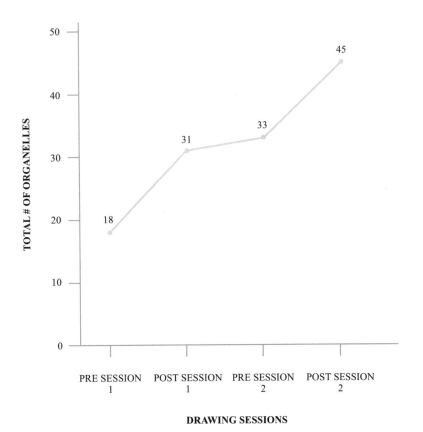

Fig. 5 Organelles present and labelled (sum of all six participants' drawings)

Participants 1, 2, and 4 had a larger change in the number of drawn organelles when they were given a goal. Participants 3, 5, and 6 had a larger change in the number of drawn organelles when they were told to explore. The patterns suggest that neither goal or explore, nor the sequence of when they had the treatments (goal 1st, explore 2nd or goal 2nd, explore 1st), was clearly better than the other.

We found students were more inclined to prefer the second version of the task they were given; all six participants stated that they preferred the second learning task, suggesting a recency effect, "a cognitive bias in which those items, ideas, or arguments that came last are remembered more clearly than those that came first" (Turvey & Freeman, 2012). Because of the recency effect, students may be inclined to believe they learned more from the most recent version of the task. Another common theme that four of the six participants mentioned during the short semi-structured interviews was VR's ability to strengthen participants' spatial awareness of where organelles were located relative to other organelles and the entire cell. When asked what they learned from being in VR, one of the participants stated, "I

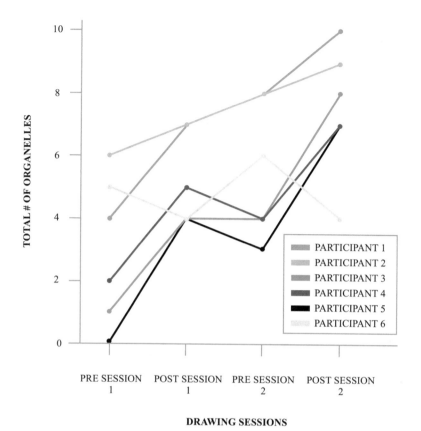

Fig. 6 Organelles present and labelled

think it reinforced the spatial arrangement of some elements in the cells ... like the proximity of the endoplasmic reticulum to the nucleus."

One participant who was new to using VR explained that an explore-based approach to learning reduced the cognitive load and demand experienced compared to the previous week's goal-based approach to learning: "The pacing made me feel more comfortable and like I had more time to explore [and] look around." The participant's experience suggests that students may need time to adapt to the VR environment before trying to accomplish certain tasks in VR.

When asked which activity they enjoyed better, a participant explained,

> I enjoy this week's more, but just because, last week I got the chance to explore, because otherwise this week I wouldn't be able to ... control, where I was going as well as last week. So, although I enjoy it more, I think last week was important to just explore so I can get used to the area [e.g., virtual environment].

The interview suggests that having multiple learning sessions helped the participant adapt better to the virtual environment, thus giving them more control and agency over their learning experience (Makransky & Petersen, 2021).

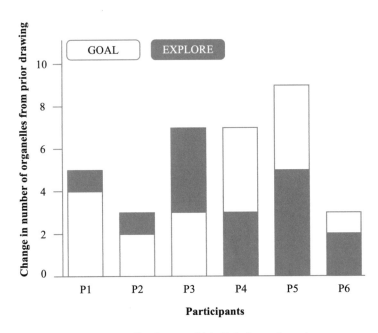

Fig. 7 Total number of new organelles drawn and labelled after each session

The results of this small study are of interest to educators planning to implement VR in their classrooms. Evidence from participants' drawings suggest that they continued to learn more about the cell from multiple sessions in *Cellverse*. Participants' feedback from the interviews underscores the value of having more than one VR experience. From both perspectives, we recommend that educators incorporate virtual experiences multiple times to give students more than one chance to explore and learn from the virtual environment. Results also suggest that learners benefit from both goal-oriented and explore-oriented framing for the activity. In the next section, we bring together the results from this study with the literature to establish strategies for implementing immersive experiences.

Strategies for Implementation of Design

Based on our experiences using *Cellverse* with learners, we present five strategies for implementing VR experiences in classrooms: pretraining, providing explore-oriented and goal-oriented segmenting (PEGS), selecting experiences that leverage presence and agency, and offering multiple opportunities for participants to engage with the VR experience.

- **Pretraining: Prepare users for what to expect in VR.** Virtual worlds are exciting and content-rich and can be overwhelming to new learners in a domain.

Pretraining—providing a framework—will help learners navigate while in VR by allowing them to see key topics or features of the virtual world before they enter. In the case of *Cellverse*, a cell schematic helps students know what they can expect to see while in the cell. Pretraining also helps learners manage cognitive load by introducing some information outside of the experience.

- **Explore-oriented and Goal-oriented: Give students time to explore freely and then time with a clear learning goal.** Consider multiple approaches when framing the VR activity. Exploration can help learners appreciate the environment without the burden of having specific ideas to remember. In exploring the world, both exploration and goal orientation require the student to look at the virtual world from a different perspective. While students may have a preference, we found that both setups resulted in learning gains. We suggest including time for exploration and goal-oriented learning.
- **Segmenting: Break the experience into smaller parts.** Find opportunities in the experience to give the learners a chance to step away from the virtual world by dividing the experience into parts. Segmenting the experience allows learners to absorb what they just viewed and integrate that information into their mental models. Since VR is still a relatively new technology, many learners may not have significant experience with VR. Providing breaks from the VR experience also helps the learners avoid nausea.
- **Selecting for presence and agency.** Select experiences with rich and representative environments that can promote the feeling of being in the environment (presence). These experiences draw upon the unique ability for VR to transport learners into new places and into situations that would otherwise be impossible, such as inside a cell. Ensure that the animation in the environment has a high refresh rate to avoid a disconnect between what the learner is doing and what the learner sees, as that disconnect can result in nausea. Select highly interactive experiences that leverage VR's unique ability to allow the learner to interact with the environment (agency). Interaction with the environment enables learners to become more engaged with the material and can transform abstract topics, such as cellular organelles, into hands on learning opportunities.
- **Planning for multiple sessions in VR.** Any VR experience is an investment in technological tools and resources, and so it makes sense to plan for students to have more than one chance to try the experience. Learners may gain a sense of the environment during the first session and in subsequent visits, focus on the relationship between the structure and the function of a specific organelle (like the nucleus). The participants in our study continued to gain knowledge each time they tried the game, as shown by their drawings of cells. Incorporating virtual experiences multiple times gives students more than one opportunity to explore and learn from the virtual environment.

Conclusion

Incorporating VR into classrooms comes at a cost: the technology to access the medium and the time it takes to learn about the technology and keep track of the materials (Kaser et al., 2019). Yet, VR can be an excellent tool for motivating learners and expanding the reach of the curriculum beyond the classroom. When compared to other technologies, VR has the unique ability to engage the learner in context-rich, interactive environments.

In this chapter, we explored different criteria for selecting experiences and provided some strategies educators can use for integrating VR experiences into their classes. The concept for implementation can be remembered as PEGS: pretraining, exploration, goal-oriented, segmenting. PEGS can be used before, during, or after the VR experience and can help maximize learning and mitigate cognitive load among learners. VR has the capacity to expand learning experiences into exciting new directions of space and time. We hope that these practical and easily implementable strategies will help educators and their students gain the greatest learning benefits from VR.

References

Bailenson, J. (2018). *Experience on demand: What virtual reality is, how it works, and what it can do*. WW Norton & Company.

Checa, & Bustillo, A. (2019). A review of immersive virtual reality serious games to enhance learning and training. *Multimedia Tools and Applications, 79*(9–10), 5501–5527. https://doi.org/10.1007/s11042-019-08348-9

Cook, M., & Thompson, M. (2021). Immersive learning: Current understandings and strategies for success: Guest editorial. *Information and Learning Sciences, 122*(7/8), 433–441. https://doi.org/10.1108/ILS-07-2021-262

Kaser, D., Thompson, M., & Grijalva, K. (2019). *Envisioning virtual reality: A toolkit for implementing virtual reality in the classroom*. ETC Press.

Klepsch, M., Schmitz, F., & Seufert, T. (2017). Development and validation of two instruments measuring intrinsic, extraneous, and germane cognitive load. *Frontiers in Psychology, 8*, 1997. https://doi.org/10.3389/fpsyg.2017.01997

Makransky, G., & Petersen, G. B. (2021). The cognitive affective model of immersive learning (CAMIL): A theoretical research-based model of learning in immersive virtual reality. *Educational Psychology Review, 33*, 937–958. https://doi.org/10.1007/s10648-020-09586-2

Makransky, G., Terkildsen, T. S., & Mayer, R. E. (2019). Adding immersive virtual reality to a science lab simulation causes more presence but less learning. *Learning and Instruction, 60*, 225–236. https://doi.org/10.1016/j.learninstruc.2017.12.007

Mayer, R. E. (2005). Cognitive theory of multimedia learning. In R. E. Mayer (Ed.), *The Cambridge handbook of multimedia learning* (pp. 31–48). Cambridge University Press. https://doi.org/10.1017/CBO9780511816819.004

Mayer, R. E. (2020). Cognitive foundations of game-based learning. In J. L. Plass, R. E. Mayer, & B. D. Homer (Eds.), *Handbook of game-based learning* (pp. 83–110). MIT Press.

Mayer, R. E., & Moreno, R. (2003). Nine ways to reduce cognitive load in multimedia learning. *Educational Psychologist, 38*(1), 43–52. https://doi.org/10.1207/S15326985EP3801_6

Meyer, O. A., Omdahl, M. K., & Makransky, G. (2019). Investigating the effect of pre-training when learning through immersive virtual reality and video: A media and methods experiment. *Computers & Education, 140*, 103603. https://doi.org/10.1016/j.compedu.2019.103603

Parong, J., & Mayer, R. E. (2018). Learning science in immersive virtual reality. *Journal of Educational Psychology, 110*(6), 785–797. https://doi.org/10.1037/edu0000241

Pellas, N., Dengel, A., & Christopoulos, A. (2020). A scoping review of immersive virtual reality in STEM education. *IEEE Transactions on Learning Technologies, 13*(4), 748–761. https://doi.org/10.1109/TLT.2020.3019405

Rey, G. D., Beege, M., Nebel, S., Wirzberger, M., Schmitt, T. H., & Schneider, S. (2019). A meta-analysis of the segmenting effect. *Educational Psychology Review, 31*(2), 389–419. https://doi.org/10.1007/s10648-018-9456-4

Slater, M., & Sanchez-Vives, M. V. (2016). Enhancing our lives with immersive virtual reality. *Frontiers in Robotics and AI, 3*. https://doi.org/10.3389/frobt.2016.00074

Tapal, A., Oren, E., Dar, R., & Eitam, B. (2017). The sense of agency scale: A measure of consciously perceived control over one's mind, body, and the immediate environment. *Frontiers in Psychology, 8*, 1552. https://doi.org/10.3389/fpsyg.2017.01552

Thompson, B. M., (2018, November 1). Making virtual reality a reality in today's classrooms. *THE Journal*. https://thejournal.com/articles/2018/01/11/making-virtual-reality-a-reality-in-todays-classrooms.aspx.

Thompson, M., Uz-Bilgin, C., Angelli, C., & Webster, R. (2021a). *Cellverse*: Using virtual reality to learn about cells from the inside out. In D. Seelow (Ed.), *Teaching in the game-based classroom* (pp. 74–81). Eye on Education.

Thompson, M., Uz-Bilgin, C., Tutwiler, M. S., Anteneh, M., Meija, J. C., Wang, A., Tan, P., Eberhardt, R., Roy, D., Perry, J., & Klopfer, E. (2021b). Immersion positively affects learning in virtual reality games compared to equally interactive 2d games. *Information and Learning Sciences, 122*(7/8), 442–463. https://doi.org/10.1108/ILS-12-2020-0252

Turvey, B. E., & Freeman, J. L. (2012). Jury psychology. In V. S. Ramachandran (Ed.), *Encyclopedia of human behavior* (2nd ed., pp. 495–502). Academic.

Vlaardingerbroek, B., Taylor, N., & Bale, C. (2014). The problem of scale in the interpretation of pictorial representations of cell structure. *Journal of Biological Education, 48*(3), 154–162. https://doi.org/10.1080/00219266.2013.849284

Vorderer, P, Wirth, W., Gouveia, F. R., Biocca, F., Saari, T., Jäncke, F., Böcking, S., Schramm, H., Gysbers, A., Hartmann, T., Klimmt, C., Laarni, J., Ravaja, N., Sacau, A., Baumgartner, T. & Jäncke, P. (2004). *MEC spatial presence questionnaire (MECSPQ): Short documentation and instructions for application*. Report to the European Community, Project Presence. http://www.ijk.hmt-hannover.de/presence.

Camila Lee is a senior at Wellesley College majoring in computer science. Her past research experiences with the Wellesley College Human-Computer Interaction Lab and the Massachusetts Institute of Technology Scheller Teacher Education Program have led her to design studies that seek to understand how to optimize learning with different model mediums, such as immersive virtual reality. Lee's past teaching experiences have brought valuable insights about instructional design and the learning experience to her education technology research. She is particularly interested in researching the role of emotions in the process of learning and hopes to design enjoyable learning experiences for students.

Meredith Thompson draws upon her background in science education and outreach as a Research Scientist and Lecturer for the Scheller Teacher Education Program. Her research interests are collaborative learning, STEM educational games, and using virtual and simulated environments for learning STEM topics. She has a bachelor's degree in chemistry from Cornell, a master's in science and engineering education from Tufts, and a doctorate in science education from Boston University. She has done work on collaborative learning environments in virtual reality, multi-user virtual environments (MUVEs) in learning ecology, and how AI powered apps can enrich parent and child learning strategies. She also creates and implements simulations to help pre-service and in-service teachers learn key skills in teaching. Thompson uses those games and simulations when she teaches the STEP course: *Understanding and Evaluating Education.*

Interactive Storytelling Through Immersive Design

Lorelle VanFossen and Karen Gibson-Hylands

Abstract Linking strong narratives and play, this chapter helps educators and designers take their first steps into immersive education using the DEW Concept Model. The focus is on designing and selecting virtual worlds that break through rigid classroom structures and offer immersive experiences that enhance learning through discovery, exploration, and wonder.

Keywords AltspaceVR · DEW Model · Discovery · Exploration · Play · Story · Wonder · World building

Introduction

From early drawings in the deepest caves to tales told around campfires, storytelling has preserved human history. Stories are powerful tools in education—transcending generations, cultures, and languages. Essential to making social connections and creating communality, stories generate healing and overcome differences and often defenses (Gargiulo, 2006). Integral to storytelling is the concept of play, offering students interesting and entertaining experiences for learning in an exciting, stress-free environment (Acar & Cavas, 2020; Yamada-Rice, 2021). Sun and Cheng (2009) found that interactivity and "perceived playfulness could serve as a motivator to raise learner intention to engage with 3D VR systems" (p. 1). The power of the user to influence the story, and thus their learning experience, especially through play

L. VanFossen (✉)
Educators in VR, Oregon, USA
e-mail: lorelle@educatorsinvr.com

K. Gibson-Hylands
Educators in VR, Lairg, UK
e-mail: karengibsonhylands@gmail.com

© The Author(s), under exclusive license to Springer Nature Switzerland AG 2022
P. MacDowell, J. Lock (eds.), *Immersive Education*,
https://doi.org/10.1007/978-3-031-18138-2_14

and role-playing in virtual reality (VR), provides an intense learning experience that manifests the adventures of the Star Trek holodeck with the freedom to travel through space and time, whether visiting ancient Egyptian pyramids or floating untethered around the International Space Station.

Nature photographer, author, and educator George Lepp (1995) explained in his photography workshops that to get someone's attention, you must either show them something they have never seen before or show it in a way they have never seen. Educational virtual worlds tap into the familiar by changing the perspective in a way the student has not experienced. Drawing a three-dimensional (3D) cube in art class is a classic lesson to help students understand perspectives. Drawing the same cube in a 3D environment causes dissonance when students move around the cube, and realize their 3D cube was drawn using 2D methods. When students step into a virtual world for learning, perspectives are challenged and imagination is unleashed. Learning is now an adventure.

From our first-hand experiences, when VR worlds integrate interactive storytelling and a sense of wonder, the experience evokes the body's natural responses and widens the mind's perspective on a subject. These experiences tap into Oppenheimer's (1982) "discovery of unexpected novelty" and Bruner's (1983) theories on play and scaffolding. The struggles teachers face with students with attention difficulties, behaviour issues, and resistance to learning tend to fade into the background; indeed, studies have shown increased motivation and improved focus when learning in VR environments, especially when storytelling and play are integrated into the experience (Cho et al., 2002; Huang & Liaw, 2018; Yamada-Rice, 2021). Creating spaces for play in the learning process is theorized to increase memory retention, and researchers are finding that VR has an even greater significant effect on long-term memory recall and retention (Yamada-Rice, 2021; Yildirim et al., 2019; Yip & Man, 2013).

This chapter introduces the DEW (Discovery, Exploration, Wonder) Concept Model, a framework designed to help educators and students understand key concepts in virtual worlds that combine storytelling narratives to achieve academic goals. A variety of existing virtual world experiences in VR apps and metaverse platforms support easy-to-use world building techniques such as the drag-and-drop technology of the free immersive social VR platform, AltspaceVR, which enables the creation of simple virtual worlds that are no more complicated to build than learning how to create a Microsoft PowerPoint presentation. Even with these easy tools, teachers often don't know where to begin integrating immersive education into the classroom. The DEW Concept Model is designed to help with the selection and development of VR-based educational worlds.

We begin with defining and outlining the DEW Concept Model, then the second section explores important characteristics of educational worlds to help designers and educators in selecting or creating an immersive experience. The third section introduces eight virtual-world model layouts that represent the building blocks of educational worlds ready for applying the DEW model. The fourth section applies

DEW model characteristics to the world models, demonstrating their use in education across diverse pedagogies. The last section explores world building for individual and collaborative student homework projects to expand the educational experience and implement the DEW Concept Model as a learning tool.

Vignette

In 2019, Gibson-Hylands and VanFossen collaborated on Earth Day projects to represent marine pollution as an educational experience free of traditional educational tools. VR was the perfect medium to convey our message, enabling the experience to 1) be interactive, immersive, and experiential; 2) overcome the dullness of facts and statistics to inspire curiosity and change attitudes; and 3) tap into the wonder and awe effect to stimulate conversation and engagement.

"The Ocean" (Fig. 1) is a visually interactive world that conveys the impact of society's garbage on marine creatures. Students swim among marine animals that mistake pieces of floating plastic for food and become entangled in debris, causing distress, injury, and eventually death. The experience often evokes an emotional response that leads to interactive discussions that meet the goal of inspiring curiosity and motivate action in day-to-day lives. The response to this experimental world inspired the authors to explore the DEW Concept Model for use in many of their VR teaching classes and workshops, test the model, and develop it as a case study for educational world building techniques.

Fig. 1 Students swimming in "The Ocean" to learn about water pollution (Gibson-Hylands, 2019)

Fig. 2 DEW Concept
Model

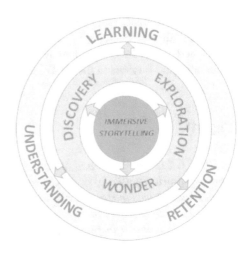

Introducing the DEW Concept Model

The desire to explore is natural for humans from birth. Each new discovery generates wonder, encouraging humans to continue the experimental exercise called *play*
(Bruner, 1983). The continuous interactive progression of exploration and discovery, accompanied by wonder, leads to enhanced learning, understanding, and
retention.

The DEW Concept Model (Fig. 2) is a philosophical framework that encourages
educators to integrate immersive virtual worlds (Immersive, 2008) and experiences
into curricula for learning, understanding, and increased knowledge retention. The
DEW model is designed to help the educator make informed choices on selecting or
designing a VR experience or world, as well as encourage students to create project-
based virtual worlds. The key principles of the DEW model balance the amount of
scaffolding needed to facilitate navigation through an educational virtual world with
the amount of freedom to encourage exploration, leading to the discovery of unexpected novelty (Oppenheimer, 1982).

Worlds with a clear narrative immerse the student into the story and the learning
experience. Such worlds have a clear sense of purpose, focus, and a path to follow.
If students land in a virtual underwater world, the story begins with life underwater,
and instinctively they start swimming, becoming part of the narrative. Through
exploring the world as a guided or self-guided experience, learning becomes an
adventure through discovery, exploration and wonder that amplifies learning, understanding, and retention.

Combined with the power of immersive reality to fool the mind with embodiment and presence, wonder is often easier to inspire. In *The Last Glacier* (VanFossen,
2019a; Fig. 3), students arrive in a glacier-covered mountainous world alongside an
iceberg-filled ocean. Students report feeling cold, even to the point of shivering, in
contrast to their ambient temperature (Yeom et al., 2019). Signs guide them to climb
over the mountain to an ice cave maze, learning about the science of glaciers and

Fig. 3 Learning about the impact of glacial warming in "The Last Glacier" (VanFossen, 2019a)

their impact on our climate and water sources, and the risk to civilization due to glacial loss over the past 20 years (Watts & Kommenda, 2021). Responses to the learning experience show students have increased curiosity and interest in learning more about glaciers and their impact on the climate. Many students surveyed over time reported fond memories of the experience even a year or two later, with some stating they started researching glaciers and seeking out ice caves near them with the hope of visiting before the caves disappear.

Exploring how the experience inspires deeper curiosity and wonder responses, we researched the concept of wonder's impact on the body, mind and memory retention through informal participant questions and surveys. Users are often changed by the immersive experience's visual, auditory, and emotional sensations, much like real world transformative experiences (Krause, 2020). The sense of presence and embodiment in VR taps into the autonomic parasympathetic nervous system associated with fight or flight responses. Some scientists believe the small boost of adrenaline—shown in increased respiration, heart rate, and dilated pupils—enables the mind to absorb and process information faster, thus improving memory retention (Allen, 2018; Fleming, 2013). The concept of play as Bruner (1983) has described is also essential to the learning process because "play provides a courage all its own" (p. 61), followed by the natural desire to share experiences with others. Indeed, students often want to share the experience, exclaiming, "Guess what I did today?" The retelling reinforces the process of scaffolding learning as students translate the experience into their version of the story, leading to learning, understanding, and increased retention (Hung et al., 2012).

We continue to investigate how these VR experiences influence the learning process to improve understanding and retention by identifying the elements of discovery, exploration, and wonder as essential in immersive educational world building. This chapter represents examples of that initial research to help educators select or create educational VR worlds with clear criteria.

Key Characteristics of Educational Worlds

Our continuing research into the DEW Concept Model shows that an educational virtual world experience has a higher success rate in meeting learning outcomes when it contains the following characteristics as part of the model's multimodal framework.

Story

"Data doesn't speak for itself; it needs a good storyteller. … Some have said data is the new oil. The findings, though, will stay buried without the help of a communicator," explained Nancy Duarte, CEO of the Durate, Inc. communications company (Wood, 2022). Storytelling structures the information in a logical or chronological order, increasing retention as the story is easier to access and play back in the student's memory (Boris, 2017). To put this another way, Katherine Cather explains:

> Further, socially minded are we, and so dependent upon social guidance, that curiosity is nowhere so keen, nor the imagination so active, as in the communication of a life situation. Any incident or accumulation of incidents that we call a plot in the experience of an individual or group of individuals, grips the mind. (Cather, 1918, p. ix)

Our experiment in developing the DEW model found that VR experiences using the *show not tell* writing principle to convey information result in increased engagement and memory retention. The more emotionally relatable the story, the greater the wonder generated. An example is the *D-Day* world (Fig. 4), which takes participants back through time to World War II on an unnamed beach in Normandy to *feel* the moment soldiers landed on the shores to face the enemy army. The memorial world offers no facts, no signs, only the sensory experience as students step off the small transport ship onto the barbed wire-lined beach accompanied by the mournful sound of the military bugle call *Taps*. With little initial discussion, students become part of the story as they explore the scene, imagining themselves as soldiers struggling past the enemy guns. Students report sadness, respect, and an increased curiosity about the history of D-Day. Psychological research found that in response to news stories about mass violence, readers need empathetic connections to deal with

Fig. 4 "D-Day World Memorial" in AltspaceVR (Tim, 2020)

large-scale suffering (Maier et al., 2017). VR experiences designed with thought-provoking empathetic narratives often create a deeper connection with the student.

Embodiment and Presence

When the virtual environment matches the lesson's goals, students report a feeling of presence, as if they are *really there*. We have found that the environment does not need to represent the real world, just allude to it. Participant surveys for the DEW Concept Model report that VR users feel as if they left their home or the classroom, experiencing sensations of heat, cold, apprehension, fear, joy, etc. in direct relationship to the immersive environment. During recent extreme heat waves, VR users in DEW research worlds reported feeling cooler when visiting snow and ice worlds and body temperatures rising when sitting in a hot jacuzzi (Yeom et al., 2019) (see Fig. 5). The greater the engagement with the virtual environment—especially the ability to move oneself, move objects, and to investigate—the more immersed and real students tend to find the experience: making it an adventure (Yamada-Rice, 2021).

Role-Playing

Instead of remaining spectators, students may become the actors and sometimes the directors in the story, leading the learning experience through role-playing (Cather, 1918). In *Designing Wonder*, Krause (2020) found that VR allows users to become

Fig. 5 "Winter Jacuzzi" in AltspaceVR (VanFossen, 2019b).

Fig. 6 Role-playing in the "Naboombu Sport Café" (SmartieMartie83, 2019)

the heroes, to feel both immensity and insignificance at once, essential characteristics of wonder in the DEW model. Often aided by avatar enhancements such as wings, hats, and costumes, students transform themselves into an integral part of the virtual narrative. In a coffee house in AltspaceVR, someone will naturally step behind the counter to sell coffee and cakes (Fig. 6). In a world of spies and mystery, a retina scanner had instructions to scan people's eyes before entering the security door, causing people to pause to scan their eyes before entering the room, becoming immediately immersed into the West World adventure worlds (Gust, 2021).

Inspired Curiosity

The elements of discovery and exploration inspire curiosity, creating a call-to-action response and eagerness to learn more. The information in the world does not have to answer everything about the subject; however, it should help the student feel a compelling need to know more. Students exploring the International Space Station (ISS) in AltspaceVR report a greater interest in the station. With news of the ISS disintegrating in the atmosphere after 2028 (Heilweil, 2021), students and teachers are using the ISS virtual experiences as a memorial to study the history of space exploration and research. Students visiting the *Food Waste* world by Gibson-Hylands (2020a) report that they researched and changed their food consumption and handling habits after visiting the world, realizing that small personal steps in food waste management contribute to the whole.

Emotional Response

Expressions of wonder and awe are often heard as students surge into a virtual world eager to learn and explore more. Students' emotional responses may improve their sense of connectedness to the experience, allowing them to become deeply immersed, sometimes achieving a state of self-transcendence (Chirico et al., 2016; Chirico & Yaden, 2018; Yamada-Rice, 2021). Through our research on the DEW model, we observed participants exploring the COVID-19/ACE2 recreation of the virus, complete with interactive elements and up-to-date statistics and information (Fig. 7). Participants reported feeling calmer and less anxious about the pandemic as the experience put the phenomenon into a playful and adventurous context (Laurenanti, 2020). Not every virtual educational experience is this intense; however, the eagerness to return and repeat the experience is a positive sign. Research into creativity and happiness finds that our instinct for entropy, relaxing and conserving energy, competes with our brain's programming for creativity, which Csikszentmihalyi (1997) describes as "an ability to enjoy almost anything we do, provided we can discover or design something new into the doing of it" (p. 9).

Fig. 7 Interactive "COVID-19/ACE2" models in AltspaceVR (Laurenanti, 2020)

Fig. 8 "Roller-Skating Party" with colourful hula-hoops in AltspaceVR

Shared Experiences

The DEW Concept Model relies heavily on the idea that virtual experience is shared, with student and teacher discussions increasing the student's understanding and improving their retention through repetition (Chirico & Yaden, 2018). We found that multi-player educational experiences allowing the students to help each other learn how to navigate and interact with the environment, also improved prosocial skills and altruism (Allen, 2018). Students reported they had more fun when they stepped into the teaching role, such as helping fellow students put roller skates and hula-hoops on their avatars for a fun roller-skating party (Fig. 8). Through the process of aiding others and telling stories of their adventures in VR, the students translate their experience, reinforcing the scaffolding process.

Familiarity

DEW research has found that when the narrative taps into the known or familiar, primarily through empathy, and builds from there, students engage faster and adapt more quickly to different viewpoints on a subject (Firth, 2015; Maier et al., 2017). Presenting a familiar story in an unfamiliar way often promotes greater interest in the story, such as found in the numerous derivations of fairy tales in modern novels and movies.

By better understanding the functionality behind wonder-responses in the discovery and exploration process of teaching in VR, we hope to clarify these characteristics for educational worlds to help teachers, students, and world builders make wiser choices about design and layout. In our early studies, we found that the use of virtual worlds aligning with the DEW Concept Model resulted in students making strong connections to the subject matter and led to understanding a diverse range of perspectives on a subject, with improved knowledge recall. The following section covers educational virtual world scenarios that represent implementing the DEW Concept Model for the process of selecting educational world models.

DEW World Models

The DEW Concept Model process begins with the educator selecting the virtual world's base layout and structure, called the *world model*, that reflects their teaching style or need. Next, they apply the above characteristics to help them select or build their teaching world. Since 2018, we have explored a wide variety of educational virtual world layouts supported by different pedagogies to support the DEW Concept Model. We have narrowed the list to eight core virtual world models that are the building blocks for educators and students to apply the DEW model characteristics of embodiment, role-playing, curiosity, emotional response, shared experience, and familiarity. These characteristics expand an ordinary educational experience into one based on discovery, exploration, and wonder. We tested each of these world formats extensively, teaching various classes and workshops as part of the research. Each world format offers a distinctive method of presenting educational information and may be used in combination with each other, offering educators various options.

- **Static presentation worlds**, often referred to as *event or lecture worlds*, present content in a traditional form with slides, videos, or lectures delivered in familiar teaching spaces such as classrooms, theatres, or auditoriums, with a clearly defined audience and presentation areas.
- **Progressive learning worlds** offer a step-by-step learning process, taking students through a chronological or logical sequence to aid in understanding complex topics such as sentence structure or mathematical equations.
- **Demonstration worlds** present a framework that allows the student access to the demonstration of a machine, simulation, or model to study, observe how it works, and understand its operation. In VR, the student can walk into a machine engine while it is running or travel through an assembly line.
- **Discussion or meetup worlds** are usually designed for small group discussion and often feature one or more *storytelling circles* such as campfires, rock circles, or tables.
- **Walking tours** are guided or self-guided tours through worlds of galleries, museums, theatres, and buildings or nature areas. These tours feature educational materials like posters or pictures that allow the user to physically move through a visual learning process (Fig. 9).
- **Complementary worlds** augment the subject matter visually and contextually to enhance the immersive experience. Examples are discussions on astronomy held in outer space and mythology's impact on culture surrounded by recognizable mythological creatures.

Fig. 9 Walking tour featuring "World Building Tips and Diagnostics" (VanFossen, 2019c)

Fig. 10 Workshop in the "World Building Tips and Techniques Hub" (VanFossen et al., 2019)

- **Simulation worlds** offer experiential lessons or training simulations often used in emergency services, medical training, job training, and flight simulators. In VR, simulations can be used to walk through history, science labs, math problems, and more. Students can fly an airplane or walk through a historical landmark in its heyday.
- **Hub worlds** act as a directory, a centralized location that transports students to related worlds, allowing the class to explore individually or in sequence. Hub worlds can act as a storyline, expanding the lessons into something resembling book chapters or sequels. Students collaborating through world building may create a hub to highlight topical worlds or link them to their virtual worlds as homework. An example is the *World Building Tips & Techniques Hub* (Fig. 10) with themed designs around the teleporters to tutorial worlds.

DEW World Model Scenarios

We continue to explore the DEW Concept Model affordances for world building and have found that many of these basic world models often combined formats to enhance the learning experience. Using the eight world models, we apply the characteristics of the DEW model for various educational scenarios.

Fig. 11 "Messages in the Mist" (Sammich, 2019)

Complementary World Model

An example of a simple and elegant complementary world model, *Messages in the Mist*, was created by Kawaii Sammich (2019) (Fig. 11). The AltspaceVR world is filled with quotes in text form in an all-black skybox saturated with rain and fog that complements the thoughtful intention of the messages. This simple and easy-to-build world hosts frequently changing narratives. In 2021, the world presented quotations and comments from the AltspaceVR community about their feelings of loneliness and need for social connections during the pandemic. Change the quotes to those associated with happiness, switch the weather to sunshine and blue skies, and the lesson would be instantly different.

Complementary worlds situate students deeply into the experience, which is essential to the characteristics of the DEW model. The environment feels embodied, so participants feel they are wandering through the fog searching for words of insight. If the words are theirs, students report a sense of ownership in the experience. Even if the words are not theirs, they still report an emotional connection with the words and their unknown author. A student highlighted one phrase and said, "I feel like they know me, the real me, and how I feel. I feel like I've found a friend I haven't met yet."

Simulation and Demonstration World Models

A science curriculum exploring astronomy is enhanced by virtual walks through space exploring planets, the sun, and star systems across the universe. For example, *Andy's ISS Space Walk* (Fig. 12) is a mix of simulation and demonstration world

Fig. 12 "International Space Station" (Andy, 2021)

models that allow students to float untethered around the International Space Station, replicated in extraordinary detail. Students experience a realistic experience spacewalking in bulky spacesuits, complete with the impaired view through the helmet. A teleporter relocates the students inside the Space Station, allowing them to crawl around, explore the various compartments, and float without gravity.

The wonder begins the moment when students enter the world and realize they are dressed in the bulky spacesuit and floating over the earth. Their attention is then drawn to the planet below, where many report experiencing the *overview effect* experienced by astronauts (Overview, 2022). Slowly, a few students look up and exclaim at seeing the space station overhead. Encouraging others to join them, the students fly around the station. Younger students quickly slip into role-playing as astronauts, manoeuvring in space, repairing the station, or climbing around inside, often collaborating on a space adventure story. Our surveys find participants expressing their wonder and delight with the experience, and their eagerness to share the story of their adventures months after experiencing them. Additionally, they revisited it often and brought friends and family to enjoy the experience.

Demonstration and Complementary World Models

Instead of teaching through cultural and historical stories, an option is to encourage students to research and share their own stories from their current or indigenous culture and family history, expanding the potential for inclusive learning and

Fig. 13 "First Nations Tepee Camp" (Stands With Trees, 2021)

Fig. 14 Students study the "Space Hurricane" over the ionosphere of Earth (Gill, 2021)

empathy. The *First Nations Tepee Camp* (Stands With Trees, 2021) is used for teaching diversity and inclusion workshops as well as for storytelling focused on heritage (Fig. 13). The tepees and the campfire among snowy mountains demonstrate an ancient Indigenous village in North America and also complement the storytelling experience. Virtual worlds providing demonstrations and designs that complement the stories enhance the experience more dramatically than traditional show-and-tell experiences. When students design their storytelling backdrop, the process reinforces their learning experiences due to the research, problem-solving, and collaborative nature of world building.

Complementary, Simulation, and Demonstration World Model

In April 2021, Chinese researchers identified a space hurricane over Earth's polar ionosphere (Zhang et al., 2021). This inspired Professor Mark Gill of St. Cloud State University, Minnesota, to create in AltspaceVR an orbital platform hovering over Earth above the space hurricane, thereby representing the invisible space weather phenomenon (Fig. 14). Students were filled with wonder and curiosity as they explored the central exhibit area featuring a 3D visual spatial recording explaining a space hurricane and how it is formed, then moved to a platform overlooking the spinning planet below the graphic simulation of the space hurricane above. The world does not explain all the science. Still, it creates wonder and intrigue and encourages deeper discussions. Mixing complementary, simulation, and demonstration world models in line with the DEW Concept Model builds multiple scaffolds of learning through the experience, and enhances learning modalities.

Fig. 15 "Forces of Aerodynamics" (Korff, 2021)

Simulation, Demonstration, and Progressive Learning World Models

Traditionally, aerodynamics is demonstrated in a classroom with textbooks and videos animated with arrows indicating wind patterns. In *Forces of Aerodynamics*, Richard Korff (2021) demonstrates lift and thrust to teach piloting and aerospace engineering classes by providing wand-shaped objects students can hold to direct the red arrows flowing from each wand, indicating the flow of the wind moving across the body of the plane (Fig. 15). The interactivity is a form of role-playing as the students *become the wind*, fascinated with its reactions as they move the wind over the airplane's surface. Korff (2021) found that students improved their understanding of aerodynamic mechanics. Inspired by their own curiosity, they also tested collaborative experiments with the interactive wind wands, exploring aerodynamics in ways rarely taught in traditional contexts. The teacher reported that his students showed greater interest and began to develop a variety of narratives to test their newly developed hypotheses on aerodynamics.

Progressive Learning and Discussion World Models

The *Food Waste* world by Gibson-Hylands (2020a) uses a compelling educational narrative to tap into students' lifestyles and change their hearts and minds in the process. Students begin their journey exploring the wastefulness of Western world

Fig. 16 The "Food Waste" world offers powerful conversation visuals (Gibson-Hylands, 2020a)

culture caused by over-buying and poor food management taking a different perspective, from farm to table to trash. The educational world ends with a discussion area with information on potential solutions and lifestyle changes. Throughout the educational world are powerful tableaus, scenes set against a backdrop that reinforces the lesson. For example, in a kitchen scene for a typical American meal of fast food, the fridge and food cupboards in the background frame the next part of the lesson, and the destination of the displayed food items in the landfill site is visible in the distance (Fig. 16). Each design element conveys a powerful message about the consequences of food waste and excess in the Western diet.

Carefully crafted by Gibson-Hylands (2020a), the *Food Waste* world serves as a training world for the authors as they research the DEW model. Each step inspires discussions by combining step-by-step progression, beginning with where food comes from, through the dining table and kitchen, to the landfill, to a home demonstrating composting. Those with gardening experience at home will jump in to share their experiences, personalizing the lesson, often evoking reactions of wonder from other students: "You grow your own food?" At the familiar dining table scene, many students role-play eating pizza and making slurping sounds as they pretend to drink from the sodas and milkshakes. Passing through the landfill, students begin to question the choices they and their families make, leading to discussions on problem-solving the ever-growing crisis of waste and pollution facing global communities. Recycling and composting are part of the solution, but the virtual world teaches that the process starts with the choices we make before making our food purchase decisions—telling the story in a new way.

Fig. 17 "Plastic Mountain" reveals a burning mountain of garbage (Gibson-Hylands, 2020b)

Static Presentation, Simulation, and Discussion World Models

As part of an ongoing series on global waste, Gibson-Hylands created *Plastic Mountain* (2020b)—an example of a static presentation, simulation, and discussion world model—to convey the impact of global waste on worlds far from where the rubbish was generated. As students enter the simulation, they arrive in a small building representing a static presentation, with wall posters providing key facts on the practice of Western countries shipping their garbage to other countries and the harm these landfills cause to the people and their land. The information prepares them for the experience outside the doors of the building, the simulation model for the lesson. As students exit the building, they find a beautiful Malaysian village slowly being destroyed by plastic waste from other countries (Fig. 17). Each element within the world's design plays a key role in the narrative to enhance the student learning experience with thought-provoking discussion points. The focal point of the world is a mountain of burning plastic draining chemicals and toxins into a river and killing the ecosystem on its deadly journey to the ocean, allowing students to see a direct connection and consequences of the pollution. The skybox adds a polluted yellow atmospheric haze representing the pungent toxic fumes from the burning plastic waste.

Experiencing the impact of global waste in VR emphasizes the imperatives of the situation and the desperate need for solutions, stimulating conversation very different from the classroom experience. Discussions covering pollution, excess lifestyles, recycling, culture, climate change, economies, and international politics reflect the student's emotional response combined with a natural curiosity inspired

Fig. 18 "Flooded House" features a community in the middle of a flood (Vodloc, 2019)

by the scene. As another test world for the DEW model, our surveys have found that the experience stays with the students for a long time. Students report that their interactions with the world increased their awareness of recycling options and making purchasing decisions with greener product choices in mind, for themselves and others.

Combination of World Models

The Flooded House (Vodloc, 2019) is an example of a world that hosts diverse story lessons through powerful narrative and mixed world models. The virtual world offers a learning experience challenging to reproduce in the real world. Students arrive in a typical two-story modern home in a suburban cul-de-sac to find themselves in water up to the chest of the avatar (Fig. 18). Outside, there are cars, toys, furniture, and garbage floating around them while overhead, a helicopter hovers with a rescue crew. The role-playing response is immediate as some students instinctively make their way to the roof of the house and some climb on the floating cars. Others begin playing the victims or rescue teams, while some gather to begin problem-solving, each role adding to the narrative and experience of the students. This world has been used in many lesson plans, users being inspired by the opportunity to host diverse discussion topics such as community water and sewer management, community infrastructure and prevention planning, emergency

Fig. 19 "Ancient Athens Agora" marketplace, social hub of the Greek Empire (Liberopoulou, 2020)

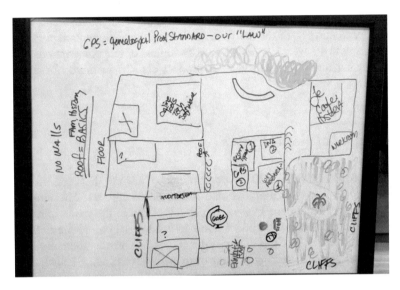

Fig. 20 Example of a virtual world plan on a whiteboard

management and responses, climate change, crisis management, and problem-solving scenarios.

As authors of the DEW Concept Model, we continue to explore virtual world models and how their characteristics may be applied to educational VR worlds. Our goal is to better understand how to break through the rigid structure of traditional classroom experiences and develop virtual educational spaces for discovery, exploration, and wonder.

World Building for Homework and School Projects

We developed the DEW Concept Model to encourage teachers to select educational worlds in VR wisely or to build their own. We found that encouraging students to design worlds in collaboration with the teacher or as homework expanded the DEW framework even further, turning discovery, exploration, and wonder into teaching-by-doing collaborative experiences.

Homeschooling programs traditionally include visits to local museums, parks, and historical sites. During the pandemic, we worked with a private homeschool program to help students create historical virtual worlds as history lessons in VR. Inspired by Liberopoulou's (2020) *Ancient Athens* collection of worlds in AltspaceVR (Fig. 19), the student project worlds had to use discovery, exploration, and wonder to encourage embodiment, role-playing, curiosity, emotional response, shared experience, and familiarity. The high school students created a hub world in AltspaceVR representing a room in a museum related to their history assignment.

They wrote up a research plan that included a sketch of their proposed world and checklist of the DEW model characteristics, and a set of guidelines limiting their choices on what they could use to build their worlds. Students were to collaborate and help each other and create the hub world. Their final project was a tour and presentation of each world representing their history museum.

This type of homework project in VR is in line with the ISTE guidelines (ISTE, n.d.) and Bloom's revised taxonomy emphasizing digital citizenship (2001). Virtual world building shows that it improves math and spatial geometry skills and develops broader competencies such as planning, research, and project management (Roman & Racek, 2019). When world building is collaborative, it teaches students to work together to create situations with a blueprint plan in hand (Fig. 20), then stretch their imagination to problem-solve the development challenges. Students learn how to follow instructions, ask for guidance when needed, and critically question concepts, thereby learning the adaptive project management principles of Agile and SCRUM instinctively as they embrace the criteria characteristics of the DEW model (Galloway, 2012; Maruping et al., 2009; Van Petegem, 2021).

Students thrive in an environment where curiosity encourages imagination, creativity, and risk-taking. The Creative, Cognitive, Qualitative model for creativity (CCQ Tool) is an example of learning with a focus on the internal mechanisms of creativity naturally arising from virtual world building (Smyrnaiou et al., 2020). In our continuing research, we find that when students take charge of the world building experience by including the DEW model characteristics supported by the CCQ Tool to create their homework worlds with a sense of immersive presence, role-playing, and curiosity, their emotional response creates a sense of shared experience and familiarity through discovery, exploration, and wonder. Overall, the students feel empowered, with a greater connection to and ownership of the lesson. They are better able to add their storytelling narrative, transforming homework projects into "personal values into stories ... and influenced by social, cultural, and ethnographic characteristics" (Smyrnaiou et al., 2020, p. 19).

Strategies for Implementation of Design Using the DEW Concept Model

We recommend the following strategies for integrating world building assignments across the curriculum, aligned with the DEW Concept Model:

- **Create a data-driven storyline**. Creating a data-driven storyline in virtual worlds naturally incorporates collaboration, teamwork, project management, leadership, and creative problem-solving.
- **Collaborate on the narrative.** Collaborating in highly visual virtual environments and focusing on the narrative to convey ideas through experiential storytelling promotes improved understanding of the topic and increased retention.

- **Facilitate critical feedback.** Generating ideas and perspectives with immersive environments increases critical feedback, especially when including emotional and experiential activities.
- **Cultivate curiosity.** World building cultivates curiosity through discovery complemented with the physical response rewards associated with exploration and wonder. To create the virtual worlds, students need to know more. As they know more about the subject, they want to learn more.
- **Foster accomplishment and achievement.** Tapping into a vast range of skill-building techniques improves students' sense of accomplishment, self-confidence, and self-efficacy, especially combined with the pride students feel when they are eager to show off their worlds to others and share their experiences.

Conclusion

As teachers and authors of this chapter, we strive to find better ways to translate material into tangible, relevant, and engaging learning experiences by mixing and matching the characteristic ingredients to apply to the eight world models. We help educators and students select or create educational worlds that are interactive, immersive, and experiential, that tap into wonder and awe to increase engagement, and that challenge traditional teaching methods often filled with dull facts and statistics. Our goal is to go further in our research to identify how to develop virtual educational experiences that change hearts and minds to truly define a quality educational virtual world.

VR offers a transcendental teaching experience that involves storytelling and play to deliver facts and data through story, taking the student on a learning adventure. In this chapter, we explored the world models that serve as the building blocks, to which educators and world builders may add embodiment, role-playing, curiosity, emotional responses, collaboration, and familiarity grown naturally out of discovery, exploration, and wonder, ingredients that bring educational virtual worlds to life. We are continuing our experiments aimed at developing a teaching toolkit to help educators select and build educational worlds and encourage students to use virtual world building as homework, especially as collaborative experiences.

We invite educators and students to integrate virtual worlds into their pedagogy using free immersive platforms such as *AltspaceVR, Mozilla Hubs*, and *Frame VR*. Our DEW (Discovery, Exploration, Wonder) Concept Model is a starting foundation for learning how to facilitate teaching in VR, filling virtual worlds with storytelling techniques and the right ingredients to take learners on an adventure of change and influence. VR can educate on diverse topics, from simple grammar lessons to computer science, history, and beyond. It can positively affect our world by immersing participants in the consequences of human history, greed, pollution, and war. By showing students a topic in a way they have never seen before, complemented by the adventures made possible by discovery, exploration, and wonder, VR is disrupting education with innovative immersive learning experiences and environments.

References

Acar, A. & Cavas, B. (2020). The effect of virtual reality enhanced learning environment on the 7th-grade students' reading and writing skills in English. *Malaysian Online Journal of Educational Sciences, 8*(4), 22–33. https://mojes.um.edu.my/article/view/26395

Allen, S. (2018). The science of awe. *John Templeton Foundation.* https://ggsc.berkeley.edu/images/uploads/GGSC-JTF_White_Paper-Awe_FINAL.pdf

Andy [djvivid, Avatar Username]. (2021). Andy's ISS Space Walk. *AltspaceVR.* https://account.altvr.com/worlds/1252273247668404326/spaces/1632256964002054419

Bloom, B. S. (2001). *Taxonomy of educational objectives, handbook 1: Cognitive domain* (2nd ed.). Addison-Wesley Longman Ltd.. (Original work published 1956).

Boris, V. (2017, December 20). What makes storytelling so effective for learning? *Leading the Way.* Harvard Business Publishing. https://www.harvardbusiness.org/what-makes-storytelling-so- effective-for-learning/.

Bruner, J. (1983). Play, thought, and language. *Peabody Journal of Education, 60*(3), 60–69. https://doi.org/10.1080/01619568309538407

Cather, K. D. (1918) Educating by story-telling; showing the value of story-telling as an educational tool for the use of all workers with children. *World Book Company.* Retrieved from the Library of Congress, https://www.loc.gov/item/18017423/

Chirico, A. & Yaden, D. (2018). Awe: A self-transcendent and sometimes transformative emotion. In H. C. Lench (Ed.), *The function of emotions: When and why emotions help us* (pp. 221–233). Springer. https://doi.org/10.1007/978-3-319-77619-4_11

Chirico, A., Yaden, D. B., Riva, G. & Gaggioli, A. (2016). The potential of virtual reality for the investigation of awe. *Frontiers in Psychology, 7,* 221–233. https://doi.org/10.3389/fpsyg.2016.01766

Cho, B.-H., Ku, J., Pyojang, D., Kim, S., Lee, Y. H., Kim, I. Y., Lee, J. H. & Kim, S. I. (2002). The effect of virtual reality cognitive training for attention enhancement. *Cyberpsychology & Behavior, 5*(2), 129–137. https://doi.org/10.1089/109493102753770516

Csikszentmihalyi, M. (1997, October). Happiness and creativity: Going with the flow. *The Futurist, 31*(5), S8–S12.

Firth, P. (2015, July 16). Wired for empathy: Why we can't resist good narrative. *Firesteel.* http://firesteelwa.org/2015/07/wired-for-empathy-why-we-cant-resist-good-narrative-2/

Fleming, D. (2013). An educational leadership perspective: Managing and revealing the DNA of wonder in teaching and learning. In K. Egan, A. I. Cant, & G. Judson (Eds.), *Wonder-full education* (pp. 178–189). Routledge.

Galloway, P. (2012). Playpens for mind children: Continuities in the practice of programming. *Information & Culture: A Journal of History, 47*(1), 38–78. https://doi.org/10.1353/lac.2012.0006

Gargiulo, T. L. (2006). Power of stories. *The Journal for Quality and Participation, 29*(1), 4–8.

Gibson-Hylands, K. (2019). The Ocean. *AltspaceVR.* https://account.altvr.com/worlds/111040940543154666/spaces/1199136371516638093

Gibson-Hylands, K. (2020a). Food Waste. *AltspaceVR.* https://account.altvr.com/worlds/111040940543154666/spaces/1437234598701432973

Gibson-Hylands, K. (2020b). Plastic Mountain. *AltspaceVR.* https://account.altvr.com/worlds/111040940543154666/spaces/1255057002795630764

Gill, M. (2021). Space Hurricane. *AltspaceVR.* https://account.altvr.com/worlds/1721842406464160506/spaces/1721856039940260830

Gust, D. [VRDarrenG, Avatar Username]. (2021). West World. *AltspaceVR.* https://account.altvr.com/worlds/1504097368616730662/spaces/1780238772152042377

Heilweil, R. (2021, December 25). The space station race. *Vox.* https://www.vox.com/recode/22839485/space-station-iss-orbit-satellites

Huang, H.-M. & Liaw, S.-S. (2018). An analysis of learners' intentions toward virtual reality learning based on constructivist and technology acceptance approaches. *International Review of Research in Open and Distributed Learning, 19*(1), 91–115. https://doi.org/10.19173/irrodl.v19i1.2503

Hung, C.-M., Hwang, G.-J. & Huang, I. (2012). A project-based digital storytelling approach for improving students' learning motivation, problem-solving competence and learning achievement. *Journal of Educational Technology & Society, 15*(4), 368–379.

Immersive virtual reality. (2008). In B. Furht (Ed.), *Encyclopedia of multimedia* (pp. 345–346). Springer. https://doi.org/10.1007/978-0-387-78414-4_85

ISTE. (n.d.). *International Society for Technology in Education (ISTE) standards for students.* https://www.iste.org/standards/iste-standards-for-students

Korff, R. (2021). Forces of Aerodynamics. *AltspaceVR.* https://account.altvr.com/worlds/1672091550936465431/spaces/1676109105606951480

Krause, C. (2020). *Designing wonder: Leading transformative experiences in virtual reality* (Kindle). https://caitlinkrause.com/mindfulbydesign/

Laurenanti, J. (2020). Covid19/ACE2. *AltspaceVR.* https://account.altvr.com/worlds/1355452616871510998/spaces/1442927460000727719

Lepp, G. (1995). *George Lepp imaging and nature photography workshops.* Wildlife Photography Workshop, Olympic National Park, Washington.

Liberopoulou, L. (2020). Ancient Athens Agora. *AltspaceVR.* https://account.altvr.com/worlds/1470947035065614383/spaces/1470952585497150056

Maier, S. R., Slovic, P. & Mayorga, M. (2017). Reader reaction to news of mass suffering: Assessing the influence of story form and emotional response. *Journalism, 18*(8), 1011–1029. https://doi.org/10.1177/1464884916663597

SmartieMartie83, S. [Luscious_Lynn, Avatar Username]. (2019). Naboombu sport cafe. *AltspaceVR.* https://account.altvr.com/worlds/1085981172908950287/spaces/1160960835086975068

Maruping, L. M., Venkatesh, V. & Agarwal, R. (2009). A control theory perspective on agile methodology use and changing user requirements. *Information System Research, 20*(3), 377–399. https://www.jstor.org/stable/23015471

Oppenheimer, F. (1982, June 21). Exploration and discovery: Acceptance speech for the AAM distinguished service award. *Exploratorium.* https://www.exploratorium.edu/files/frank/exploration_discovery/exploration_discovery.pdf

Overview effect. (2022, May 25). In *Wikipedia.* https://en.wikipedia.org/w/index.php?title=Overview_effect&oldid=1089748779

Roman, T. A. & Racek, J. (2019). Virtual reality as a pedagogical tool to design for social impact: A design case. *TechTrends, 63*(1), 79–86. https://doi.org/10.1007/s11528-018-0360-z

Sammich, K. [Yunji, Avatar Username]. (2019). Messages in the Mist. *AltspaceVR.* https://account.altvr.com/worlds/1004132374591570815/spaces/1004132375094887297

Smyrnaiou, Z., Georgakopoulou, E. & Sotiriou, S. (2020). Promoting a mixed-design model of scientific creativity through digital storytelling—The CCQ model for creativity. *International Journal of STEM Education, 7*(1), 25. https://doi.org/10.1186/s40594-020-00223-6

Stands With Trees. (2021). *First Nations Diversity.* Educators in VR Private Event World.

Sun, H.-M. & Cheng, W.-L. (2009). The input-interface of webcam applied in 3D virtual reality systems. *Computers & Education, 53*(4), 1231–1240. https://doi.org/10.1016/j.compedu.2009.06.006

Tim [timfarm1, Avatar Username]. (2020). D-Day. *AltspaceVR.* https://account.altvr.com/worlds/1406192320948207713/spaces/1488709513853796709

Van Petegem, W. (2021). The future digital scholar. In W. Van Petegeme, J. P. Bosman, M. De Klerk, & S. Strydon (Eds.), *Evolving as a digital scholar: Teaching and research in a digital world* (pp. 159–174). Leuven University Press. https://doi.org/10.2307/j.ctv20zbkk0.12

VanFossen, L. (2019a). The Last of the Glaciers. *AltspaceVR.* https://account.altvr.com/worlds/1085593780330955061/spaces/1184218728842134150

VanFossen, L. (2019b). Winter Jacuzzi. *AltspaceVR*. https://account.altvr.com/worlds/1004233404394242649/spaces/1471104759443226759

VanFossen, L. (2019c). World Building Tips: Diagnostics. *AltspaceVR*. https://account.altvr.com/worlds/1141587974610223946/spaces/1503185773795475905

VanFossen, L., Gibson-Hylands, K. & Dimond, M. (2019). World Building Tips and Techniques Hub. *AltspaceVR*. https://account.altvr.com/worlds/1141587974610223946/spaces/1476995568956867487

Vodloc, M. (2019). Flooded House. *AltspaceVR*. https://account.altvr.com/worlds/1205461343847579984/spaces/1237246223853813931

Watts, J. & Kommenda, N. (2021, April 28). Speed at which world's glaciers are melting has doubled in 20 years. *The Guardian*. https://www.theguardian.com/environment/2021/apr/28/speed-at-which-worlds-glaciers-are-melting-has-doubled-in-20-years

Wood, C. (2022, January 13). How to tell an effective data story: Tips from Nancy Duarte. *MarTech*. https://martech.org/how-to-tell-stories-using-data/

Yamanda-Rice, D. (2021). Children's interactive storytelling in virtual reality. *Multimodality & Society, 1*(1), 48–67. https://doi.org/10.1177/2634979521992965

Yeom, D., Choi, J.-H. & Kang, S.-H. (2019). Investigation of the physiological differences in the immersive virtual reality environment and real indoor environment: Focused on skin temperature and thermal sensation. *Building and Environment, 154*, 44–54. https://doi.org/10.1016/j.buildenv.2019.03.013

Yildirim, G., Yildirim, S. & Dolgunsoz, E. (2019). The effect of VR and traditional videos on learner retention and decision making. *World Journal on Educational Technology: Current Issues, 11*(1), 21–29. https://doi.org/10.18844/wjet.v11i1.4005

Yip, B. C. B. & Man, D. W. K. (2013). Virtual reality-based prospective memory training program for people with acquired brain injury. *NeuroRehabilitation, 32*(1), 103–115. https://doi.org/10.3233/NRE-130827

Zhang, Q.-H., Zhang, Y.-L., Wang, C., Oksavik, K., Lyons, L. R., Lockwood, M., Yang, H.-G., Tang, B.-B., Moen, J. I., Xing, Z.-Y., Ma, Y.-Z., Wang, X.-Y., Ning, Y.-F. & Xia, L.-D. (2021). A space hurricane over the Earth's polar ionosphere. *Nature Communications, 12*(1), 1207. https://doi.org/10.1038/s41467-021-21459-y

Lorelle VanFossen is a long-time educator in digital technology and Director of Educators in VR, a membership organization dedicated to integrating immersive technology into education, business, training, research, and more. VanFossen teaches a variety of VR event production and world building workshops and has built over 100 virtual educational worlds.

Karen Gibson-Hylands has over 25 years' senior management experience in quality assurance and service improvement. Working from home in a remote area of the Scottish Highlands, Gibson-Hylands spends her spare time moderating educational events and building virtual worlds on the immersive social platform *AltspaceVR*. She is also learning Scottish Gaelic.

A Classroom Model for Virtual Reality Integration and Unlocking Student Creativity

David Kaser

Abstract Recent studies have shown immersive technology has a positive impact on learning. However, implementation and oversight remain major obstacles for school districts. This chapter explores a practical model for implementing virtual reality technology in a high school setting and shows how student contribution promotes a positive learning environment.

Keywords Collaboration · Facilitator · Near-peer classroom · Peer assisted learning · Student-led · Student ownership · Virtual reality implementation

Introduction

Sticker shock, educational value, and equipment management. Those three issues cause K–12 school districts with limited resources to hesitate about purchasing virtual reality (VR) equipment, and understandably so. While the release of stand-alone headsets such as the Quest 2 have increased affordability, it is easy to understand why many tech departments would be quick to dismiss the idea. Their budgets are already limited with the rollout of one-to-one initiatives, ongoing replacement cycles, and rising content subscription costs. Besides, isn't VR just for games anyway? In the high-stakes testing world that defines education, administrators and technology coordinators are quick to question the classroom value of immersive technologies (Metcalf et al., 2013), particularly in the face of rising costs. However, an increasing amount of research suggests immersive technologies can be effective and affordable when compared to non-immersive approaches (Wu et al., 2020).

D. Kaser (✉)
Barberton City School District, Wadsworth, OH, USA
e-mail: dkaser@barbertonschools.org

© The Author(s), under exclusive license to Springer Nature Switzerland AG 2022
P. MacDowell, J. Lock (eds.), *Immersive Education*,
https://doi.org/10.1007/978-3-031-18138-2_15

In this chapter, I examine how a suburban Ohio high school designed a course to teach and train students as VR experts. The new course consisted of 15–20 students with academic abilities ranging from normal to gifted. The course addressed concerns of both administrators and technology coordinators regarding implementation and equipment oversight, while providing a valuable outlet for student creativity and leadership. First, I lay out how a near-peer classroom model can have a positive effect on both the VR expert and the learner. Second, I describe how the core student group is empowered through responsibility and oversight, fostering a sense of ownership that in turn leads to increased classroom engagement. Lastly, I look at how instructional methods are improved by tapping into immersive technology and student creativity. In doing so, students are involved in the design process from beginning to end, making the activities personal. The chapter challenges us to reconsider traditional classroom roles by making students partners in the educational process and turning teachers into facilitators. If done successfully, this process creates school-wide access to the world of VR by placing the responsibility of training on a group of students, rather than on staff.

Vignette

As class was winding down one early winter day, one of David's students approached him with a suggestion, "We should get VR equipment for the STEM room." It was an absurd request on the surface. Could an emerging technology, stereotyped as a gaming device, really be used as an educational tool? David's initial reaction softened as possibilities were explored. It sparked conversations over the next several months—conversations that were student led, prompting research and brainstorming sessions. They resulted in the design of a student-driven high school course where the students became the teachers, and in many instances, the teachers became the students. Student expertise became the creative driving force. David's students designed lessons for core classes and assisted peers, teaching them to use VR technology while experiencing content. All David had to do was relinquish classroom control and become the guide rather than the source of knowledge.

The Argument for Using a Near-Peer Model

An ancient Japanese proverb says, "To teach is to learn." Over time, *near-peer* has been known by several different names: peer-assisted learning (PAL), team-based learning, peer tutoring, education through student interaction (ETSI), and peer mentoring (Evans & Cuffe, 2009; Lockspeiser et al., 2006; Ten Cate & Durning, 2007a, b). Through all the re-labelling, there exists a common theme; a student with more knowledge is put in a position alongside another to teach, assist, and help them gain understanding. For the sake of clarity, for the remainder of this chap. I use the terms teacher, near-peer tutor (NPT), and near-peer learner (NPL) to refer to the participants.

On the surface, it seems this model benefits the near-peer learner, but research shows both parties benefit in a near-peer setting. NPLs find NPTs more approachable and relatable than older instructors (Velez et al., 2011; Williams & Fowler, 2014), creating a more relaxed atmosphere where an NPL is more apt to admit they need assistance in clearing up misconceptions (McLelland et al., 2013; Ten Cate & Durning, 2007a, b; Topping, 2005). This relaxed relationship and understanding of learning difficulties between the two appear to exist because of more recent experience with the subject matter (Brueckner & MacPherson, 2004; Lockspeiser et al., 2006). Learners cited this cognitive congruence as a factor allowing NPTs to relay information at an appropriate level (Lockspeiser et al., 2006; Rashid et al., 2011; Ten Cate et al., 2012).

Research demonstrates that the near-peer model benefits the NPT by enhancing understanding, cultivating communication skills, and helping future career development (Evans & Cuffe, 2009; Williams & Fowler, 2014). Additionally, it offers them the chance to "learn twice" as teaching requires deeper learning of subject matter (Annis, 1983). Teaching a topic requires better cognitive organization to improve retrieval during instruction. Karpicke's (2012) research suggested that a group who studied content with the purpose of teaching retained 45 to 60% more information after one week than a group who studied it for the same amount of time without the expectation of teaching. Gregory et al.'s (2011) results support this finding and went one step farther by examining the knowledge gains of a group of medical students in a peer-teaching environment. The students were assigned two topics to teach. Then on instruction day, they were asked to teach only one of the topics. Peer tutors showed increased learning for both topics prepared, but they demonstrated more significant gains in the content they taught. When re-tested 60 days later, the learning gains were still present (Gregory et al., 2011).

When focusing on classroom climate in a near-peer setting, observations and survey responses from both groups perceived positive social interaction and a change in classroom dynamics. Class discussion increased and became more interactive. There was more laughing, smiling, and exchanging of ideas throughout the lesson than in a traditional setting. The improved climate encouraged a freer exchange of ideas. Research also shows that participants on both the teaching and learning sides appreciated the opportunity to make the material more creative. Near-peer learners remarked on how doing more hands-on work and applying what they had been learning makes it more interesting and engaging (Velez et al., 2011; Williams & Fowler, 2014).

There may be lasting benefits for NPTs as well. They develop an awareness of their individual learning styles through the planning and teaching process (Velez et al., 2011). A near-peer model also yields a deeper processing of information, which improves conceptual understanding. These two advantages combine to improve self-monitoring and comprehension when faced with new material in other areas (Benè & Bergus, 2014).

The most difficult aspect of incorporating a near-peer model lies with instructors since it requires us to relinquish control and take on the role of facilitator (Velez et al., 2011; Williams & Fowler, 2014). Most have been trained and taught in an educational setting where the instructor is the disseminator of information. But when the research surrounding near-peer instruction demonstrates increased knowledge gains for both parties, we need to be willing to embrace a more student-centred approach to teaching. Incorporating this student-centred model to unlock the potential of immersive technology reduces the need for schoolwide professional development while tapping into a valuable resource we all have sitting at desk: students.

Spencer (2019) proposes a shift from simply engaging students to empowering them. To do this, we as educators must recognize our job has shifted from being a fountain of knowledge to teaching students to think critically. Teachers should become facilitators within the classroom; they may shape the direction by asking leading, open-ended questions meant to guide thinking, but ultimately, they let students dictate the overall direction. When students share ideas or present findings, educators can offer perspectives that the students had not considered and ideas that perhaps come only with life experience or professional training. Yet educators must be willing to acknowledge and honour what students bring to the table. The facilitator mindset fits nicely with the near-peer model. Students still share their proficiency in a given subject with the gentle guidance from the instructor working in the background. This dynamic promotes student ownership of their education while giving them the autonomy to explore new ideas without the dark cloud of failure lurking overhead.

Student Empowerment from Conceptualization to Realization

In spring 2019, 18 high school students filed off a yellow school bus, backpacks over one shoulder and a laptop under the other arm. All were dressed in jeans and a plain black T-shirt. Three other students unloaded a wooden box, three large buckets of sand, and a desktop computer from the back of a minivan and onto a cart. The group made its way past the LeBron James Family Foundation logo painted on the sidewalk, toward the entrance of the I Promise School in Akron, Ohio. Inside the entrance, their eyes fixed on the walls bordering the spiral staircases, showcasing game shoes worn by James himself. But the group had to move on. They weren't there for a tour of the school; they were there to work. They made their way down the steps, walking past murals on the wall depicting James and other influential figures from history, into the *Think Tank*. There was a sense of excitement mixed with confidence as they transformed the large room into 15 VR stations: 15 spaces where each high school student would be paired with one fourth grader. Over the next two days, 110 fourth graders would be exposed for the first time to immersive technology and the worlds it opens.

The high school students had been preparing for these two days since the fall semester, learning how to use the equipment and troubleshoot problems that inevitably pop up from time to time. They had become adept at walking new users through the basics using effective verbal communication. Up until now, their knowledge had been refined with peers, community members, and adults at educational conferences. But for the next two days, their communication skills would be put to the test on a group of inner-city fourth-grade students.

How did those two days come about in the first place? We need to rewind our story back two years, when the idea of using high school students as near-peer teachers with immersive technology was initiated. Our plunge into the VR world began when an intelligent, yet quirky student asked me if we could purchase some VR headsets for our STEM classroom. Like anyone who thinks they understand how education views video games in the classroom, I immediately dismissed the idea. I cited my lack of knowledge, funding issues, and supposedly nonexistent educational value as the top reasons as to why VR could never work. But that one interaction set into motion a series of brainstorming sessions. Out of it came a course designed to not only use VR technology, but one that fashioned a space where students would create lessons using VR and assist classroom teachers in implementing it.

Any time a district decides to make a significant technology purchase, there must be a plan in place for equipment oversight and teacher training. Spend a little time talking to technology coordinators and educators, and you will hear stories of their districts investing significant amounts of money on technology and/or software, only to see it collect dust or end up damaged. There are many reasons: a lack of professional development, a convincing salesperson followed by poor customer support, compatibility issues, poor quality, etc. We were determined to avoid the same pitfalls. Incorporating immersive VR equipment is an easy step for those who are proficient at using technology but challenging for people who are unsure. We needed to guard against the outcome of broken equipment destined to live in locked cabinets.

The first priority of the course was equipment management and oversight. The initial investment was steep and demonstrated an act of trust by the Alcoa Corporation, our grant funder. We purchased 15 Oculus Rift VR headsets, 15 gaming laptops, and all the peripherals that went with them. Oversight included creating 15 online accounts for Oculus and STEAM, software updates, firmware updates, dealing with account issues, sanitization, repairs, software installation, and organization. All are aspects that would overwhelm a single teacher and put a time strain on their schedule. But by instilling the idea of ownership with a group of students, training them in the technology, and giving them responsibility for a single VR station, the task becomes manageable.

I witnessed student leadership emerging from the outset. Students are intelligent, unique, and many times have skill sets that quietly reside beneath the surface. Given the opportunity, they jump at the chance to showcase what they can do. I stepped back and let them do their thing. Some oversaw operating system and graphics-card updates, others handled equipment repairs, a few solved sound issues, and others made sure everything was organized and properly sanitized after each class. They learned and taught each other, themselves becoming the source of knowledge and no longer relying on me. They took pride in properly handling the equipment, updating it, and keeping it in pristine operating condition. What was once a daunting task for a single educator, lining up 15 computers and running updates one at a time, was now entrusted to a group of increasingly motivated teenagers. The foundations for a near-peer environment were well established moving forward.

Instructional Creativity Driven by Students

Once technology oversight is established, phase two is designing meaningful educational lessons. Bloom's revised framework for educational goals lists evaluation and creation at the apex of cognitive skills to help students learn (Wilson, 2016). Unfortunately, many classes are designed to have students enter, sit in a seat, absorb information, but never engage in higher-order thinking skills such as analyzing, reasoning, and evaluation. Students routinely complain about how boring school is and how the assignments are time fillers. Our goal was to change this.

Our approach to VR implementation puts students in control. It challenges them to transform ordinary topics into dynamic lessons. Students, our NPTs, are tasked with the responsibility of evaluating existing VR experiences. The process goes as follows: first, they search out, test, and create reviews of educational apps. These already exist in an app store and are either free or paid for using classroom supply funds provided by our district. The tested VR apps can be associated with any concept taught in one of our high school courses. Second, groups present their findings and opinions on the learning value of their selected VR experience. After discussion and deliberation, the class selects one app on which to focus, based on the criteria established by the class. Third, once the VR experience is selected, groups meet and brainstorm ideas for the activity structure. Fourth, these activity ideas are presented to the class. The class explores the positives and negatives about each, during which time we discuss aspects of meaningful instruction. Fifth, the class decides on a single concept to develop. Finally, they shape the activity structure and delivery, determine how information within the VR app is collected and applied, and formulate a plan to keep their peers engaged in the learning process. Out of this process comes an activity to accompany the virtual experience that reinforces core class concepts and furthers discussion. This series of steps engages the NPTs with the upper two levels of Bloom's framework: evaluation and creation.

Here is an illustration using the application *eXPerience: Colorblindness*. This teaches users about types of colour-blindness and has them complete tasks through the eyes of people with varying types (Fig. 1). A simplistic approach for integrating this experience into the curriculum would involve parading biology students through the app. They would each spend 30 minutes in a VR headset, interact with their virtual environment, and then return to their respective biology classrooms where it seems the entire experience was a disconnected field trip. In essence, it would be akin to having the students watch a glorified video on the topic, never diving deeper into how it relates to the curriculum. This is a missed opportunity to tap into one of

Fig. 1 Activity screenshots from eXPerience: Colorblindness

the most powerful facets of VR—embodied learning, combining psychomotor learning with cognitive engagement. One empirical analysis of embodied learning studies showed significant gains in student learning when this method was used in comparison to a control group (Georgiou & Ioannou, 2019).

In an effort to maximize knowledge acquisition and retention, the NPTs created an accompanying student guide (Appendix), asking the NPLs to gather factual information, guiding them through color-blindness tasks, documenting results, and reflecting on the challenges each one posed. They also made a guide for the class-room teacher that explains the activity design, proposes a timeline, and provides teachers with answers to all the questions. This near-peer learning experience is designed to be done during a genetics unit within a biology class. Having the NPT on hand is a benefit because they are always in close proximity to the NPL, able to provide rapid content and technology support when needed. Overall, the experience enriches the learning by having the NPL undergo daily virtual tasks with different types of colour-blindness. The NPT will learn more from creating materials and teaching others, while the NPL will learn more from practicing and doing kines-thetic activities.

Other examples of student-created lessons in combination with VR experiences include the following: live tweeting during an immersive reading of the "The Raven" (Fig. 2), creating postcards from the past after getting a glimpse of the civil rights movement in "I AM A Man," interacting with detailed human anatomy in *Organon3D* (Fig. 3), and marketing molecules in social media posts after using *Nanome,* a VR application for molecular construction. Other VR experiences are excellent launch-ing points for discussion about social issues and developing empathy. NPTs used Bloom's higher-order thinking skills to create activities. Within these activities, they used higher-order question-stems to construct discussion questions centred on top-ics such as race, homelessness, human impact on global warming, and disabilities. These question-stems urge students to analyze, evaluate, or create opinions.

Fig. 2 Screenshot from "The Raven" VR and a tweet template for students

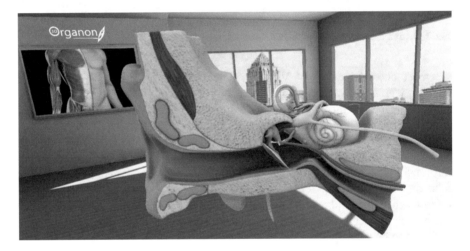

Fig. 3 Detailed human anatomy in Organon3D

Ultimately the design decisions are left to the students. They decide which immersive experiences they want to delve into, and the types of activities designed to complement them. It allows them to create meaningful lessons they would want to do in a classroom. A collection of student-created lessons can be found visiting envisionxr.net or scanning this QR code:

The Near-Peer Classroom in a Virtual World

The initial vision was to enhance the learning experience in classrooms by creating a model where students would assist with the technology, thus removing that hurdle from classroom teachers. There are some very practical advantages to using such a model for the integration of immersive technology. If we invested funds into VR equipment, designed accompanying lessons, but never let them leave our four walls, the technology and educational impact would be limited to a single class. But by incorporating a near-peer model, we are able to increase technology exposure.

In the weeks and days leading up to the actual VR experience, a typical engagement with the VR class involves NPT-led meetings between the near-peer tutors and the traditional classroom teacher. These meetings cover activity designs, modification suggestions, and a demo of the experience for the teacher. On the day(s) of the near-peer VR activity, a crew conducts an early morning setup of all the equipment. The NPTs assigned to each period know every aspect of the app to be used and can walk users through most issues with effective oral communication, something we practice and discuss. This enables keeping the user in the headset without the NPT needing to don the headset themselves. The role of the classroom teacher is simply to discuss content and ask probing questions; all the technology and VR-experience questions are answered by the near-peer tutor. At the end of the day, the setup crew comes back in to take down and pack up all the VR equipment, laptops, and electrical cords.

This model has proved highly effective and popular in our school. We have run demonstrations for community stakeholders, staff meetings, technology conventions, and other school districts. With each event or classroom collaboration, I see the confidence and communication skills grow among my students—but not without work. Much like Evans and Cuffe (2009), who concluded they should increase feedback opportunities in future trials, we recognize the need to do the same to improve the near-peer experience for the learners. These feedback opportunities prompt meaningful reflective discussions on initiating engagement, troubleshooting flowcharts, modifying activities, and increasing overall efficiency. We have had sessions where our delivery techniques were ineffective. NPLs shared that help was not always near, or NPTs struggled to effectively guide them through the application. This feedback told us where we needed to focus our efforts and make improvements.

My high school students were confident working with teenagers and adults, but what about impatient fourth graders who had never donned a headset? We had very detailed plans. Each student knew their role, from setup to tear down and everything in between. What happened those two days was amazing. I watched as my students executed the near-peer model. Each fourth grader spent 30 minutes in a one-on-one setting with one of my VR students (Fig. 4). They travelled the Earth, identifying and exploring landforms (Fig. 5), took a deep ocean dive with marine life, and played a basic game created by two of my computer programming students (Fig. 6).

Once the VR experience ended, small groups of students used an AR sandbox to create some of the same landforms they learned about in science class. They watched

Fig. 4 High school students working with fourth graders at the I Promise School

Fig. 5 Examples of different landforms explored in Google Earth

Fig. 6 Game created by high school students and played in VR

topographic lines change in real-time and virtual rainwater run down slopes and collect in low-lying areas. Those two days were remarkable to watch, from the awe and wonder in the expressions of 10 and 11-year-olds to the transformation I saw in my students as they worked with each one. Not only did these high school kids help bolster knowledge in the fourth graders, but by preparing to teach them, they also reinforced science topics that some had not covered in their own coursework in a few years.

Strategies for Implementation of Design

Educators may consider the following four pedagogical strategies when implementing virtual technologies in their classroom. It is important to know the audience and adapt as needed.

- **Expand your collaborative strategy repertoire**. Allowing peers, both NPT and NPL, to work together has several benefits. One aspect easily overlooked with respect to technology is varying comfort levels. Select small groups two to five students. The smaller groups reduce hiding spots for a student less willing to participate. Within the groups, designate roles such as a content evaluator, creative mastermind, and manager. With pairs or small groups, students with some anxiety toward technology are freer to learn at their own pace without feeling pressured. Groups often interact with more humour, placing everyone at ease.
- Tapping into this potential requires careful lesson design. Begin with a complex learning activity (Burns, 2016): a task that is too simple promotes independent work and allows some students in the group to contribute little to the cause, whereas a complex task promotes collaboration because it is too involved for one student to handle. One way to do this is by incorporating real-world problems for students to remedy. This problem may be solving a technical issue, designing engaging content to accompany VR experiences, or establishing a set of coherent procedures for a user to follow. It requires students to focus on a problem, conduct research, debate, and develop a working solution. During the collaborative process, build in opportunities to come back together as a collective group and share, using techniques such as round table, fishbowl debate, conver-stations, back-channel, or snowball (Gonzalez, 2015). Sharing and exchanging ideas intermittently can further spark creativity and progress as well as keep each group focused along the way. The instructor's role should include checking in on students, providing feedback, and asking probing questions.
- **Incorporate brainstorming sessions**. Immersive technology is more than a tool; its existence in the classroom should initiate critical thinking. Use the creative minds sitting at desks in your class to devise ways to transform the technology into a meaningful resource. Unlock the technology's potential through brainstorming, before the planned immersive session takes place. Provide the technology, the content standards, the freedom to ask "What if" questions, and the time to conceive and explore solutions. Begin by establishing a safe environment where students can share and discuss ideas without the fear of failure. Teach your students that with brainstorming, there are no right or wrong answers, just ideas. Be mindful that most class discussions are dominated by the loudest and most confident students, so one method of combating this tendency is brainwriting: introduce the topic ahead of time and allow individual students to con-

tribute anonymously. In-class brainstorming sessions should be structured. Set time limits. Divide students into small groups where they spend short amounts of time generating ideas, followed by time vetting those ideas, then repeat. Doing so keeps ideas flowing and forms connections. Another in-class option to ensure every voice is heard is the "card method." Each student lists their ideas on a card, then passes it to the person next to them. The student on the right adds to the idea or asks a clarifying question. Continue this process until each student has seen every card. Also, consider choosing a format that requires all students to contribute and then share. This discourages anchoring from taking place, where the first few suggestions sway the direction of all future discussions.

- **Empower students as designers**. A common complaint of students is a lack of connection between assigned tasks and the real world. The design process we implement in my VR course requires students to use metacognitive awareness as they think critically about a problem. At the top of Schlechty's Levels of Engagement (2011) is engagement, meaning that students have high attention and commitment because they associate the task with a result that has value, resulting in a willingness to persevere through challenges. To achieve this, instructors need to hand over control and encourage students' creativity to shine. First, challenge them to think and create content that is outside the box or beyond what is usually expected. Second, give students the latitude to make decisions about how immersive technology is implemented or assessed. Third, let them design the change they want to see. Fourth, let them create a product that has value and represents how they learn best. Finally, promote self-examination to determine how they learn best and apply that to lesson design (Schlechty, 2011). The International Society for Technology in Education (ISTE) provides guidance for implementing technology in the classroom. Empowering students as designers fits in perfectly with ISTE standards 4A and 6D. These require students to know and use a design process for generating ideas and creating innovative artifacts, and then publishing or presenting content that customizes the message and medium for their intended audiences (ISTE, 2016). Since some students will struggle in the beginning, start by inviting them to collaborate with you. This allows them to have concepts reinforced while learning to work independently. Encourage creative risk-taking, where failures are welcomed as learning experiences. In the end, students will have a sense of ownership over their learning, a greater understanding of content, and a blueprint for transforming from consumers to creators (Spencer, 2019).

- **Look for incidental learning opportunities**. Constructivism is essential to education. The belief that new knowledge is constructed on the foundations of existing knowledge is important because our students come to us with different backgrounds and life experiences. The wider range of life experiences a student brings to class means potentially a larger foundation on which to build. Help students increase their base knowledge by giving them open-ended tasks that allow them to explore and investigate. Instead of giving them all the answers, push them to research information and solutions. The incidental learning through these assignments may not only help them relate to new topics in class but allow them to draw natural connections in other classes. In researching new VR applications, students in my class gained incidental knowledge in a wide range of areas, including types of colour-blindness, the Memphis sanitation strike, racial issues related to travel in the 1960s, geography, geology, medical terminology, medical conditions, empathy, and more. Their exposure to these topics can lead to class discussions and further investigation. These topics are not routinely covered, but they help students develop deeper empathy or increase their general knowledge of the world.

Conclusion

There is more to good teaching than technology. It does not take long to realize that investing in the latest software or gadget without investing in professional development means a closet full of unrealized potential. Immersive technology will not in itself revolutionize education, but creativity will. Successful implementation requires a plan that includes maintenance and professional development. In our district, this meant designing a course for students with leadership and creativity as key aspects. As a result, students became more fluent using technology and learning content through a variety of avenues, while applying the design process to improve technology integration.

For a program like this to be successful, educators must lead by example. In our case, we demonstrated being lifelong learners in a rapidly changing world. We took risks and pursued the unknown to move past the status quo. This provided an alternate educational experience and challenged traditional boundaries. Our students witnessed both our successes and failures during our plunge into VR integration. The technologies we were implementing did not exist when we entered the teaching profession; they were the fantasies and lore of science fiction. Without a roadmap, we were destined to have a few mishaps along the way, but those obstacles gave opportunities for group discussion and problem solving. The course involved students in real-world collaboration, showing them that not every endeavour produces success—just a learning opportunity. Moving forward, ideally our example will inspire educators and students to be relational, risk-takers, and lifelong learners in whatever field they choose.

Appendix: Instructional Guide Created by the Near-Peer Tutors

EXPERIENCE COLORBLINDNESS VR EXPERIENCE

OVERVIEW

Students will go through the "eXperience Colorblindness" VR app. They will work in pairs going through the app and collecting information in their student activity worksheets.

MATERIALS

- Oculus Rift or Rift S
- Oculus Touch controllers
- Student activity worksheet

SYNOPSIS

The eXperience: Colorblindness VR experience takes students on a deeper dive into the causes and types of colorblindness. It aims to educate and erase common misconceptions through interactive activities. These activities include daily tasks using filters to simulate what it is like to have the different types of colorblindness. These activities include sorting fruit and painting. The application finishes by giving them a colorblind test with results to see if they have any deficiencies.

TIMELINE

This activity is designed to take be completed in three-45 minute sessions.

✓ For added depth, use this activity in conjunction with the "eXperience Colorblindness VR and Discussion" activity to promote further discussion of what the students learned.

CREATED BY THE BARBERTON HIGH SCHOOL VR TEAM

TIMELINE

Day 1
- The teacher puts students into pairs and hands out the "eXperience Colorblindness" worksheets.
- Students take turns completing each segment of the VR application. The partner inside the headset should communicate information to be recorded by the partner outside of the headset.

Day 2
- Continuation of the previous day's activities.

Day 3
- Students will finish up the worksheet and should have time to answer the reflection questions at the end of the packet.

STANDARDS

Biology:
  Heredity
- An altered gene may be passed on to every cell that develops from it. The resulting features may help, harm, or have little or no effect on the offspring's success in its environment.
- Gene mutations can be passed on to offspring.
- Mendel's laws of inheritance.
- Employ the Punnett Square to determine results of monohybrid and dihybrid crosses to determine genotype and phenotype.

CREATED BY THE BARBERTON HIGH SCHOOL VR TEAM

EXPERIENCE: COLORBLINDNESS ACTIVITY

OPENING QUESTIONS

Fill in the blanks as Qbee describes how we see color. Restart if needed.

- The color we see is based off of incoming _____ of _____.

- Eyes use _____ different types of _____ to see color:

    o One for _____ wavelengths

    o One for _____ wavelengths

    o One for _____ wavelengths

- Color blindness occurs when one cone is either _____ or

    _____.

CREATED BY THE BARBERTON HIGH SCHOOL VR TEAM

ONTO THE GARDEN

Write down a description of each type of colorblindness as Qbee explains them.

Deuteranomaly	
Protanomaly	
Tritanomaly	
Monochromacy (Chronomaly)	

FRUIT STORE

In the fruit store, sort the fruit and write down your results.

- **Partner 1:** How many did you get right? _____   How many did you get wrong? _____
  - **Bonus math question:** What is your percentage? _____

- **Partner 2:** How many did you get right? _____   How many did you get wrong? _____
  - **Bonus math question:** What is your percentage? _____

CREATED BY THE BARBERTON HIGH SCHOOL VR TEAM

THE MUSEUM

Once you've finished the colorblind experience and you're in the museum, take some time to look at the different paintings using different colorblindness filters.

- Which type of colorblindness do you find to be the **least** disruptive to sight?

- Which type of colorblindness do you find to be the **most** disruptive to sight?

COLORBLINDNESS TEST

Now take the color blindness test. (have your partner record your results)

- Partner 1: _____
- Partner 2: _____

How did your results compare with those of your partner's?

PAINT A PICTURE

Take a moment to try and paint a picture of a supreme pizza or a fruit stand or a rainbow or something that requires using many different colors. Try doing it with each type of color blindness.

- Which type was the hardest to paint with and why?

- Which was the easiest and why?

CREATED BY THE BARBERTON HIGH SCHOOL VR TEAM

HUE SORTING ACTIVITY

Let's try the hue sorting activity. Take a couple minutes and see if you can finish.

- Were either of you able to finish?

- What made this activity difficult?

REFLECTION

After you are finished with the activities above, discuss with your partner how each type would make everyday life difficult and what they could to make adjustments.

- What are some of the difficulties people with colorblindness encounter on a daily basis?

- What are some possible solutions to help combat these difficulties?

CREATED BY THE BARBERTON HIGH SCHOOL VR TEAM

EXPERIENCE COLORBLINDNESS VR & DISCUSSION ACTIVITY

OVERVIEW

Students will go through the "eXperience Colorblindness" VR app. Using the material covered by the experience and any other supplemental materials or information covered in the class, students will engage in discussions.

MATERIALS

- Oculus Rift or Rift S
- Oculus Touch controllers

CREDITS

www.cultofpedagogy.com/speaking-listening-techniques/

www.grinnell-k12.org

SYNOPSIS

The eXperience: Colorblindness VR experience takes students on a deeper dive into the causes and types of colorblindness. It aims to educate and erase common misconceptions through interactive activities. These activities include daily tasks using filters to simulate what it is like to have the different types of colorblindness. These activities include sorting fruit and painting. The application finishes by giving them a colorblind test with results to see if they have any deficiencies.

Upon completion of the activities, use one of the two suggested discussion formats described on the next page. This is meant to engage students in thoughtful conversation about the VR experience and colorblindness. You will find sample questions on the third page to get the conversation started.

TIMELINE

This activity is designed to take be completed in three-45 minute sessions.

CREATED BY THE BARBERTON HIGH SCHOOL VR TEAM

DISCUSSION FORMAT SUGGESTIONS
Gallery Walk

a.k.a. Chat Stations

Basic Structure: Stations or posters are set up around the classroom, on the walls or on tables. Small groups of students travel from station to station together, performing some kind of task or responding to a prompt, either of which will result in a conversation.

Variations: Some Gallery Walks stay true to the term gallery, where groups of students create informative posters, then act as tour guides or docents, giving other students a short presentation about their poster and conducting a Q&A about it. In Starr Sackstein's high school classroom, her stations consisted of video tutorials created by the students themselves. Before I knew the term Gallery Walk, I shared a strategy similar to it called Chat Stations, where the teacher prepares discussion prompts or content-related tasks and sets them up around the room for students to visit in small groups.

Socratic Seminar

a.k.a. Socratic Circles

Basic Structure: Students prepare by reading a text or group of texts and writing some higher-order discussion questions about the text. On seminar day, students sit in a circle and an introductory, open-ended question is posed by the teacher or student discussion leader. From there, students continue the conversation, prompting one another to support their claims with textual evidence. There is no particular order to how students speak, but they are encouraged to respectfully share the floor with others. Discussion is meant to happen naturally and students do not need to raise their hands to speak. This overview of Socratic Seminar from the website *Facing History and Ourselves* provides a list of appropriate questions, plus more information about how to prepare for a seminar.

Variations: If students are beginners, the teacher may write the discussion questions, or the question creation can be a joint effort. For larger classes, teachers may need to set up seminars in more of a fishbowl-like arrangement, dividing students into one inner circle that will participate in the discussion, and one outer circle that silently observes, takes notes, and may eventually trade places with those in the inner circle, sometimes all at once, and sometimes by "tapping in" as the urge strikes them.

CREATED BY THE BARBERTON HIGH SCHOOL VR TEAM

DISCUSSION QUESTIONS

- What were the 3 main types of colorblindness? Which one do you think is the worst variation of colorblindness?
- What makes the ability to see the world in a new way important? (Empathy)
- What would one task be that would be harder for people that are colorblind than people that aren't?
- What would you try and come up with to help the colorblind people navigate daily tasks?

STANDARDS

Biology:
   Heredity
- An altered gene may be passed on to every cell that develops from it. The resulting features may help, harm, or have little or no effect on the offspring's success in its environment.
- Gene mutations can be passed on to offspring.
- Mendel's laws of inheritance.
- Employ the Punnett Square to determine results of monohybrid and dihybrid crosses to determine genotype and phenotype.

CREATED BY THE BARBERTON HIGH SCHOOL VR TEAM

References

Annis, L. F. (1983, April). *The processes and effects of peer tutoring* [Paper presentation]. The annual meeting of the American Educational Research Association, Montreal, Canada. https://eric.ed.gov/?id=ED228964

Benè, K. L., & Bergus, G. (2014). When learners become teachers: A review of peer teaching in medical student education. *Family Medicine, 46*(10), 783–787. https://pubmed.ncbi.nlm.nih.gov/25646829/

Brueckner, J. K., & MacPherson, B. R. (2004). Benefits from peer teaching in the dental gross anatomy laboratory. *European Journal of Dental Education, 8*(2), 72–77. https://doi.org/10.1111/j.1600-0579.2003.00333.x

Burns, M. (2016, November 22). 5 Strategies to deepen student collaboration. *Edutopia.* https://www.edutopia.org/article/5-strategies-deepen-student-collaboration-mary-burns

Evans, D. J. R., & Cuffe, T. (2009). Near-peer teaching in anatomy: An approach for deeper learning. *Anatomical Sciences Education, 2*(5), 227–233. https://doi.org/10.1002/ase.110

Georgiou, Y., & Ioannou, A. (2019). Embodied learning in a digital world: A systematic review of empirical research in K-12 education. In P. Díaz, A. Ioannou, K. Bhagat, & J. Spector (Eds.), *Learning in a digital world. Smart computing and intelligence* (pp. 155–177). Springer. https://doi.org/10.1007/978-981-13-8265-9_8

Gonzalez, J. (2015, October 15). The big list of class discussion strategies. *Cult of Pedagogy.* https://www.cultofpedagogy.com/speaking-listening-techniques/.

Gregory, A., Walker, I., Mclaughlin, K., & Peets, A. D. (2011). Both preparing to teach and teaching positively impact learning outcomes for peer teachers. *Medical Teacher, 33*(8), e417–e422. https://doi.org/10.3109/0142159x.2011.586747

ISTE. (2016). *ISTE Standards for Students.* https://www.iste.org/standards/iste-standards-for-students

Karpicke, J. D. (2012). Retrieval-based learning: Active retrieval promotes meaningful learning. *Current Directions in Psychological Science, 21*(3), 157–163. https://doi.org/10.1177/0963721412443552

Lockspeiser, T. M., O'Sullivan, P., Teherani, A., & Muller, J. (2006). Understanding the experience of being taught by peers: The value of social and cognitive congruence. *Advances in Health Sciences Education, 13*(3), 361–372. https://doi.org/10.1007/s10459-006-9049-8

McLelland, G., McKenna, L., & French, J. (2013). Crossing professional barriers with peer-assisted learning: Undergraduate midwifery students teaching undergraduate paramedic students. *Nurse Education Today, 33*(7), 724–728. https://doi.org/10.1016/j.nedt.2012.10.016

Metcalf, S. J., Kamarainen, A. M., Grotzer, T., & Dede, C. (2013). Teacher perceptions of the practicality and effectiveness of immersive ecological simulations as classroom curricula. *International Journal of Virtual and Personal Learning Environments, 4*(3), 66–77. https://doi.org/10.4018/jvple.2013070105

Rashid, M. S., Sobowale, O., & Gore, D. (2011). A near-peer teaching program designed, developed and delivered exclusively by recent medical graduates for final year medical students sitting the final objective structured clinical examination (OSCE). *BMC Medical Education, 11*(1). https://doi.org/10.1186/1472-6920-11-11

Schlechty, P. (2011). *Engaging students: The next level of working on the work.* Jossey-Bass.

Spencer, J. (2019, March 18). Making the shift from student engagement to student empowerment. *John Spencer.* https://spencerauthor.com/empowerment-shifts/.

Ten Cate, O., & Durning, S. (2007a). Peer teaching in medical education: Twelve reasons to move from theory to practice. *Medical Teacher, 29*(6), 591–599. https://doi.org/10.1080/01421590701606799

Ten Cate, O., & Durning, S. (2007b). Dimensions and psychology of peer teaching in medical education. *Medical Teacher, 29*(6), 546–552. https://doi.org/10.1080/01421590701583816

Ten Cate, O., Van de Vorst, I., & Van den Broek, S. (2012). Academic achievement of students tutored by near-peers. *International Journal of Medical Education, 3*, 6–13. https://doi.org/10.5116/ijme.4f0c.9ed2

Topping, K. J. (2005). Trends in peer learning. *Educational Psychology, 25*(6), 631–645. https://doi.org/10.1080/01443410500345172

Velez, J., Cano, J., & Whittington, S. (2011). Cultivating change through peer teaching. *Journal of Agricultural Education, 52*(1), 40–49. https://doi.org/10.5032/jae.2011.01040

Williams, B., & Fowler, J. (2014). Can near-peer teaching improve academic performance? *International Journal of Higher Education, 3*(4), 142–149. https://doi.org/10.5430/ijhe.v3n4p142

Wilson, L. O. (2016). Anderson and Krathwohl Bloom's taxonomy revised: Understanding the new version of Bloom's taxonomy. https://quincycollege.edu/wp-content/uploads/Anderson-and-Krathwohl_Revised-Blooms-Taxonomy.pdf.

Wu, B., Yu, X., & Gu, X. (2020). Effectiveness of immersive virtual reality using head-mounted displays on learning performance: A meta-analysis. *British Journal of Educational Technology, 51*(6), 1991–2005. https://doi.org/10.1111/bjet.13023

David Kaser earned his Bachelor's and Master's degrees from the University of Akron. He has taught for over 20 years, the last 10 focused on STEM education. This role allows him to design and implement different programs for his students. In 2019, he was a finalist for both the State of Ohio Teacher of the Year and the PAEMST Award.

Conclusion: The Future of Immersive Learning: Designing for Possibilities

Paula MacDowell and Jennifer Lock

Abstract This chapter summarizes the book's main themes and contributions to immersive education. It calls attention to new pedagogical frameworks and design strategies for creating or implementing high-quality immersive learning experiences in K–12 and higher education contexts. Future research and development recommendations are offered, including immersive learning technologies created collaboratively and governed responsibly.

Keywords Immersive education · Immersive learning · Immersive pedagogy · Immersive technology · Metaverse

Introduction

Nick Clegg's essay, *Making the Metaverse,* analyzes the impact of ground-breaking technologies on transforming everyday human communication. He explains how quickly the Internet will evolve to be more human, physical, and interactive:

> When Facebook started 18 years ago, we mostly typed text on websites. When we got phones with cameras, the Internet became more visual and mobile. As connections got faster, video became a richer way to share things. We've gone from desktop to web to mobile; from text to photos to video. In this progression, the Metaverse is a logical evolution. It's the next generation of the Internet — a more immersive, 3D experience. Its defining quality will be a feeling of presence. (Clegg, 2022, para. 3–4)

P. MacDowell (✉)
College of Education, University of Saskatchewan, Saskatoon, SK, Canada
e-mail: paula.macdowell@usask.ca

J. Lock
Werklund School of Education, University of Calgary, Calgary, AB, Canada
e-mail: jvlock@ucalgary.ca

© The Author(s), under exclusive license to Springer Nature Switzerland AG 2022
P. MacDowell, J. Lock (eds.), *Immersive Education,*
https://doi.org/10.1007/978-3-031-18138-2_16

Presence is one of the main affordances of immersive education, as first-person perspective experiences make learning more engaging, authentic, and meaningful. Other unique affordances include increased agency to interact with the learning environment and the ability to make abstract ideas into tangible representations that students can manipulate. Immersive technologies offer a new medium for teaching and learning in K–12 and higher education. Predicted to generate $5 trillion in value by 2030, the Metaverse is rapidly developing and too significant for educators to ignore (McKinsey & Company, 2022). From empathetic climate change lessons to managing cognitive load for teaching complex topics, immersive learning experiences are being designed and implemented to address real-world educational problems in today's complex contemporary classrooms (e.g., Lee & Thompson, 2022; MacDowell, 2022; Savickaite & Simmons, 2022). *Immersive Education: Designing for Learning* prepares teachers and designers for the journey ahead toward a safe, respectful, inclusive, accessible, inspiring, and thriving immersive learning classroom.

This chapter summarizes the book's central themes and contributions, looking toward future needs for designing high-quality immersive learning experiences that are aligned with K–12 and higher education goals, values, and curricular outcomes. The book brings together leaders in immersive education to provide practical examples of immersive learning innovation in their courses or classrooms. Uniquely, each chapter offers an illustrative vignette to contextualize a problem of learning in a real-world educational setting. The authors synthesize their technical and pedagogical knowledge to evidence the effectiveness of extended reality (XR) in enhancing curriculum and instruction at educational institutions worldwide. Readers will benefit from the design strategies and pedagogical guidelines for creating or implementing a meaningful immersive learning experience (Lock & MacDowell, 2022). We close with a mindful call to action for a new dawn of immersive education that includes designing for accessibility, facilitating shared experiences and social connection, and shifting learning into the global classroom.

Vignette

After a year of working with colleagues and students and engaging in professional learning about immersive education, Teri took a moment to reflect on her own learning. It did not seem that long ago when she nervously designed and facilitated an augmented reality (AR) activity using tablets. She remembered the lesson that did not go well, given the lack of scaffolding for the learning experience and how she had to redesign the lesson. Gaining confidence over time with both using immersive technologies and designing the learning, she advanced the degree of immersion from AR to virtual reality (VR). She found she was thinking differently about the curriculum outcomes as she created opportunities for students to explore unique immersive environments and learn through experiences not otherwise possible to have in school. As Teri stepped into the classroom, she smiled and lifted a head-mounted display to be used in today's VR field trip to the aquarium.

Designing Immersive Learning in K–12 Education

A major contribution of section one, *Designing Immersive Learning in K–12 Education,* is its rich description of pedagogical strategies involved in designing a learning experience for the immersive context. Collectively, the five chapters provide an up-to-date understanding of when, why, and how to integrate XR technologies in teaching and learning. Chapters contributed by Wöessner (2022) and Brenner et al. (2022) demonstrate how immersive approaches impact learning and offer experiences that would otherwise be inaccessible, emphasizing the need for educators to prepare pre-activities and participatory activities that extend through to the post-activities (e.g., guided reflection and journaling). Instructional planning is more than the immersive experiences facilitated by technology; it is about the meaningful and purposeful integration of pedagogy and technology. A critical component of this work is to check educators' and designers' assumptions. Wang's (2022) chapter maintains that instructional designers and developers should not assume that students are technologically capable of working and learning in an immersive environment. Rather, thorough assumption-checking and iterative design processes are required to ensure appropriate development and integration of the new technology. Beaumier and Koole's (2022) chapter adds a postdigital perspective for educators to consider in their lesson planning, integrating XR in ways that question human/technology relationships. The authors offer valuable information on the instructor's role in designing the immersive experience, assessing the learning, and facilitating reflection about how technologies are co-shaping our lives and physical/ virtual worlds. Further, the concept of psychopedagogy by design introduced by Perriguey (2022) ensures that the emotional impact of immersive learning is healthy, especially for experiences that simulate dangerous situations such as seismic risk preparedness.

From engaging STEM education (Brenner et al., 2022; Wang, 2022) to simulating dangerous learning situations (Perriguey, 2022) to teaching the human impact on water ecosystems (Beaumier & Koole, 2022) to intercultural language learning (Wöessner, 2022), experts in immersive education report how they use XR to enhance learning in K–12 classrooms and museum settings. New learning technologies require new means of assessment. XR technologies enable the collection of data beyond what was previously possible, which brings forth many questions: What kinds of data and learning analytics are helpful to support meaningful assessment? What counts as learning in an immersive experience? Traditional assessment practices (e.g., pre- and post-assessments) may not be appropriate when learning occurs within an immersive context. As designers and educators, how might we think differently about assessing student learning in immersive environments? How do we evaluate the subject matter or content knowledge, skills and competencies, and personal attributes? How do we measure the complexity and creativity that is part of the student learning experience?

As we look to the future of immersive education, Beaumer and Koole (2022) recommend a backward-design approach wherein teachers and designers first consider the learning goals and evidence needed for assessment purposes. Once these are carefully identified, the learning activities and instructional strategies can be successfully determined. Brenner et al. (2022) recommend integrating companion resources like a Digital Science Journal (DSJ) with activities and questions related to the XR experiences, which has the additional benefit of managing the increasing cognitive load when students use new technologies. Teachers can use the DSJ to provide students with immediate, ongoing, and contextualized assessments. Perriguey (2022) cautions that students may wonder if their behaviour is being observed and assessed in virtual environments, leading to increased anxiety that may negatively impact their learning. Student roles and expectations must be well-defined and understood to promote safe, empowering, and positive immersive learning experiences.

Designing Immersive Learning in Higher Education

The book's second section, *Designing Immersive Learning in Higher Education,* advocates for empowering instructors with XR technologies and the knowledge of how to use them in meaningful ways. Lessons learned from the well-documented history of educational technology reveal that *cool new* technologies are often over-sold, underused, and purchased without the necessary funds for training or plans for professional development. There is a need to intentionally support, inspire, and invite instructors to experiment with XR; otherwise, immersive education will fail, do harm, or not be used to its full potential. Chapters by Lane and Havens-Hafer (2022) and MacDowell (2022) share examples of how to empower and support teachers as designers of immersive education. They lead and analyze training initiatives designed for pre-service and in-service teachers to explore the affordances and constraints of XR for learning. Both chapters offer a valuable blueprint for teacher education programs and administrators seeking to support educators in developing their confidence and competence as facilitators of immersive learning and designers of entirely new virtual worlds. In shifting from traditional instructor roles to being designers and facilitators of immersive learning, instructors will need to change their expectations of themselves and students. That may mean learning from the students and championing their gifts and talents. It may require different instructional and technical skills to lead the immersive learning experience and facilitate connection and reflection with the course materials.

As Lane and Havens-Hafer (2022) and MacDowell (2022) evidence, instructors need more opportunities to explore and play with XR technologies and align learning outcomes with meaningful and unique experiences that immerse students in specific content areas. This hands-on training approach will build knowledge and capacity for instructors to evaluate the practicality, merit, and effectiveness of immersive learning in the classroom, now and into the future. Additionally, there is a need for interdisciplinary collaboration and further inquiry to discern how XR can help or hinder learning, including technical and pedagogical impacts. For example,

Lane and Havens-Hafer analyze the rapid evolution of head-mounted displays, concluding that today's headsets are still too bulky, heavy, expensive, and unsustainable for mainstream educational use. Savickaite and Simmons (2022) contribute to building the pedagogical literature by studying the impact of using VR to teach complex and abstract concepts in developmental psychology. Their initial findings demonstrate the unique affordances of immersive technologies that allow interactive learning opportunities in safe and controllable virtual worlds. Students have a high affinity for and curiosity about XR. However, Savickaite and Simmons caution that some are not ready for the metaphysical aspects of learning and socializing as avatars. There is also a need to prepare for the cultural changes that will occur as colleges and universities expand their programming and build digital twins (fully spatial 3D replicas of campuses) in the Metaverse (Clegg, 2022; McKinsey & Company, 2022).

Alongside the rapid advancement of immersive technologies, the scope of immersive learning research must increase as we are only beginning to realize the uses and effects of XR in diverse educational settings. Dengel et al. (2022) and Lion-Bailey et al. (2022) have developed well-grounded theoretical models that apply to both K–12 and higher education. Dengel et al. (2022) contribute a comprehensive and holistic model that examines the macro-, meso-, and micro-levels of teaching and learning with immersive media. Their model provides a solid foundation for understanding the technological and pedagogical complexity of integrating immersive learning in educational programs. The authors outline the organizational structures, policies, and administrative challenges to consider, demonstrating how key stakeholders must work collaboratively to address internal and external factors related to the immersive education process. The XR-ABC Framework developed by Lion-Bailey et al. (2022) provides a structure for understanding how learning happens in immersive environments and serves as a guide for integrating immersive learning in classrooms. The XR-ABC Framework, which builds on practice and learning theory, offers a common language for researchers and educators to study and communicate the educational impacts of XR. The framework includes three aspects: Absorb, Blend, and Create (ABC), which depict the technological pedagogical content knowledge required for integrating XR technologies to enhance teaching and learning.

Teachers and Students as Designers of Immersive Learning

The book's third section focuses on *Teachers and Students as Designers of Immersive Learning*. Four chapters give the reader a greater understanding of how immersive technologies offer powerful new ways to engage students as partners and designers in the learning process (Kaser, 2022; Lee & Thompson, 2022; Southgate, 2022; VanFossen & Gibson-Hylands, 2022). Kaser (2022) focuses on achieving deep understanding by unlocking student creativity through VR assignments that challenge them to develop innovative solutions to real-world problems. He demonstrates a near-peer classroom model for implementing VR in a high school setting where senior students are responsible for training the junior students. This approach empowers students by giving them agency to take on teaching and leadership roles. Further, Kaser (2022) shows how peer mentoring promotes a positive learning environment and facilitates engagement with the whole school community. Southgate (2022) highlights how students can meet learning outcomes and creatively demonstrate their knowledge by designing virtual environments that share their ideas and views. She advises teachers to include student VR content creation as part of the curriculum. Southgate calls for more educational research conducted in natural school settings. While rigorous lab studies are essential, they do not sufficiently address the complexities, tensions, and impacts of immersive learning within classrooms.

VanFossen and Gibson-Hylands (2022) describe how education in VR is defined by compelling narratives and visual storytelling, providing a familiar learning context for teachers and students to be designers and world builders. The authors contribute a wealth of world building strategies to foster immersive learning through discovery, exploration, and wonder (the DEW Concept Model). They offer examples to show how teachers can design culturally responsive and customized virtual worlds to meet the learning needs of students and discipline areas, rather than working within the confines of what is available online. Teachers can create authentic immersive environments rooted in local issues and locations. Hence, students can engage with the course content in a personalized and contextualized way, and as a result, retain the information as a memory from a shared immersive experience. Lee and Thompson (2022) describe how educators and designers need to think differently about creating, facilitating, and evaluating learning in virtual environments. They recommend selecting immersive experiences that foster presence and agency to provide opportunities unavailable in traditional classrooms. XR technologies have the capacity to expand learning experiences and to include students who are differently abled (e.g., in terms of mobility or cognitive impairments). With managing cognitive load an ongoing concern, Lee and Thompson contribute a well-defined strategy for educators and designers to minimize cognitive load and maximize learning by considering four interconnected elements: pretraining, exploration, goal orientation, and segmentation (PEGS).

As we look to the future of immersive education, there is a pressing need for easy-to-use authoring technologies that teachers and students can use efficiently and creatively to design immersive learning and virtual worlds (Southgate, 2022; VanFossen and Gibson-Hylands, 2022). Further, we need to build community amongst educators and designers to support each other and share knowledge of what works. For example, the Educators in VR (https://educatorsinvr.com) network promotes standards of open, global, cross-platform collaboration amongst researchers, educators, and designers. Open pedagogy and open design standards are essential for achieving a sustainable and diverse immersive future: enabling sharing of instructional resources and 3D assets across platforms and promoting inclusivity by welcoming diverse representation and multiple perspectives. Addressing issues of accessibility will be an integral part of developing XR applications that can serve as assistive technologies to help students reduce physical barriers and cognitive impairments in the real world.

Conclusion

While the new wave of immersive technologies holds great promise for enhancing student learning, we are only beginning to understand effective pedagogical strategies and design principles that are inclusive and sustainable. This edited book is relevant and timely to identify how immersive education lives in practice. The book's development began as universities, colleges, and K–12 classrooms worldwide needed to adopt a range of digital communication technologies, online pedagogies, and learning methods in response to the global COVID-19 pandemic. Post-pandemic students will have increased expectations, given their experiences with remote learning. Demand for interactivity and engagement will be strong as students are more informed learners and know what they want and don't want as their learning experience. Instructors will need to design more creative, collaborative, and experiential learning environments for tomorrow's students. Well-designed immersive experiences can increase options for teaching and learning across the lifespan and address some of the challenges experienced in today's physical and digital learning spaces, such as inclusion and diversity.

To fully appreciate the opportunities for XR in education, we need to understand the impact of other powerful technologies such as using artificial intelligence to offer personalized learning, 5G networks for increased speed and connectivity, and blockchain (and related digital currencies) to manage intellectual property assets of all kinds. These technologies depend on each other to provide security, privacy, efficiency, scalability, and flexibility in future immersive learning scenarios. Alongside the rapid development of XR technologies, we also need to establish values, norms, and policies to govern immersive learning and social interaction in virtual worlds, which span hundreds of different platforms, apps, and devices. Who is responsible for setting the standards that will guide students to have healthy and empowered engagements with immersive learning technologies?

We hope educators and designers will benefit from this book's practical examples and evidence of immersive learning and immersive teaching that works; and what needs to be improved. Promising future research directions for immersive education include designing for accessibility, developing shared experiences, and shifting learning into the global classroom where people from around the world can safely and creatively engage in immersive environments together. Immersive education research needs to move beyond isolated lab studies and be situated in today's complex contemporary classrooms to understand how learning outcomes are influenced by technology *in* interaction *with* pedagogy, or what Fawns (2022) identifies as the mutual entanglements of technology and pedagogy.

Immersive education is a source and reason for innovation, inspiration, and change. As educators and designers engage with various levels of immersion, more will be learned to inform research, design, and pedagogical practice. As evidenced in this book, developing high-quality immersive learning experiences and environments takes a community of experts. Collectively, the authors of these chapters have contributed their pedagogical and design strategies for utilizing immersive technology in meaningful ways to support student learning. We advocate for productive partnerships among universities, industry, and government to lead the forward thinking necessary for advancing the future of immersive education in K–12 and higher education and guide its impact on learning.

References

Beaumier, A., & Koole, M. (2022). Augmented and virtual reality in the classroom: Adding a postdigital perspective to backward design lesson planning. In P. MacDowell & J. Lock (Eds.), *Immersive education: Designing for learning* (pp. 31–50). Springer Nature. https://doi.org/10.1007/978-3-031-18138-2_3

Brenner, C., Ochoa Hendrix, J., & Holford, M. (2022). See it and be it: Designing immersive experiences to build STEM skills and identity in elementary and middle school. In P. MacDowell & J. Lock (Eds.), *Immersive education: Designing for learning* (pp. 89-103). Springer Nature. https://doi.org/10.1007/978-3-031-18138-2_6

Clegg, N. (2022). *Making the Metaverse: What it is, how it will be built, and why it matters.* https://nickclegg.medium.com/making-the-metaverse-what-it-is-how-it-will-be-built-and-why-it-matters-3710f7570b04

Dengel, A., Buchner, J., Mulders, M., & Pirker, J. (2022). Levels of immersive teaching and learning: Influences of challenges in the everyday classroom. In P. MacDowell & J. Lock (Eds.), *Immersive education: Designing for learning* (pp. 107–122). Springer Nature. https://doi.org/10.1007/978-3-031-18138-2_7

Fawns, T. (2022, April 2). An entangled pedagogy: Looking beyond the pedagogy-technology dichotomy. *Postdigital Science and Education.* https://doi.org/10.1007/s42438-022-00302-7

Kaser, D. (2022). A classroom model for virtual reality integration and unlocking student creativity. In P. MacDowell & J. Lock (Eds.), *Immersive education: Designing for learning* (pp. 249–272). Springer Nature. https://doi.org/10.1007/978-3-031-18138-2_15

Lane, B., & Havens-Hafer, C. (2022). Teaching the teachers with immersive technology: Preparing the next generation of educators at Ithaca college. In P. MacDowell & J. Lock (Eds.), *Immersive education: Designing for learning* (pp. 153–170). Springer Nature. https://doi.org/10.1007/978-3-031-18138-2_10

Lee, C., & Thompson, M. (2022). PEGS: Pretraining, exploration, goal orientation, and segmentation to manage cognitive load in immersive environments. In P. MacDowell & J. Lock (Eds.), *Immersive education: Designing for learning* (pp. 205–220). Springer Nature. https://doi.org/10.1007/978-3-031-18138-2_13

Lion-Bailey, C., Lubinsky, J., & Shippee, M. (2022). The extended reality ABC framework: Fostering immersive learning through augmented and virtual realities. In P. MacDowell & J. Lock (Eds.), *Immersive education: Designing for learning* (pp. 123–134). Springer Nature. https://doi.org/10.1007/978-3-031-18138-2_8

Lock, J., & MacDowell, P. (2022). Meaningful immersive learning in education. In P. MacDowell & J. Lock (Eds.), *Immersive education: Designing for learning* (pp. 1–12). Springer Nature. https://doi.org/10.1007/978-3-031-18138-2_1

MacDowell, P. (2022). Teachers designing immersive learning experiences for environmental and sustainability education. In P. MacDowell & J. Lock (Eds.), *Immersive education: Designing for learning* (pp. 1–12). Springer Nature. https://doi.org/10.1007/978-3-031-18138-2_11

McKinsey & Company. (2022). *Value creation in the metaverse.* https://www.mckinsey.com/business-functions/growth-marketing-and-sales/our-insights/value-creation-in-the-metaverse

Perriguey, G. (2022). Student emotions in virtual reality: The concept of psychopedagogy by design. In P. MacDowell & J. Lock (Eds.), *Immersive education: Designing for learning* (pp. 51–70). Springer Nature. https://doi.org/10.1007/978-3-031-18138-2_4

Savickaite, S., & Simmons, D. (2022). From abstract to concreate: How immersive virtual reality technology enhances teaching of complex paradigms. In P. MacDowell & J. Lock (Eds.), *Immersive education: Designing for learning* (pp. 135–152). Springer Nature. https://doi.org/10.1007/978-3-031-18138-2_9

Southgate, E. (2022). Teachers facilitating student virtual reality content creation: Conceptual, curriculum, and pedagogical insights. In P. MacDowell & J. Lock (Eds.), *Immersive education: Designing for learning* (pp. 189–204). Springer Nature. https://doi.org/10.1007/978-3-031-18138-2_12

VanFossen, L., & Gibson-Hylands, K. (2022). Interactive storytelling through immersive design. In P. MacDowell & J. Lock (Eds.), *Immersive education: Designing for learning* (pp. 221–247). Springer Nature. https://doi.org/10.1007/978-3-031-18138-2_14

Wang, Q. Q. (2022). Designing an interactive science exhibit: Using augmented reality to increase visitor engagement and achieve learning outcomes. In P. MacDowell & J. Lock (Eds.), *Immersive education: Designing for learning* (pp. 15–30). Springer Nature. https://doi.org/10.1007/978-3-031-18138-2_2

Wöessner, S. (2022). Immersive intercultural language learning at the crossroads of virtual reality. In P. MacDowell & J. Lock (Eds.), *Immersive education: Designing for learning* (pp. 71–87). Springer Nature. https://doi.org/10.1007/978-3-031-18138-2_5

Paula MacDowell, PhD, is an Assistant Professor in the College of Education, University of Saskatchewan. Her area of specialization is Educational Technology and Design (ETAD) with research interests in immersive education, emerging technologies, instructional design, and education for social and environmental change. Paula serves as the Practitioner Chair for the Immersive Learning Research Network (iLRN).

Jennifer Lock, PhD, is a Professor and Vice Dean in the Werklund School of Education, University of Calgary. Her area of specialization is in the Learning Sciences. Dr. Lock's research interests are e-learning, change and innovation in education, scholarship of teaching and learning in higher education, and learning in makerspaces.

Index

© The Editor(s) (if applicable) and The Author(s), under exclusive license to
Springer Nature Switzerland AG 2022
P. MacDowell, J. Lock (eds.), *Immersive Education*,
https://doi.org/10.1007/978-3-031-18138-2

Printed in the United States
by Baker & Taylor Publisher Services